LEVITATION

Levitation

FROM ANTIQUITY TO
JOSEPH OF CUPERTINO & BEYOND

An Examination of the Evidence

BY OLIVIER LEROY

"And as Credulity is the cause of Error,
so Incredulity oftentimes of not enjoying Truth."
Pseudodoxia Epidemica, Bk. I., Ch. V.

Angelico Press

For information, address:
Angelico Press, Ltd.
169 Monitor St.
Brooklyn, NY 11222
www.angelicopress.com

Paperback: 979-8-88677-062-9
Cloth: 979-8-88677-063-6

NIHIL OBSTAT:
GEORGIUS D. SMITH, S.T.D.,
Censor deputatus

IMPRIMATUR:
EDM. CAN. SURMONT,
Vicarius generalis

WESTMONASTERII,
Die 17a *Octobris,* 1928

Cover design
by Michæl Schrauzer

INTRODUCTION

1. ACCORDING to an ancient, uninterrupted and almost general tradition, the human body is able, with certain persons, at certain moments, to be raised from the ground, to remain suspended in mid-air without any visible prop, and sometimes move about in it, without the traceable action of any physical force. The phenomenon is now called *levitation*.

2. I thought the fact singular enough to examine the reasons of those who assert it. If it is imaginary—as, indeed, daily experience suggests—a searching inquiry into these reasons may be sufficient to get rid at last of such a gross mistake or of such a persevering imposture.

Some will object that it is vain to test the value of traditions contradictory to the data of experimental science. I do not wish to discuss the point just now, but simply observe that facts apparently chimerical, when they have been so long and continuously on record, deserve the attention of the psychologist, sociologist, and historian, who want to know how such legends are originated, crystallised, and diffused. Nothing seems better fitted to enlighten them than a careful inquiry into some definite fact such as the strange phenomenon which it is the object of the present book to study.

3. To expose the facts handed down by tradition—outside and inside Christianity, among uncivilised and civilised peoples, in antiquity and in modern times; to scrutinise the evidence on which the traditions are founded; to weigh the arguments of those who deny the facts, of those who accept and attempt to account for them, is the threefold end I have in view.

4. The word *levitation* often means both the uplifting of the human body and of any inanimate object above the earth. I am concerned here only with the first acceptation, and ignore the motion of distant objects, which in metapsychics is termed *telekinesis*. I want to deal solely with what is sometimes called for precision's sake *autolevitation*.

INTRODUCTION

5. The word *levitation* was first used in England, and with reference to spiritualism. Its usage, according to Murray's dictionary, does not date further back than 1875. It has now been commonly adopted among Catholic theologians. There was no term, before, to designate the phenomenon. The Latin of the Bollandists had to resort to periphrases whenever it wanted to allude to it: *haerebat a terra, in aera ferebatur, a terra levabatur, corporaliter elevatus est*, etc.; and he who wants to find out, in the *morales indices* of the *Acta Sanctorum*, references to the levitations of the saints, should look for such cognate words as *raptus, oratio, extasis*, etc.

French theologians and hagiographers also used, not very long ago, quite an approximate and variable terminology. The Abbé J. Ribet, in the different editions of his well-known treatise, speaks of *suspension, ascension, vol extatique*, but never of *levitation*. The expression *extase ascensionnelle* is also to be found in some authors (Dr. Imbert-Gourbeyre, Mgr. Farges), or, again, *extase d'élévation, ravissement corporel*. None of these was comprehensive enough.

So, despite some protests,[1] *levitation* was generally accepted (Vacant's *Dictionnaire théologique, s.v. extase*; Tanquerey's *Précis de théologie*; Poulain's *Les graces d'oraison*, etc.). The word was obviously needed.

To this day the word *levitation* has not been usually used in the plural. This common usage seemed to me so unhandy at times— maybe from my not being accustomed to it in my mother tongue— that I have made so bold as to infringe it in the course of the present book whenever I felt shackled by it. I hope the liberty will not scandalise English readers too much.

6. The subject of levitation, as a whole, in its various bearings has never—as far as I know—been methodically treated. The levitation of the saints is but lightly touched upon in textbooks of mystical theology; one chapter at most is given up to the matter. Besides, the few cases—always the same—which are quoted in them are accepted without discussion, and this deliberate lack of criticism is capable of creating a disgust for the marvellous in many a serious mind. To give but one instance of this, Mgr. Farges, in his work, *Les phénomènes mystiques*, mentions St Francis of Assisi as " the first ecstatic whose spontaneous upliftings above the ground have

[1] Father de Bonniot thought the word looked queer, and supposed it had been coined with the special purpose of explaining away the supernatural element in this phenomenon (*Le miracle et ses contrefaçons*, p. 366, n. 1).

vi

been officially ascertained."[1]   Now, as we shall see (bk. ii, ch. iii, par. 3), not only were Francis's levitations never officially attested, but it is impossible to find the least historical foundation for them. . . .

7. The only essays of some extent where the phenomenon is studied are, to my knowledge, the following:
(a) An anonymous article published in 1875 in the *Quarterly Journal of Science: Human Levitation, illustrating Certain Historical Miracles*.
(b) A book by A. de Rochas, published in 1897, under the title of *Recueil de documents relatifs à la lévitation du corps humain*, and completed in 1901 by an article in the *Annales de Sciences psychiques: La lévitation du corps humain* (pp. 17-47).
(c) An article by Mgr. Elie Méric in the *Revue du Monde invisible* (March, April, June, 1899), the title of which is *Le vol aérien des corps*.
(d) An article published by the Rev. Father Herbert Thurston in the numbers for April and May, 1919, of the *Month*.
Other works on the subject may have been published, but I do not know them.
In the first three essays the same grave deficiency is to be found as in textbooks of mystical theology; all the quoted instances are presumed authentic, or, at least, no attempt is made at discriminating their respective credibility. That which is apparently the most important, A. de Rochas's little book, is in fact rather poor.   Without meaning any disparagement of a work which, after all, in the beginning of my inquiry, pointed out some available directions to me, and which formed, at the time of its publication, a pretty handy compendium of mediumistic levitation, its deficiencies cannot be passed over in this critical essay; the more so, as some writers have evinced some partiality to it.   " Rochas," says M. R. Sudre in his *Introduction à la métapsychique humaine*, " has collected on the subject (levitation) a complete documentation."[2]   And, according to Dr. C. Richet, the same work is " a capital little memoir full of wisdom and erudition."[3]
Practically the hagiographic part of the question, which is fundamental both from the bulk of the documents and the exceptional value of some of them, has been manifestly neglected by de Rochas.   What is not mere repetition of Abbé Ribet's textbook was borrowed from the article of the *Quarterly Journal of*

[1] Vol. ii, p. 272.   [2] P. 247.
[3] *Traité de métapsychique*, ch. iv, p. 692, n. 2.

Science. Indeed, no reference is made to it, but some peculiar mangling undergone by several saints' names in the French transcription of them shows quite obviously the source from which they were drawn.[1] Lastly, this incomplete and unclassified compilation does not afford any critical view of the matter, and even expounds with exaggerated seriousness the most fanciful theories on the mechanism of levitation. Not only the book is not what we were told above, but it should be regarded at best as a rough sketch which has not even the merit of suggesting a methodical arrangement of the subject.

An essay of more modest scope, but original, critical, and most suggestive, is that of the Rev. Father H. Thurston. Deliberately, the author has treated but a few points, but he has done it with exceptional sagacity. Besides, he has brought to light several cases which are very little known and quite interesting. The article is almost exclusively hagiographical, and leaves out the causal side of the question. Limited as it is, it has been very useful.

8. The preceding remarks are not intended to impress the reader's mind with the excellence of the present work, but, on the contrary, to serve me as an excuse, if I have been unable to make an untilled ground yield more and better fruit. My attempt is not towards a final treatment, but a first clearing up of the question, and I think I may claim not to be censured too harshly for the deficiencies of my information or the weaknesses of my method.

I am afraid the reader will sometimes find monotony in this work, especially in the part of it where the traditions of the Catholic Church regarding levitation are dealt with; monotony in the matter, but also in the style; speaking always of the same things, I could not always vary the diction, especially in a language which is not my own. Some will say that I had no need to recite this never-ending line of hagiographic facts. I had but to collect the more characteristic and circumstantial. I preferred to enter promiscuously all the

---

[1] For instance, the saint called in French Luc le Jeune is named Luke de Sotherium, from the English Luke of Soterium; Ambrose of Siena (of the Sansedoni family) is called Ambroise Santédonius because the English text reproduced the Latin Sansedonius; St Lutgard has remained without a final " e " (Lutgarde), according to the English spelling, etc., etc. The author shows again how unfamiliar he is with the question by referring to the numbers of the volumes of the *Acta Sanctorum* corresponding to the months without mentioning the months themselves; which is a form of reference practically useless, since there are several numbered volumes in each month.

available facts under the head *traditions*, and to sift my matter publicly afterwards, or rather to show by some illustrations how the sifting should be done. The method smacks of carelessness, and makes the book cumbrous, but I thought it a slight blemish in an essay of the kind, where the first need is to give the reader a feeling of safety, and, maybe, to enable him to perform the same task over again in his own way.

For the same reason—that this essay might serve as a working instrument—I did not hesitate in loading the bottom of my pages with bulky Latin quotations. Giving thus the full passages of the biographies in the Bollandists, I was at liberty, in the text itself, to deal directly with the main things. They who care more for details, or would like to check the accuracy of my version, will do so without difficult researches.

9. The First Book of this essay is strictly descriptive. I relate in it, with perfect indifference to rational probability or historical veracity, whatever was available as to levitation. The number of pages devoted to this or that saint is no token of the value I set on what is recorded of him. It simply marks a greater quantity of matter without any implication of quality.

10. Several more years, much labour, and leisure that I do not enjoy were needed for the book I aimed at. I made up my mind to publish this one, despite its shortcomings, in the hope that it may serve as a basis and frame for a more important work, richer in facts, evidences, and suggestions. It could be done if readers will kindly correct any mistakes or omissions they may notice. Therefore I solicit criticism, and I shall be thankful for any suggested amendment of the pages that follow.

11. I wish, before closing this introduction, to express my hearty gratitude to those who have helped me in any way in writing the present essay. They are too many to be mentioned by name.

CONTENTS

CONTENTS

BOOK II
THE FACTS

CONTENTS

BOOK I
THE TRADITIONS

PART I

SOME NON-CHRISTIAN TRADITIONS

CHAPTER I

ANTIQUITY AND THE ORIENT

§ 1. GREEK BELIEFS

NEITHER the documents of ancient Egypt nor those of Assyria or Chaldea reveal anything, to my knowledge, of a possible belief, in the magic or religion of those countries, in facts of levitation. Nor does classical Greece seem to have commonly fancied that man might occasionally be freed from the force that fastens him to the ground. Further, according to S. Reinach, the Greek mind evinces its positive bias by denying the gods themselves the power of winging the air without the help of some contrivance.[1] Hermes, before he takes his flight, should lace the gold-winged sandals to his ankles:

> *Primum pedibus talaria nectit*
> *Aurea. . . .*

and if Aphrodite can fly through the air, it is on a chariot drawn by doves or swans. Far less could a simple mortal like Abaris, the Hyperborean magician, have deserved to be called αἰθροβάτης, without the gold arrow given him by Apollo.[2]

But is it safe to infer the more esoteric belief of the Greek soul from this popular imagery ? Most probably not. The winged socks of Mercury or the chariot of Cypris do not tell us any more what the mystics' notion about levitation was than the pinions of angels disclose the doctrine of Catholic theology regarding the agility of glorified bodies. How, then, are we to believe that the initiates of the sects, so confident of the theurgical virtue of asceticism, were such prejudiced positivists ? Could, for instance, the Pythagoreans, imbued as they were with occultism, have been

---

[1] *Cultes, mythes et religions*, vol. ii., pp. 49-50.
[2] *Iamblichi de Pythagorica Vita*, xxviii.

3

LEVITATION

unacquainted with the Indian traditions on the yogi's power, when his body, etherealised by mortification, is lifted from earth in ecstatic rapture ? Had not the master of the sect himself, according to Porphyry and Iamblichus,¹ enjoyed the power of transporting himself through the air ?

In the beginning of the Christian era, Damis, a disciple of Apollonius of Tyana, not only believed in levitation, but says he himself had seen Brahmins " lifted up in mid-air, two cubits above the earth . . . because, they said, everything they do in honour of the sun, at some distance from the earth, is still worthier of the god."² In another passage of the Life of Apollonius, Brahmins are seen again floating in the air, during a ritual ceremony: " They came to a fountain which, according to Damis, who saw it later on, is like the Dirce spring in Bœotia. First they undressed, and rubbed their heads with a perfume like amber; this heated them so much that their bodies were steaming and perspiring as if they had been in a hot bath. Then they jumped into the water and, after washing, proceeded towards the holy ground, with crowns on their heads, singing hymns with all their heart. Next, they made a ring and formed a choir which Iarchas led, and they struck the ground with their rods; and the earth swelled like waves, and they were raised two cubits above the ground. Meanwhile they sang a chant like the paean of Sophocles which is sung in Athens in honour of Aesculapius."³ In the same century a sign of the same belief— though with a different connotation—is to be found in Lucian. The satirist is far from believing in such marvels himself, but one of his characters, Kleodemos, maintains that he saw a Hyperborean wizard uplifted in the air, in full daylight, and walking on the water.⁴

Iamblichus mentions levitation among the signs of divine possession,⁵ and himself, according to Eunapius, was seen by his servants, raised more than ten cubits above the ground, as he prayed, with his body bathed in a bright golden light.⁶

¹ *Porphyrii de Vita Pythagorae*, xxvii.; *cf.* Iamblichus, *ibid.* According to these authors, Pythagoras showed himself on the same day to his disciples at Metapontum and Tauromenium. They do not specify that he was bodily carried over, and it might be supposed that a bilocation is referred to, but the fact that the event is mentioned in connection with Abaris' faculty of flying through the air makes the first supposition preferable. (*Cf.* the quotation in Murray's Dictionary: *Levitation as old as Pythagoras*, *s.v.* Levitation.)
² Philostratus, *Apollonius Tyaneus*, bk. iii, ch. xv.
³ *Ibid.*, bk. iii, ch. xvii.   ⁴ *Philopseudes*, 13.
⁵ *De mysteriis*, sect. iii, § 5.
⁶ Eunapius, *Life of Iamblichus*, in *Vitae Sophistarum*, p. 13, §§ 22-25.

4

Lastly, Julian the Apostate is said to have been raised into the air on the day of his initiation into the mysteries of Diana, at Ephesus, in the crypt of the ruined temple, by Maximus his initiator. This is how the scene is described by E. Lamé: " . . . Then Maximus, as if he had embraced an invisible being, spread out his arms, bent his head backward, and rising in the air, remained suspended, motionless, wrapped in an effulgent cloud. . . . Julian walked steadfastly towards him, as if drawn by an overwhelming force. . . . Maximus clutched his hair at once, dragged him to himself, and they began whirling round the cave, some feet above the ground, with increasing rapidity."[1]

§ 2. BUDDHISM, YOGIS, FAKIRS

The Indian traditions on the levitation of ascetics were, as it was shown above, known by the Greeks in the time of Apollonius. There is no doubt that they were known far earlier. These traditions are very old. Gotama and his ancestor Maha Sammata could rise in the air. The Buddhist ascetic, once arrived at perfection (*irdhi*), has the power of levitation. He is lifted up over the ground at will or through ecstatic rapture (*udwega prîti*).[2] The same power is obtained by the yogi as a result of the breathing exercise known as *prâyânâma*.

If the stories of modern travellers are to be trusted, the ascetics of modern India are no less gifted than Buddha himself. L. Jacolliot, a French magistrate, who lived in India (he was " procureur impérial " at Pondicherry in 1866), says that he saw a fakir, Covindassamy, raised two feet above the earth. The fakir had come from Trivandrum in Travancore, and was spending some time in Benares. He had taken shelter in a hut near the Ganges, at a small distance from Jacolliot's house, and he lived there given up to fasting and contemplation. One day the author saw him suspended in the air, on the terrace of his house, with only the prop of a stick, on the top of which he laid his hand after pronouncing some magic formulas, and he remained thus twenty minutes, with legs folded in the Oriental way. Another time, the phenomenon took place without any support: " At the moment when he left me for lunch

---

[1] *Julien l'Apostat*, pp. 48 ff.
[2] R. S. Hardy, *Manual of Buddhism*, pp. 38, 126, 150; *Eastern Monachism*, pp. 272, 285, 382; Eug. Burnouf, *Introduction à l'histoire du Bouddhisme indien*, vol. i, pp. 183, 250, 312; H. Oldenberg, *Le Bouddha*, ch. iv, p. 183.

LEVITATION

. . ., the fakir stopped in the doorway opening from the terrace into the backstairs, and folding his arms, he was lifted—or so it seemed to me—gradually, without visible support, about one foot above the ground. I could determine the exact height, thanks to a landing mark upon which I fixed my eyes during the short time the phenomenon lasted. Behind the fakir hung a silk curtain with red, golden and white stripes of equal breadth, and I noticed that the fakir's feet were as high as the sixth stripe. When I saw the rising begin, I took my watch out. From the time when the magician began to be lifted until he came down to earth again, about ten minutes elapsed. He remained about five minutes suspended without motion."[1]

De Rochas, from whom I borrow the quotation, mentions other facts of the kind from accounts published in the *Theosophist* of Madras in 1880.[2]

Lastly, everybody knows the classical tale of the rope-trick where a fakir is seen to vanish mysteriously with his boy, by climbing up a rope he has thrown into the air.[3]

§ 3. TAOISM AND CHINESE BUDDHISM

According to Taoist books, through a special ascetic training the sage's body grows so fluid as to be lighter than air. It is what happened to the famous disciple of Lao-chang, Lie-tzeu, when, after nine years' exercise, he had conquered the state of perfect indifference.[4]

The traditions of Chinese Buddhism are like those of Indian Buddhism; the ascetic, on attaining the fourth degree of contemplation, wins the power of rising and flying through the air as Buddha himself did when he betook himself to Kapilavastu to attend his father's death.[5]

The Tibetan adepts of the yoga system of asceticism profess, like the Indian yogis, that their training renders their bodies so light that they can sit on the top of a corn-stalk without bending it. The proper degree of lightness is obtained by the *maljorpa* (anchorite)

[1] L. Jacolliot, *Voyage au pays des fakirs charmeurs*, p. 61; quoted by de Rochas, *Recueil de documents relatifs à la lévitation du corps humain*, pp. 8 ff.
[2] *Ibid.*, pp. 11 ff.
[3] E. G. Browne, *A Literary History of Persia*, vol. i, p. 431; Hadland Davis, in the *Occult Review*, December, 1905. A recent version is to be found in R. Schmidt's *Fakire und Fakirtum*, pp. 167-168.
[4] L. Wieger, *Histoire des croyances religieuses et des opinions philosophiques en Chine*, p. 190.
[5] *Ibid.*, pp. 426, 482.

6

when he is able to jump out of his *cham kang* (anchoret's dwelling) through a narrow aperture in the roof.[1] The notion of aerial transport through supernatural ways is also to be found in China in the nondescript traditions that Father L. Wieger labels as hybrid folk-lore. To the latter belongs, among others, the story of Kia cheu-fang, who was snatched up to heaven by a *tao-cheu*. " Shut your eyes, take my arm and be not afraid !" said the bonze. Kia cheu-fang felt himself raised off the earth. The wind was whistling, and from beneath he could hear the roaring of the waves. After spending a short while in heaven, Kia cheu-fang was conveyed back to his village by the *tao-cheu*.[2]

Sometimes the power of levitation does not depend on a certain way of living, but on the possession of a charm. One should swallow the charm, think of the place where one wants to go, and one is carried there. Such is the doctrine of Keue-houng, a celebrated theorist of Taoist magic.[3]

§ 4. ISLAMIC MYSTICISM

The belief in the levitation of the ascetic is a well-established tradition of Islamic mysticism. In one of his opuscules, the *Minhâj al-abidin* (The Safe Way of the Devout), Al-Gazzali mentions levitation and walking on the water among the gifts with which God favours his faithful servant,[4] and an old Sufic treatise says that the pious *Santon* enjoys the power of " traversing great distances in a short time."[5]

The Sheikh Jîlâni (Bagdad, twelfth century) was said to be lifted in the air during ceremonies very much like mediumistic séances.[6] The Persian poet and mystic Jalálu d'Din Rûmi (†1273) tells us in his *Masnaví* that a certain sheikh, suspected of having

---

[1] *Le Thibet mystique*, by Madame Alexandra David-Neel (in *Revue de Paris*, l. 5, ii, 1928, pp. 869-870). The author, who has lived fourteen years in Tibet specially to observe the lives of the ascetics, speaks in rather ambiguous terms of their preternatural feats. Referring to the results obtained in this respect by the *maljorpas*, as an effect of their respiratory exercises, she says that she has witnessed different phenomena, but does not expressly mention levitation among them.

[2] L. Wieger, *ibid.*, p. 632.

[3] *Ibid.*, p. 401.

[4] Asin Palacios, *Une introduction musulmane à la vie spirituelle*, p. 40.

[5] Al-Hujwirî, *The Kashf al-Mahjûb*, translated by R. A. Nicholson, p. 231.

[6] Carra de Vaux, *Les penseurs de l'Islam*, vol. iv, p. 244 (quoting D. S. Margoliouth).

stolen pearls, proved his innocence by an impressive levitation performed out at sea, on board a ship.[1] Jalálu Rûmi himself enjoyed from childhood similar gifts. One day, as he was playing with some children on the roof of a house, one of his comrades asked him if it were possible to jump from there on to the roof of another house. Jalálu Rûmi answered this was fit for cats, but not for men. " Let us rather leap towards heaven !" he said, and bounding into the air, he vanished from the view of the children, who began crying with fear. A moment after, Rûmi appeared again. He said he had been carried away by celestial beings, who had brought him back to earth.[2] According to the tradition of the Order he has founded (the *mawla-wîyah*, the whirling darvishes), Rûmi, every time he was absorbed in contemplation, was lifted off his seat and began whirling in mid-air.[3]

The same prodigy is attributed to Al-Hosayn-Ibn-Mansur, surnamed Al-Hallaj (†992), whose life was studied by L. Massignon in a most erudite monograph. A former disciple of Al-Hallaj, Al-Sâmarrî, who was afterwards witness for the prosecution in the proceedings that ended in the execution of the mystic, declared to vizir Hâmid that he had seen his master floating in the air.[4]

[1] *The Masnaví*, by Jalálu d'Din Rûmi, bk. ii, translated by C. E. Wilson, vol. i, p. 304.
[2] J. P. Brown, *The Darvishes*, p. 250.
[3] *Ibid.*, p. 255.
[4] L. Massignon, *Al-Hallaj*, vol. i, p. 263.

CHAPTER II

WIZARDS AND DEMONIACS

§ 1. Traditions among Savages

(a) Wizards

AUSTRALIAN wizards, according to the somewhat confused stories collected by ethnographers, are believed to possess the power of journeying through space to the celestial abode where magical virtues are conferred on them. More exactly, these aerial voyages are performed through the help of protector spirits, unless the wizards hoist themselves up there by means of a rope which is thrown down to them from the sky, or, after the Theddora's tradition, they eject from their mouth, like spiders or caterpillars, a kind of filament by which they climb up.[1]

Others, once they have grown *bangal*, can be levitated, thanks to their feathers. Such is the notion of the Boandik, West Arunta, and Mungaberra.[2] Among the Kurnai, the *birraark* is initiated by *mrarts*, or ghosts, who convey him to the clouds, holding him by the bone peg he wears through the septum of his nose; or, again, he is lifted hanging to a *marrangrang*, which is described as being either like a rope or else something on which the *birraark* can sit. Having been thus introduced to the land of ghosts, the initiate can return there at will. He simply has to call on the *mrarts* to carry him.[3] A native gave A. W. Howitt the account of one of the manifestations of a celebrated *birraark* of the Brabalung clan named Mundauin. That man said he had become a *birraark* by dreaming three times he was a kangaroo. From this time he began to hear the *mrarts* drumming and singing up aloft, and then one night they came and carried him away:

" In the night his wife shouted out, ' He is gone up.' Then we heard him whistling up in the air, first on one side of us and then on the other, and afterwards sounds as of people jumping down

---

[1] A. W. Howitt, *The Native Tribes of South-East Australia*, pp. 388-389.
[2] M. Mauss, *L'origine des pouvoirs magiques dans les sociétés australiennes*, pp. 22 ff.
[3] A. W. Howitt, p. 391.

on the ground. After a time all was quiet. In the morning we found him lying on the ground, near the camp where the *Mrarts* had left him. There was a big log lying across his back, and when we woke him and took the log off, he began to sing about the *Mrarts*, and all he had seen up there."[1]

" In another account of a *séance* by Mundauin," writes Howitt, " the same account was given of his departure in the night. Then his voice was heard shouting to them, and then noises of people in the tree-tops, and then of them jumping down on to the ground. The *Mrarts* answered questions put to them, as to the movements of the Brajerak and the *Lohan* (white men), and whether the former were pursuing them. Finally the ghosts said, ' We must now go home (*Mellagan*), or the west wind might blow us into the sea.' In the morning the *Birraark* was found lying on the ground outside the camp, and round him were the footprints of the *Mrarts*.

" A third account of one of these *séances* I give in the words of my informant: ' I was once at Yunthur at the Lakes, and the *Dinna-birraark* Brewin was there with his wife. In the night she woke up and shouted out that he was gone up to the *Mrarts*. We all got ready, and soon someone shouted out, " Where are you?" He replied, " Here I am; I am coming down." He said that he had heard the *Mrarts* having a great *Gunyeru* and making a great noise, and he had gone up to them. Then the *Mrarts* came down with him, and conversed with us as to where the other mobs of the Kurnai were, and whether any Brajerak were coming after us. When the *Mrarts* went away, we found Brewin lying, as if asleep, where we had heard them speaking to us. The *Mrarts* talked in very curious voices.' "[2]

At the end of another séance, the *birraark* " was found in the top of an almost inaccessible tree, apparently asleep, where he said the *Mrarts* had left him when they went away."[3]

Howitt found the same kind of beliefs in other tribes of the Wotjobaluk group. In one of these tribes was a female seer " who went up aloft, being supported, as it was believed, by ghosts, from whom she gleaned information as to the dead."[4]

Among the Indians of North America, the wizards were thought to enjoy similar powers. Not only the ghosts controlled their mind by possession, but carried their bodies off the ground.[5] A

[1] *Ibid.*, p. 390.
[2] *Ibid.*, pp. 390-391.
[3] *Ibid.*, p. 391.
[4] *Ibid.*, p. 393.
[5] J. F. Lafitau, *Mœurs des sauvages américains*, etc., vol. i, p. 383.

French missionary, Father Papetard, Superior of the African Missions in Nice, told Dr. Imbert-Gourbeyre that during his stay in Oregon " he had seen, more than once, wizards lifted two or three feet above the earth and walking on the top of the tufts of grass."[1]

In the Congo, members of the secret society *Bwiti* say that some of them during certain ceremonies remain suspended for about ten minutes one yard from the ground.[2] Father H. Trilles also says he witnessed an initiation into the secret society *Ngil*, among the Fân, and saw three neophytes raised on the end of a pole, in a way that makes this uplifting very much like a levitation.[3]

With the traditions about levitation is connected the belief in the nocturnal aerial transport of sorcerers to their meetings or in order to perform some malefic operation. It is to be found among nearly all nations, and it is particularly current among the Bantu tribes. However, the connection between the two classes of facts is slender enough; indeed, we have no longer to deal here, generally, with a material removal of the human body, but with the travelling of a fluid substance severed for a time from the entranced body, which will assume, as a rule, the shape of a will-o'-the-wisp, globe of fire, bird or other animal.[4]

(b) Demoniacs

Sometimes the carrying up is not supposed to be dependent on a particular power or on the assistance of a guardian spirit, but to be worked by a malignant spirit who possesses or obsesses the levitated person. African negroes say that some of them are thus snatched away up to the top of the highest baobabs, where they are found tightly lashed with lianas. Father Picarda, a mis-

[1] Imbert-Gourbeyre, *Les stigmatisées*, vol. ii, p. 246.
[2] Le Scao, *Au pays de Sette Cama*, quoted by H. Trilles, *Le totémisme chez les Fân*, p. 51.
[3] H. Trilles, *La sorcellerie chez les non-civilisés*, pp. 181-182. *Cf.* the description of the same scene with schematic illustration in Leroy's *La raison primitive*, p. 170.
[4] H. Trilles, *Le totémisme chez les Fân*, p. 455; R. H. Nassau, *Fetichism in West Africa*, p. 123; H. A. Junod, *Les Ba-Ronga*, p. 428; B. Malinowski, *Argonauts of the Western Pacific*, p. 238 *ff.*; C. G. Seligmann, *The Melanesians of British New Guinea*, p. 640.

LEVITATION

sionary in Zanguebar, has given a detailed report of his investigation
in a case of the kind, and thinks he has ground to believe there was
something mysterious in it.[1]

§ 2. TRADITIONS AMONG CIVILISED PEOPLES

(a) Wizards

In Europe, traditions regarding the aerial travelling of sorcerers
do not differ from those of savage nations. Now the wizard is
supposed to fly through the air by means of some apparatus or
agency, now he does it by purely magical power. Or else it is but
his spirit which leaves his body and moves freely through space
towards its goal. All this is very well known, and I simply refer
the reader to classical treatises on demonology.[2]

A famous instance where a magician is said to have been lifted
materially in the air is that of Simon Magus, who collapsed in his
flight and was smashed up on the ground at Nero's feet.[3]

Another case of levitation ascribed to demonolatry is that of
Mary Magdalen of Cordova, a Franciscan abbess contemporary
with St Teresa. Mary Magdalen was regarded for forty years
as a saint. Prelates and princes visited and revered her. Charles
the Fifth's wife called her " dear mother." One day, during an
illness, she declared that as a child she had signed a diabolical pact,
the source of all her magic powers. Among these was levitation,
and during some religious ceremonies she was seen raised three
cubits and more above the ground.[4]

Of Margaret Pajot, who was executed in 1576 at Tonnerre,
J. Bodin says, in his Démonomanie des Sorciers, that whenever she
wanted she could rise into the air, and that she did it in public.[5]

The same thing happened to a servant of the President of the
" election " of Brioude, initiated into witchcraft by his master. He
was sometimes lifted off the earth, at church in sight of everyone.[6]

[1] Autour de Madéra: Notes sur l'Ouzigoua, pp. 272-273.
[2] Del Rio, Disquisitionum magicarum . . ., l. ii, q. xvi; Görres, La
mystique divine, naturelle et diabolique, vol. v, ch. xvii.
[3] Const. apost., l. 6, Migne, P.G., vol. i, col. 930; Arnobius, Adversus
Gentes, l. 2, n. 12, Migne, P.L., vol. v, col. 828; Sulp. Sev., Hist., l. 2, c. 28,
Migne, vol. xx, col. 145. Cf. H. Schlarick, De Simonis magi fatis romanis
commentatio historica et critica.
[4] Acta Sanctorum, vol. vii, October, p. 569 B: In solemni pompa festorum
dierum ad tres et amplius cubitos in sublime efferebatur. Other details, ibid.,
pp. 151 A, 227 EF, 687.
[5] Quoted by L. A. Cahagnet, Magie magnétique, p. 134.
[6] Fléchier, Mémoires sur les Grands Jours tenus à Clermont en 1665, p. 63.

(b) Demoniacs

As regards demoniacs properly so called—possessed or obsessed persons—there are more abundant and explicit accounts. Here are some facts drawn from pretty well-known documents. My aim is neither to be complete nor novel. I only want to produce a few samples of the literature on the matter.

Describing how St Martin exorcised demoniacs, Sulpitius Severus writes: " I saw, when Martin approached him, a demoniac raised from the earth and remain suspended in the air, with his arms stretched out, without touching the ground with his feet. . . . You could see the wretched people whirled about in different ways: some were uplifted and floated in the air with their feet upwards, neither did their clothes hang down on their faces or discover their bodies in any immodest way."[1] Similar quotations might be drawn from St Hilary or St Paulinus.[2] We read also in the Life of St Geneviève,[3] and in that of St Vincent Ferrer,[4] that demoniacs brought to their presence remained suspended in the air or began flying about.

The levitations of a possessed girl of Louviers, Françoise Fontaine, exorcised in 1591, were recorded in an official report, the original of which is in the Bibliothèque Nationale of Paris.[5] One can read in it that Françoise, in the presence of Provost Morel, his clerk and other persons, was " lifted into the air upright about two feet above the ground," then having fallen back flat to the ground, she was dragged thus through the room to the great amazement of everybody.[6]

---

[1] Sulp. Sev., *Dial.* iii, c. vi, Migne, P.L., vol. xx, col. 215.

[2] S. Hil., *Lib. contra Const.*, Migne, P.L., vol. x, cols. 584-585; S. Paul., *In Natal. S. Fel.*, 70; *De vita S. Martini*, 8, Migne, vol. lxi, col. 1090.

[3] *Acta Sanctorum*, vol. i, January, p. 140.

[4] R. P. Fages, *Histoire de S. Vincent Ferrier*, vol. i, p. 214.

[5] *Original d'vn procès-verbal, fait pour deliurer vne fille possédée par le malin esprit à Louuiers où il y a de grandes preuues d'vne véritable possession du démon*, MS. No. 24122, fonds français.

[6] *Ibid.*, p. 25: " And having entered the said court, the door of which is under the porch and in the passage of the said prison, the said Françoise walked but six paces into the said court, and we together with our clerk entered the office where the judge's chair is and the sitting is held, and as our clerk was beginning to write the present report, that we were dictating to him, he cried out and showed us the said Françoise, who was near the door of the said court, whom we saw raised about two feet off the floor, upright, and at once she fell down on the ground, flat on her back, with her arms spread out crosswise, and afterwards she was dragged, with her head foremost, still on her back, along the said court, without anybody touching

13

LEVITATION

At another moment, as the Provost read the Gospel of St John to her as an exorcism, the possessed girl, who was stretched on her back on the floor, was raised three or four feet above the ground, and thus carried horizontally towards the extempore exorcist, who was so horrified that he fled incontinently into his office. This is how the scene is told in the report:

" Then, the said Françoise had again fallen backwards on to the floor, and twisted her body about; which seeing we bethought ourself of reading the Gospel according to St John, as it is more powerful against devils; and lest the said Françoise should see what we intended to do, we covered our face with our cloak, pulling it over our eyes; having approached the said Françoise, we crossed ourself before and behind, as they use to do when they say the gospel at church, and begin to say: *Initium sancti Evangelii secundum Johannem. In principio erat Verbum*; and as we continued to read the said gospel, the body of the said Françoise, who was then lying on the ground, with her face upwards and her arms stretched out crosswise, began to crawl along, head foremost, all dishevelled and bristly, and all at once the body of the said Françoise was raised off the floor, three or four feet high, and borne horizontally, face upwards, along the court, without anything to support her. When we saw the said body making straight for us, thus suspended in mid-air, it threw us into such fright that we withdrew into the office of the court, locking the door behind us and reading the said Gospel of St John down to the end. But the said body kept following us through the air up to the office, against the door of which it struck with the soles of its feet, and then was carried back through the air, with the face upwards and head foremost out of the court; which gave such a fright to the gaoler, his servants, our archers and many prisoners who were present with several inhabitants of Louviers, that they fled, some into the prison, some into the street, after shutting the doors behind them; and the body of the said Françoise was carried away out of the said court and remained in the passage of the said prison, between the door of it and the street-door, which the fugitives had shut; which we considered with great astonishment, till one Desjardins and other prisoners opened the door of

---

her, or standing near her, as witnessed the said La Prime, gaoler, the said Nicolas Pellet, servant of the said gaoler, his wife and several prisoners who came into the said court, a thing which amazed me much." (*The lack of clearness of the present translation should not be ascribed to the translator but to the impossible style of Provost Morel, which is not at all easier to make out in the original French.*)

14

the prison and said they would help us, which enabled us to get out of the said office and court, having thus found the said Françoise lying on the ground, close to the said prison door."[1]

Later on, as curé Pellet wanted to give her the Sacrament, Françoise was raised again several times, and even carried away with her head downwards through the church, like the demoniac of Sulpitius:

" . . . And the said Françoise kneeling down had been most alarmingly carried away, without being able to take the Sacrament, opening her mouth, rolling her eyes in her head in such a horrible way that it had been necessary, with the help of five or six persons, to pull her down by her dress as she was raised into the air, and they had thrown her down on the floor. . . . Then the said curé had presented the holy Host again to the said Françoise, who had knelt down; but she was again snatched off the floor, higher than the altar, as if she had been taken by the hair, in such a strange way that the bystanders were much amazed, and would never have thought of witnessing so frightful a thing, and they all knelt down and began saying prayers. . . ."[2]

At a new attempt of curé Pellet to give her Communion, " she had been for the third time prevented from taking it, having been for the third time carried over a large bench that was before the altar where Mass was said, and lifted up into the air towards where a glass had been broken, with her head downwards and her feet upwards, without her clothes being upset, through which, before and behind, was belching forth much water and stinking smoke, and she was then tormented more frightfully than before . . . and for some time thus carried through the air, till at last seven or eight men had taken hold of her and brought her down to the ground."[3]

At last the same scene took place again when they tried to shave her head, as the custom was in such cases:

" And as the said Beaugeois Gautier passed his razor for the third time over the crown of her head, the said Françoise had been snatched out of his hands and those of our archers who held her fast, who were obliged to catch her again, to run after her, carried through the air, and brought her again to the ground by her clothes. . . . The said ' curé ' Pellet had then exorcised the said Françoise, thrown holy water over her and conjured the said malign spirit; as the said Beaugeois Gautier had resumed the shaving of the hair of the said Françoise, who had come to herself, the latter had been lifted up very

[1] *Ibid.*, pp. 27-28. [2] *Ibid.*, pp. 59-60. [3] *Ibid.*, p. 61.

15

high into the air, with her head downwards and her feet upwards, without her clothes being upset. . . ."[1]

The levitations, no less lively, of a Jansenist " convulsionnaire," Mademoiselle Thévenet, have been described by Dom La Taste, with details that deserve to be set down here:

" She was sometimes raised seven or eight feet high up to the ceiling, and then could carry two persons pulling her down with all their might three feet above the ground. . . . Something still more prodigious took place, something horrible indeed; while Mlle. Thévenet was lifted up, with her head upwards, her skirt and chemise were turned up over her head. . . . Now and then, when she was lying down, her head and feet would be lifted up together several feet high."[2]

As regards the famous possessed Sisters of Loudun, those who have inquired into the matter do not agree together. Abbé Leriche says that during the exorcisms two of the demoniacs were twice seen raised above the floor.[3] According to Abbé H. Bremond, there was no such uplifting.[4] On the other hand, a physician of Poitiers, François Pidoux, reports a fact in connection with levitation. Some of the Sisters, he says, when lying down at full length on the floor, would come to their feet without bending their bodies, as if they had been pulled up with invisible strings: *aliae humi jacentes nec articulatim, sed erecto quasi trunco et rigido corpore, se ipsis assurgunt.*[5]

Sometimes demoniacs are rather snatched away than levitated, like the servant-girl Mary Longdon, mentioned by Glanvil, who would be transported by an invisible power to the top of the house, and there " laid on a board betwixt two sollar beams."[6] Görres in his classical treatise mentions a number of such facts,[7] some instances of which are still to be met with in stories by missionaries. I will only recall here what the Rev. Father Bouchet, a missionary in Madura, reported: " A great number of idolaters are tormented by the evil spirit, and they cannot be set free unless they have

---

[1] *Ibid.,* p. 68.
[2] Dom La Taste, *Lettres théologiques,* vol. ii, pp. 1312-1313.
[3] Leriche, *Étude sur les possessions,* p. 197.
[4] H. Bremond, *Histoire littéraire du sentiment religieux en France,* vol. v, p. 182.
[5] *In actiones Joliodunensium virginum,* p. 37 (*ap.* Figuier, vol. i, p. 231).
[6] *Sadducismus Triumphatus* (ed. of 1726), quoted by F. Podmore, *Modern Spiritualism,* vol. i, p. 23.
[7] *La mystique,* vol. iv, ch. xix.

implored the help of the Christians. . . . Will anybody say that the prodigies that we ascribe to the Devil are only due to the power of the imagination ? Is it by imagination that some are snatched off from one place to another, from their village to a far-distant wood or unknown path ?"[1] And the author specifies that one of his neophytes " was suddenly carried away from the road to church to another."[2] But he does not say he witnessed the fact, as is stated by several writers who mention the anecdote.[3]

Calmeil, in his treatise on lunacy,[4] quotes a letter from a missionary containing a curious account of a levitation ascribed to demoniacal influence:

" It occurred to me," says the missionary, " in an exorcism to order the devil in Latin to carry him (the possessed native) up to the ceiling of the church, with the feet upward and the head downward. His body stiffened at once, and he was dragged through the church to a column, and there, with legs together, without helping himself with his hands, he was lifted up in the twinkling of an eye to the ceiling, like an inert weight drawn up from above. He remained suspended, with his feet stuck to the ceiling, his head downward, and I compelled the devil to confess, as I intended, that the pagan religion was false. . . . I kept him in the air more than half an hour, and as I had not the endurance to keep him longer there, being much frightened by the sight, I ordered him to send him back down to my feet without hurting him. . . . He flung him down at once like a bundle of dirty clothes without harming him."

In some instances no suspension in the air is referred to, but only an exceptional agility, such as was reported in the so-called hystero-demonopathic epidemic of Morzines.[5] In March, 1857, two girls of Morzines (Haute-Savoie) were taken with strange fits which some people considered demoniacal. The disease became infectious and was caught by twenty-seven persons, seventeen of whom were cured by exorcisms.[6] At the end of 1860 the number

[1] *Lettres édifiantes et curieuses*, vol. vii, p. 303.
[2] *Ibid.*, p. 305.
[3] De Mirville (*Des esprits*, p. 264) quotes thus the missionary's words: " JE VIS un Indien que j'allais baptiser, transporté. . . ." And he was careful to write the interpolation (*je vis*) in capital letters. The same version is to be found in de Rochas (*Recueil*, p. 25).
[4] *De la folie*, vol. ii, p. 417 (quoted by de Bonniot, *Le miracle et les sciences médicales*, p. 92).
[5] A. Maury, *La magie et l'astrologie*, pp. 330 *ff.*
[6] *Ibid.*, p. 331.

LEVITATION

of the possessed persons had so much increased that the Home Office had the matter inquired into by the General Inspector of Lunacy. The magnetist Lafontaine, who visited the place in 1858, reports that the young possessed girls climbed up trees with amazing swiftness, but were quite at a loss how to climb down if the fit subsided when they were at the top. One of them, Victoire Vuillet, sixteen years old, not only could climb up and down trees with great rapidity, " but again, when on the top of the highest, sprang from one pine on to another, just as a squirrel or monkey might have done.[1]" Of the same facts Hippolyte Blanc gives the following details:

" Several of these children's performances seem plainly against natural laws, as, for instance, when they climbed with unusual easiness and rapidity up to the topmost branch of trees forty or fifty metres high, leapt from there with a somersault on to another tree several metres off, climbed down with their heads downwards, stood with one foot on the very top of a tree and with the other on another."[2]

" T. Joseph," reports the same author, " twelve years old, in good physical condition, a very clever boy, began having fits. . . . As he was coming back from his father's funeral he had one, during which he climbed up a huge fir-tree. . . . When he was on the top, he broke the end of the uppermost branch, and set himself upright on it with his head downward, singing and moving about. . . . His brother ordered him to come down, saying it was not the proper time to amuse himself when he had just buried his father. At this the boy seemed to awake, and when he found himself there, he was much afraid and shouted for help. The brother bethought himself then to cry out, " Devil take that boy quick again, so that he may come down." The fit caught him again; he stopped crying and climbed down with his head downwards as fast as a squirrel.[3]

According to several authors, levitation is pointed out to exorcists by the ritual as one of the signs of possession.[4] Such is not the case. The official text only says that one of the said signs consists in showing powers above one's age and condition: *vires supra aetatis seu condi-*

[1] C. Lafontaine, *Mémoires d'un magnétiseur*, vol. ii, p. 344.
[2] H. Blanc, *Le merveilleux dans le jansénisme, le magnétisme, le méthodisme et le baptisme américains, l'épidémie de Morzine, le spiritisme*, p. 290 (Report of Dr. Arthaud).
[3] *Ibid.*, p. 291.
[4] *Cf.* J. E. de Mirville, *Des esprits*, pp. 469-470; de Rochas, *Recueil*, p. 29; Dr. C. Hélot, *Névroses et possessions diaboliques*, p. 146; L. Figuier, *Histoire du merveilleux.* vol. i, p. 28.

tionis naturam ostendere. On the other hand, an old book, the nature of which is not liturgical, the *Manuale Exorcistarum*, by Candido Brognoli, mentions among evident " signs of a diabolical presence " the transport and uplifting of the body against the patient's will, without it being possible to see that which carries it.[1]

Possibly levitation was mentioned as a sign of possession in ancient rituals; it is the first one referred to by de Saint-André in his *Lettres au sujet de la magie* (1725). De Saint-André was physician to the king, and his book was published with the approval of ecclesiastical authority.[2]

[1] P. 90, art. 26: *Deportatio corporis, et illius elevatio contra voluntatem patientis, et non videtur a quo deportatur, signum est evidens diabolicae praesentiae.*

[2] This is the passage: "1. The lifting up into the air of obsessed or possessed persons, remaining thus suspended for a considerable time, without the help of any art." (Quoted by Garçon and Vinchon, *Le diable*, p. 184.)

CHAPTER III

MEDIUMS AND MAGNETISED SUBJECTS

§ 1. MEDIUMS

' LEVITATION," says Dr. Charles Richet, " is an exceptional phenomenon, even among very powerful mediums."[1]
I will sum up in this chapter the most remarkable cases
of this phenomenon recorded in the annals of spiritualism or metapsychics.

The famous medium Daniel Dunglas Home had, according to
William Crookes, no less than a hundred levitations observed by
different witnesses.[2] The first time Home experienced levitation
was on August 8, 1853, at South Manchester (Connecticut), at the
Ward Cheneys', where he was spending some time on his recovery
from an illness.
This is the account of the incident as given by the Rev. S. B.
Brittan:
" On the 8th of August, 1853, several gentlemen were assembled
at the residence of Ward Cheney, Esq., Manchester, Conn., where
in the course of the evening very remarkable demonstrations
occurred. One of the editors of the *Hartford Times* was present,
and from his account of the exhibition, as published in that paper,
I cut the following paragraph:
" ' Suddenly, and without any expectation on the part of the
company, the medium, Mr. Hume, was taken up in the air![3] I
had hold of his hand at the time, and I felt of his feet—they
were lifted a foot from the floor ! He palpitated from head to foot
with the contending emotions of joy and fear which choked his
utterance. Again and again he was taken from the floor, and the
third time he was carried to the ceiling of the apartment, with which

---

[1] *Traité de métapsychique*, p. 692.
[2] " There are at least a hundred recorded instances of Mr. Home's
rising from the ground, in the presence of as many separate persons "
(*Quarterly Journal of Science*, January, 1874).
[3] His name used to be spelled in this way at this time.

his hands and feet came in gentle contact. I felt the distance from the soles of his boots to the floor, and it was nearly three feet! Others touched his feet to satisfy themselves.' "[1]

This took place in the dark.[2]

A similar feat occurred seven years later at a séance at Mrs. Marshall's rooms in Red Lion Street. It has been described by the dramatist Robert Bell, who was present, in the August, 1860, number of the *Cornhill Magazine*. Thackeray, then the editor of this publication, vouched for the good faith of his contributor, who had not signed his article, *Stranger than Fiction*. This is the passage of it referring to levitation:

" Mr. Home was seated next the window. Through the semi-darkness his head was dimly visible against the curtains, and his hands might be seen in a faint white heap before him. Presently he said in a quiet voice, ' My chair is moving—I am off the ground —don't notice me—talk of something else,' or words to that effect. It was very difficult to restrain the curiosity, not unmixed with a more serious feeling, which these few words awakened; but we talked, incoherently enough, upon some indifferent topic. I was sitting nearly opposite Mr. Home, and I saw his hands disappear from the table, and his head vanish into the deep shadow beyond. In a moment or two more he spoke again. This time his voice was in the air above our heads. He had risen from his chair to a height of four or five feet from the ground. As he ascended higher he described his position, which at first was perpendicular, and after-wards became horizontal. He said he felt as if he had been turned in the gentlest manner, as a child is turned in the arms of a nurse. In a moment or two more, he told us he was going across the window, against the grey, silvery light of which he would be visible. We watched in profound stillness and saw his figure pass from one side of the window to the other, feet foremost, lying horizontally in the air. He spoke to us as he passed, and told us that he would turn the reverse way, and recross the window; which he did. His own tranquil confidence in the safety of what seemed from below a situation of the most novel peril gave confidence to everybody else; but, with the strongest nerves, it was impossible not to be conscious of a certain sensation of fear or awe. He hovered round the circle for several minutes, and passed, this time perpendicularly over our heads. I heard his voice behind me in the air, and felt something lightly brush my chair. It was his foot, which he gave me leave to

[1] Quoted from F. Podmore's *Modern Spiritualism*, vol. i, pp. 244-245.
[2] *Ibid.*, p. 245.

touch. Turning to the spot where it was on the top of the chair,
I placed my hand gently upon it, when he uttered a cry of pain,
and the foot was withdrawn quickly, with a palpable shudder. It
was evidently not resting on the chair but floating; and it sprang
from the touch as a bird would. He now passed over to the farthest
extremity of the room, and we could judge by his voice of the alti-
tude and distance he had attained. He had reached the ceiling,
upon which he made a slight mark, and soon afterwards descended
and resumed his place at the table. An incident which occurred
during this aerial passage, and imparted a strange solemnity to it,
was that the accordion, which we supposed to be on the ground under
the window close to us, played a strain of wild pathos in the air from
the most distant corner of the room."[1]

W. Crookes says that he himself was a witness of Home's levitation:

" On three separate occasions have I seen Mr. Home raised
completely from the floor of the room: once sitting on an easy
chair, once kneeling on his chair, and once standing up. On each
occasion I had full opportunity of watching the occurrence as it
was taking place."[2]

Of these three cases two have been recorded in detail by the
famous physicist. One instance took place on July 30, 1871, in
a séance where a subdued light had been substituted for gas light:

" Mr. Home walked to the open space in the room between
Mr. I.'s chair and the sideboard, and stood there quite upright
and quiet. He then said, ' I'm rising, I'm rising,' when we all saw
him rise from the ground slowly to a height of about six inches,
remain there for about ten seconds, and then slowly descend. From
my position I could not see his feet, but I distinctly saw his head,
projected against the opposite wall, rise up, and Mr. Walter Crookes,
who was sitting near where Mr. Home was, said that his feet were
in the air. There was no stool or other thing near which could
have aided him. Moreover, the movement was a continuous glide
upwards."[3]

The record for the séance of April 21, 1872, is as follows:

" A message was given, ' Try less light.' The handkerchief
moved about along the floor visible to all. Mr. Home nearly dis-

[1] Quoted from Podmore, vol. ii, pp. 49-50.
[2] *Notes of an Inquiry into the Phenomena called Spiritual*, quoted in
D. D. Home, p. 298.
[3] *Proc. S.P.R.*, vol. vi, pp. 118, 119; quoted by Podmore, vol. ii, pp.
254-255.

appeared under the table in a curious attitude; then he was (still in his chair) wheeled out from the table, still in the same attitude, his feet out in front off the ground. He was then sitting almost horizontally, his shoulders resting on his chair. He asked Mrs. Walter Crookes to remove the chair from under him, as it was not supporting him. He was then seen to be sitting in the air, supported by nothing visible."[1]

The Earl of Crawford (then Lord Lindsay) has given an account of the most noteworthy séance in Home's career, which took place on December 13, 1868,[2] at 5, Buckingham Gate, London, in the presence of Lord Lindsay himself, of Lord Adare and his cousin, Captain Charles Wynne. This is his description of the event:

" I was sitting with Mr. Home and Lord Adare and a cousin of his. During the sitting Mr. Home went into a trance, and in that state was carried out of the window in the room next to where we were, and was brought in at our window. The distance between the windows was about seven feet six inches, and there was not the slightest foothold between them, nor was there more than a twelve-inch projection to each window, which served as a ledge to put flowers on. We heard the window in the next room lifted up, and almost immediately after we saw Home floating in the air outside our window. The moon was shining full into the room; my back was to the light, and I saw the shadow on the wall of the window-sill, and Home's feet about six inches above it. He remained in this position for a few seconds, then raised the window and glided into the room feet foremost and sat down."[3]

From Lord Adare's testimony it appears that the feat was repeated another time. This is his account:

" Wynne and I went over to Ashley House after dinner. There we found Home and the Master of Lindsay. Home proposed a sitting. We accordingly sat round a table in the small room. There was no light in the room, but the light from the window was sufficient to enable us to distinguish each other, and to see the different articles of furniture. Home went into a trance. . . .

" Lindsay suddenly said: ' Oh, good heavens ! I know what he is going to do; it is too fearful.'

" Adare: ' What is it ?'

---

[1] *Ibid.*, p. 126, quoted *ibid.*, p. 255.
[2] From later information it appears that this was the correct date, and not the 16th. *Cf. Proc. S.P.R.*, vol. xxxv, p. 151.
[3] *Psychic Power—Spirit Power : Experimental Investigation*, quoted by Podmore, *ibid.*, pp. 255-256.

"Lindsay: 'I cannot tell you; it is too horrible. A spirit says that I must tell you. He is going out of the window in the other room, and coming in at this window.'

"We heard Home go into the next room, heard the window thrown up, and presently Home appeared standing upright outside our window. He opened the window and walked in quite coolly. 'Ah,' he said, 'you were good this time,' referring to our having sat still and not wished to prevent him. 'Adare, shut the window in the next room.'

"I got up, shut the window, and in coming back remarked that the window was not raised a foot, and that I could not think how he had managed to squeeze through. He arose, and said, 'Come and see.' I went with him; he told me to open the window as it was before. I did so; he told me to stand a little distance off; he then went through the open space, head first, quite rapidly, his body being nearly horizontal and apparently rigid. He came in again, feet foremost, and we returned to the other room. It was so dark I could not see clearly how he was supported outside. He did not appear to grasp, or rest upon, the balustrade, but rather to be swung out and in. Outside each window is a small balcony or ledge, nineteen inches deep, bounded by stone balustrades eighteen inches high. The balustrades of the two windows are seven feet four inches apart, measuring from the nearest point. A string-course four inches wide runs between the windows at the level of the bottom of the balustrade; another three inches wide at the level of the top. Between the window at which Home went out and that at which he came in the wall recedes six inches. The rooms are on the third floor.

"I asked Lindsay how the spirit had spoken to him. He could scarcely explain; but said it did not sound like an audible human voice, but rather as if the tones were whispered or impressed inside his ear. When Home awoke he was much agitated; he said he felt as if he had gone through some fearful peril, and that he had a most horrible desire to throw himself out of the window. He remained in a very nervous condition for a short time, then gradually became quiet."[1]

The third witness, Charles Wynne, did not give any account of the facts, but corroborated the preceding evidence in a letter to Home, in answer to an article by Dr. Carpenter, who had assumed in the *Contemporary Review* (January, 1876) that at least Captain Wynne

[1] *D. D. Home*, p. 301.

had not shared in the illusion of the two other witnesses. The letter, dated February 2, 1877, is as follows:

" DEAR DAN,—Your letter has just come before me. I remember that Dr. Carpenter wrote some nonsense about that trip of yours along the side of the house in Ashley Place. I wrote to the *Medium* to say that I was present and a witness. Now I don't think that anyone who knows me would for one moment say that I was a victim to hallucination or any other humbug of the kind. The fact of your having gone out of the window and in at the other I can swear to; but what is the use of trying to convince men who won't believe anything—not even if they see it? I don't care a straw whether Dr. Carpenter or Mr. Hammond believe me or not—it does not prevent the fact having occurred. But this I *will* say, that if you are not to believe the corroborative evidence of *three* un-impeached witnesses, there would be an end to all justice and courts of law. . . ."[1]

Other levitations of the same medium are to be found described more or less accurately in the report of the Dialectical Society.[2]

By a notable exception in the annals of mediumship Home is said to have been levitated in full light. Among others, Mr. Enmore Jones records that he saw Home rise vertically in the air a foot above the floor by the light of a single burner and a bright fire.[3] As Lord Lindsay was asked by the Committee of the Dialectical Society whether the phenomenon of levitation invariably occurred in darkness or semi-darkness, he answered: " No, I once saw Home in full light standing in the air seventeen inches from the ground."[4] fortunately, no details regarding such full-light séances are available.

D. D. Home is even said to have possessed the faculty of pro-ducing levitation in others. There is at least one instance of it on record. The testimony is by Dr. Thomas Hawksley, who had the medium as a client and a friend.

" On another occasion," writes the doctor, " a friend, a young and highly intelligent man, asked me to introduce him to Mr. Home. I said, ' Come with me—I am just going to see him.' It was a bright summer's afternoon, about 3 p.m. We were shown into one of the ordinary sitting-rooms at Cox's Hotel, not a room occupied by Mr. Home. When the latter came in, I said to him, ' This is Sir ——, a very valued friend of mine; and he is anxious to know you,

[1] *D. D. Home*, pp. 306-307.
[2] Sittings of April 27, May 11, June 22, July 6.
[3] Podmore, vol. ii, p. 254.
[4] *D. D. Home*, p. 299.

25

and, if possible, to see something of the marvellous phenomena which take place in your presence.' Mr. Home was, as usual, most kind. ' I am always happy,' he said, ' to do anything to please a friend of Dr. Hawksley's, but he knows that I have no power of commanding them—I am obliged to accept whatever comes.' He then added, ' We will try '; and, addressing my companion, said, ' Sir ——, will you stand on that table ?' My friend stood on the table, an ordinary centre-claw table of great strength and weight. Immediately table and man rose in the air for at least eight inches from the ground. I stooped down and swept my hand freely between the castors and the carpet. After I had ended all the investigation I could give the phenomenon, the table came down to the floor and Sir —— descended from his elevation."[1]

About the same time another celebrated medium, William Stainton Moses, formerly a curate in the Isle of Man, then English master in University College School, is said to have experienced the same phenomenon. He himself has left the record of his first levitation, which occurred on June 30, 1870. In this account W. S. Moses records that he was lifted up from the floor with his chair about twelve inches high; then he was raised off the chair and glided up gently near to the ceiling. He was fully conscious of the phenomenon, and felt as if he were in a lift. He placed a pencil firmly against his chest and marked the spot opposite to him on the wallpaper. The mark was ascertained to be more than six feet from the floor.[2]

In August, 1888, Professor Ercole Chiaja wrote to C. Lombroso asking him to experiment with him with the medium Eusapia Palladino, who was in the course of time to become celebrated. " This woman," he said, " is lifted up into the air . . .; she remains thus, lying in the air, in contradiction to every law of statics, and seems to be freed from the law of gravitation."[3] In 1889, the same observer sent to the Spiritualistic Congress a detailed account of the upliftings experienced by Eusapia that year at Naples. In 1892 the medium gave séances at Milan, and according to the report drawn up by Aksakof her levitation was again ascertained. Later on the same phenomenon was witnessed in Warsaw by Ochorowicz

¹ D. D. Home, p. 188.
² Cf. Human Nature, 1874, pp. 172, 173; Proc. S.P.R., vol. ix, p. 261, quoted by Podmore, vol. ii, p. 278.
³ Grasset, L'occultisme, p. 397.

and in France by de Rochas.[1] From the different reports it appears that, with this medium, the facts were of a very vague and elusive character. This is, for instance, the report drawn up after the séance held on September 27, 1895, at l'Agnélas (Isére) at Colonel de Rochas' villa, in the presence of MM. Sabatier, doyen of the Faculté des Sciences of Montpellier, Colonel de Rochas, Comte Arnaud de Gramont, Dr. Dariex, J. Maxwell, and Baron de Watteville:

" 10.50.—MM. de Gramont, Sabatier, de Rochas are successively touched on the head, on the shoulder, on the back, on the arm. At this moment Dr. Dariex, feeling tired, leaves the room. Mr. Maxwell gives his place on Eusapia's left to de Rochas. M. de Gramont no longer supervises Eusapia's legs, and passes on to the right in the place of M. Sabatier. M. de Rochas holds Eusapia's left hand and M. de Gramont the right one.

" Eusapia asks for the table to be removed from the window, and, being taken towards the middle of the room, her hands are supervised as before; her right foot rests on M. de Gramont's left foot, her left foot on M. de Rochas' right one.

" Eusapia says several times ' *Alzare, alzare,*' that is ' Rising, rising,' meaning that she is going to try to rise. She wants MM. de Gramont and de Rochas, who hold her hands, to follow the ascending movement of her hands, but without helping her up nor hindering the ascent. After some minutes, and in a nearly complete darkness where the figures are hardly perceived, Eusapia *without support from the hands of the observers*, who simply follow her own, nor from the feet of the same observers on which her feet are resting, seems to M. de Gramont, who is holding her right hand, to be rising *in a sitting posture*, with a continuous gliding and rather rapid movement, but not with any noticeable jump, as if she were in a lift. The chair rises with her and her feet reach *about* the level of the table. The observers stand up at the same time to follow the uplifting movement. From this moment she escapes the control of the two observers, as her hands are no longer held by them. M. Sabatier, who is on the right of M. de Gramont, tries to ascertain by feeling in the dark if Eusapia, while rising, helps herself up with a knee on the table, but he could not perceive anything clearly. MM. de Gramont and de Rochas declare that Eusapia rose up with her chair not quite level with the table, without leaning on them or on their hands or feet.

" The surprise somewhat disconcerts and relaxes the supervision; it is simply ascertained that Eusapia is *standing* with her chair

[1] De Rochas, *Recueil*, pp. 82 ff.

27

on the table. She tries to rise again vertically; M. Sabatier passes his hand rapidly under Eusapia's soles and finds that her heels are raised above the surface of the table, but that Eusapia stands on tiptoe.

" Then Eusapia collapses; those at her sides receive her in their arms and seat her on the floor.

" We should add that one of those near the table nearly fainted, not with emotion, but with exhaustion, saying that he felt all his strength drawn from his body by Eusapia's exertions."[1]

More recently similar phenomena were observed by Dr. Schwab with Maria Vollhardt and by Dr. von Schrenck-Notzing with Willy Sch. The latter, according to M. René Sudre, several times rose in the air in the presence of Professors Holub and Berzé and of Herr Hans Müller in Vienna. The medium was dressed in black tights studded with phosphorescent pins; his body was quite visible by the red light. " He rose horizontally and seemed to rest on an invisible cloud. He ascended to the ceiling and remained five minutes suspended there, moving his legs about rhythmically. The descent was as sudden as the uplifting. The supervision had been perfect. Geley in his last journey to Vienna also witnessed a levitation of Willy at Dr. Holub's, and he told me he felt absolutely sure of the genuineness of the phenomenon."[2]

Among the last feats of mediumistic levitation should be mentioned those of the Brazilian Carlos Mirabelli, of whom very few details have so far been obtained. According to a pamphlet published at Sao Vincente and reviewed by the *Revue métapsychique*, this medium was levitated in the presence of different members of the Academy Cesare Lombroso, created with the special purpose of observing his manifestations. Carlos Mirabelli was fastened to an armchair; he is said to have thus risen from the ground, and to have remained two minutes suspended twelve feet over the floor. The witnesses were able to pass and repass under the levitated body. At Santos the same medium is reported to have experienced a levitation in the street, being lifted up from a motor-car for about three minutes.[3]

[1] Rochas, *Recueil*, pp. 82-84. The italics are in the original. *Cf* pp. 72 *ff.*, accounts of similar experiments with Eusapia; pp. 85 *ff.*, séances with Fontana and Ruggieri.
[2] Sudre, *Introduction à la métapsychique*, p. 248.
[3] *Revue métapsychique*, No. 2, 1927, pp. 145 *ff.*, review of a pamphlet published in June, 1926, at São Vincente by Rodolpho Mikulash.

§ 2. MAGNETIC ATTRACTION

Levitation is said to have occurred at times as the result of magnetisation. Charpignon, in his *Physiologie du magnétisme*, says that one Bourguignon of Rouen had thus lifted from the ground several of his subjects. The latter described one of his experiments as follows in a letter to Dr. Charpignon, dated June 3, 1840:

" As I had found that all his limbs could follow my movements every time I wished, it occurred to me to draw them up. After successful attempts I put my hand two or three inches over the epigastrium, and the whole body was raised and remained suspended . . . I will add that as the person I magnetise had been ill six weeks ago with inflammation of the lungs, I left off raising him horizontally lest it should tire him; I now place my hand over his head and lift him up from the floor so as to be able to pass my hand or a stick several times under his feet."[1]

This M. Bourguignon declared that he had succeeded in his experiment eight times out of ten, but he had failed with every other subject.[2]

A similar uplifting is said to have been produced by a magnetiser of Montauban, M. Théron, who succeeded in raising a somnambulist off the floor. Charpignon says he vouches for the honesty of the experimenter.[3]

Another instance of magnetic levitation may be found in the *Journal du magnétisme*, published by Ricard. The latter in his number of November, 1840, says that a Dr. Schmidt of Vienna, who wanted to magnetise his daughter for some therapeutic purpose, was very surprised one day when he found that his patient arose above her be under his passes.[4]

Dr. Justinus Kerner got the same result with Friederike Hauffe, the celebrated Seherin von Prevorst, when he magnetised her. She would then rise at a simple touch of the fingers.[5] She is also reported to have been at times so buoyant that her body would float like cork in her bath.[6]

---

[1] Quoted by de Rochas, p. 93.   [2] *Ibid.*, p. 94.   [3] *Ibid.*   [4] *Ibid.*

[5] *Die Seherin von Prevorst*, p. 43: " Allein vermochte sowohl ich als meine Frau sie, wie gegen alle Gesetze der Schwerkraft, hielten wir unsere Finger an die ihrigen und war sie vorher sich nicht aufzurichten fähig, weit in die Höhe zu ziehen."

[6] *Ibid.:* " So oft man sie (in magnetischem Zustande) in ein Bad bringen wollte, zeigte sich die sonderbare Erscheinung, dass alle ihre Glieder, auch Brust und Unterleib, in ein unwillkürliches Hüpfen, in eine völlige Elastizität kamen, die sie aus dem Wasser immer wieder austiesz. Ge-

LEVITATION

The magnetist, Ch. Lafontaine, has recorded in his *Mémoires* the case of an English girl whose fits were quite like those theoretically described by psychiatrists.[1] The patient had experienced them from the age of fourteen; she was eighteen when Lafontaine met her. When he came to see her the first time, he found her lying motionless on her bed, like a dead person. Her face was ghastly pale and covered with perspiration. Suddenly this seeming corpse became alive.

" With a bound the girl was in the middle of the room, staring with wide-open eyes, moving her arms about, standing on tiptoe and running, half naked, about the room; then she threw herself down on the floor in a fit of horrible convulsions, knocking herself everywhere and shrieking, striking the persons who tried to hold her back lest she should hurt herself. Then recovering her feet suddenly and uttering words with inarticulate sounds, she walked in a straight line and with a firm pace, and jumped to an incredible height; then writhing into impossible attitudes, she put her head between her knees, lifted up one leg and whirled on the other with amazing rapidity, keeping her head near the floor. Now she stood up, shouting as if in a great fright, now she kissed lovingly imaginary people; then she collapsed exhausted on the floor.

" A moment after, she sprang up again and ran about the apartment, putting her naked feet on the articles of furniture, on glasses, the globe of the clock, on all those brittle gimcracks that are laid on shelves, without breaking or even upsetting anything. . . . Soon after her eyes expressed an ineffable bliss; she fell on her knees, her lips moved about as if she was praying. She was entranced; she said verse, announced events that actually happened; she rose into the air as if she was going to fly up; then she sank down again on the floor, motionless, without apparent breathing. The fit was over; it had lasted two hours."[2]

Lafontaine says that after three months' magnetising he succeeded in curing the neurotic girl.

---

hilfinnen, die bei ihr waren, gaben sich alle Mühe, sie mit Gewalt in das Wasser zu drücken, aber ihre Spannkraft strebte immer nach oben, sie könnte nicht unter gehalten werden, und hätte man sie in einen Flusz geworfen, sie wäre wohl auch in diesem so wenig wie ein Pantoffelholz untergesunken."

[1] *Cf. infra*, pp. 159-160.

[2] *Mémoires d'un magnétiseur*, vol. i, pp. 284 *ff*. Lafontaine gave séances in England in 1841. Some of them were recorded in the *Manchester Times* (Nov. 13) and the *Manchester Guardian* (Nov. 13 and 17). It was by attending one of these that J. Braid was led to his explanation of hypnotism.

The same author declares that he saw another of his patients, Mme. d'A., perform a feat closely allied to levitation. It occurred in these circumstances: as he was magnetising Mme. d'A., a relative of hers, Mlle. Laure, happened to play on the piano in the adjoining room. As soon as she heard the tune the magnetised person sat up, then stood up on her bed; " presently her feet glided on to the side of the bed without any motion of the muscles, and she got slowly down, with her legs close together and unsupported, on to the carpet. . . . Her body seemed to be sustained in the air by invisible strings; her limbs were stiff. . . . When on the carpet her feet kept gliding along without the least motion or contraction. She looked like a statue set on a board and drawn by somebody or sliding on rails without any jerk."[1]

[1] *Ibid.*, vol. ii, p. 96.

PART II
CHRISTIAN HAGIOGRAPHY

SECTION I
TRADITIONS COMMON TO ALL OR SOME OF THE CHRISTIAN CHURCHES

CHAPTER I
OLD AND NEW TESTAMENT RECORDS

BEFORE giving an account of the traditions of the different Christian Churches, it may be advisable to mention some which belong to their common fund, the Old and New Testaments.

Truth to tell, no belief in levitation as a phenomenon of mystical life is to be found in these books. They rather refer to far-distant transports of the human body, where the latter seems to be quite passive, whereas in the levitation of the mystics—all reserves being made regarding the reality or causes of the phenomenon—the moral dispositions and psychic conditions of the levitated person appear to play a certain part. Besides, the translation of the body is, in the case of the mystics, exceptional.

The following Scriptural facts may be recalled here:

Enoch, according to Genesis, was borne alive from the earth.[1] Elijah, as he walked with Elisha, was suddenly taken up on a whirlwind, described by Elijah as a blazing chariot.[2] Habakkuk was carried from Judea to Babylon to bring food to Daniel in the lions' den, then carried back to Judea through the air. The angel of the Lord,

---

[1] Gen. v 24: *Ambulavitque cum Deo, et non apparuit, quia tulit eum Deus.*

[2] 4 Reg. ii 11: *Cumque pergerent, et incedentes sermocinarentur, ecce currus igneus et equi ignei diviserunt utrumque ; et ascendit Elias per turbinem in coelum.*

says the text, took hold of the top of his head and carried him by the hair, and set him in Babylon over the den in the force of his spirit; then set him back again in his own place.[1] In a similar way was Philip the deacon suddenly caught away from the road to Gaza, after he had baptised the eunuch of Candace. But here no angel is referred to; Philip is only said to have been taken away by the Spirit of the Lord, and the eunuch saw him no more.[2]

Under the same head should be mentioned the transport of Christ by Satan to the pinnacle of the temple of Jerusalem, then to the top of a high mountain.[3]

Lastly, it is by a levitation that Christ's earthly life is closed when, having taken his disciples towards Bethany, he was raised up and vanished from their view.[4] According to St Paul's teaching, it is in the same way that, at the parousia, the elect shall be taken up into the air to meet their Lord.[5]

St Paul's rapture cannot be mentioned as a case of levitation, but it proves that the notion of bodily transport was familiar at the time.[6]

The tradition according to which St Mary of Bethany had levitations during her ecstasies should also be stated here for its connection with the New Testament. In her solitude of the Sainte-Baume,

---

[1] Dan. xiv 32-38: *Et apprehendit eum angelus Domini in vertice ejus ; et portavit eum capillo capitis sui, posuitque eum in Babylone, supra lacum, in impetu spiritus sui. . . . Porro restituit Habacuc confestim in loco suo.*

[2] Acts viii 39: *Spiritus Domini rapuit Philippum.*

[3] Matt. iv 5-8; Luke iv 5-8. The second text has *duxit illum.* Some commentators have inferred from it that there is no reference to a real carrying of the body. In support of this thesis one may argue that the verb used in St Matthew (*assumere,* παραλαμβάνειν) does not imply physical transport (*cf. ibid.,* xvii 1, xxvii 27).

[4] Luke xxiv 51; Mark xvi 19; Acts i 9. A levitation of magical character is also ascribed to Christ in a scurrilous work of Hebrew origin, *Toledôth Yeshū* (Life of Jesus), composed about the sixth century, the original text of which was published for the first time in 1681 by J. Wagenseil in a collection entitled *Tela ignea Satanae.* In this book, Christ is a magician whose power is derived from the possession of the secret name of the Lord stolen by him from the Temple. Thanks to the charm, he can work all sorts of miracles in presence of the Queen; among others, his own uplifting into the clouds. But Judas, one of the Sages of Jerusalem, also in possession of the ineffable name, is able to vie with him, and even to bring him down to earth again. (*Les Evangiles apocryphes,* ed. G. Brunet, pp. 390-391).

[5] 1 Thess. iv 16: *Deinde nos, qui vivimus, qui relinquimur, simul rapiemur cum illis in nubibus obviam Christo in aera.*

[6] 2 Cor. xii 2-4.

33

the sister of Lazarus and Martha is said to have continued her life of contemplation and seven times a day was raised off the earth. The shrine called the Saint-Pilon still marks the spot where these raptures are believed to have taken place.[1]

[1] Lacordaire, *Sainte Marie-Madeleine*, Works, vol. ix, pp. 423 *ff*. Practically, the tradition of Mary's living in Provence is without serious historic grounds.

CHAPTER II

COPTIC, GREEK, AND RUSSIAN CHURCHES

St Ammon (†350).—St Antony the Great (251–†356).—St Mary the Egyptian (354–†431).—Shnudi (333–†451).—St Joannicus (†845).—St Luke the Younger (890–†946).—St Andrew Salus (†956).—Seraphinus of Sarov (†1833).

THE traditions recorded in the present chapter are remarkably incomplete. Very likely the list of the levitations mentioned in the Lives of the Saints or mystics in the Oriental Churches would have grown much longer if by linguistic ignorance I had not been debarred access to needful documents.[1] Therefore this chapter should only be considered as a pigeon-hole for future information to be lodged in, should benevolent correspondents supply me with it. For the present it may serve to show that the belief in levitation has obtained, or obtains, in the above-mentioned Churches.

Of course, several of the saints or holy persons who are mentioned below belong also to the Catholic Church, as they are prior to the Oriental schism.

As regards the Protestant Churches, I have not found any tradition as to the levitation of their mystics. It may be noticed here, in this respect, that the ardent atmosphere of revivals has not brought forth any belief of the kind—at least, to my knowledge.

＊　　　＊　　　＊　　　＊　　　＊

One might expect to find many cases of levitation in the Lives of the Fathers of the Desert, so rich in prodigies. They are, on the contrary, very few. One simply reads in the Life of St Antony the Great that one day St Ammon was miraculously carried over a tributary of the Nile.[2] As to St Antony himself, he is said to have felt lifted up into the air when rapt in ecstasy.[3]

A fact of levitation proper is reported in the Life of St Mary the Egyptian. These are the circumstances of it: St Zosimus,

[1] Like *The Lives of the Saints* by Dimitri of Rostov, which would have probably brought me some instances like that of Seraphinus.
[2] *A.S.*, Life by St Athanasius, vol. ii of Jan., ch. xx, p. 498.
[3] *Ibid.*, ch. xxii.

35

about the year 430, had crossed the Jordan to spend Lent in the wilderness. One day he came across an uncouth-looking creature, with white dishevelled hair, whose tanned naked body told of long exposure. It was Mary the Egyptian. She asked him to throw her his cloak. She wrapped herself in it and drew near. After exchanging some words they began to pray. Her prayer was so long that Zosimus at last looked up, and he was in great awe when he saw the penitent in rapture and floating in mid-air.[1]

St Pachomius was still alive when, in 343, a ten-year-old child, the son of poor fellahs, was being initiated by his uncle, the anchoret Bgul, into the coenobitic life. The child, Shnudi, was to be one of the most picturesque characters of Egyptian monachism. When Bgul died, Shnudi became the head of the monastery. His apostolic zeal often assumed violent forms; he organised regular raids with his monks against pagan temples, whose idols he destroyed. Two expeditions of the kind caused him to be prosecuted. As he was sailing under escort to Antinoe he stopped one evening near a village to spend the night there. Before going to sleep he set himself under a vine to pray and implore divine protection. Then, he said, an angel appeared to him saying: " Peace be with you; instead of speaking to the Governor from the earth, you shall speak to him from on high." The next day they landed at Antinoe. Shnudi was taken to the tribunal of the Governor of Upper Egypt to be examined. The whole town was there, pagans and Christians. Now, reports Visa, the disciple and biographer of Shnudi, when the latter answered the magistrate " he was uplifted into the air by the angels of the Lord to such a height that he could still be heard." " There is no other God than the God of our Father, the holy *anba* Shnudi !" they all cried out. Shnudi remained thus suspended over the court for some time, then he sank gradually down. As soon as he had set his feet on the ground the crowd rushed towards him and bore him in triumph on their shoulders to a church near the River Nile, where all were thronging to receive his benediction.[2]

Joannicus, first a shepherd, then a soldier, became an anchoret

[1] *A.S.*, vol. i of April, p. 80 A: *Juravit autem, sermonis sui testem appellans Deum, quod animadvertens longius protrahi orationem, oculos aliquantum a terra sustulit, viditque ipsam orare in altum sublatam, et in aere suspensam velut ad cubitum unum: quod cum vidit, majori correptus metu, multumque anxius, et omnino nihil proloqui audens, solum intra se dicebat identidem, Domine miserere.*
[2] E. Amélineau, *Les moines égyptiens. Vie de Schnoudi*, pp. 318-319.

when he was about forty. After twelve years he entered a monastery and became an abbot in Bithynia. One Eustratius, espying him as he was in contemplation, saw him twice raised two cubits above the ground.[1]

St Luke the younger, born in Thessaly about the close of the ninth century, was first a herdsman. He next entered a monastery near Athens, then retired to Mount Joannitsa (near the Bay of Corinth) to live as an anchoret. He had to flee from there at the time of the invasion by the Bulgars in 915. He lived some time in Corinth as servant of a stylite, and later went back to his retreat of Mount Joannitsa, which he left again for the wilderness of Soterion, where he died in 946. His Life was written by an anonymous monk, who says that he was his contemporary and disciple.[2] From his boyhood Luke led a life of penance and contemplation. His mother, eager to know why he used to hide himself, watched him. She saw him in ecstasy lifted off the earth. Wondering if she had not been deceived, she watched him again and ascertained the fact.[3]

Andrew Salus lived in the first half of the tenth century, and died about 948 in Constantinople. Nicephorus, a priest of St Sophia, his biographer, reports that he was seen one day in prayer, with his hands lifted up and his body raised from the earth. Nicephorus

[1] *A.S.*, vol. ii of Nov., p. 352 EF: *Inde quadam die, cum orationis gratia solus remansisset sanctus occupatusque contemplationis suavitate diutius detineretur et remoraretur abiens ut sciret causam morae ejus Eustratius vidit eum procul intentum orationi, et quibusdam quasi invisibilibus loris vel alis duobus cubitis a terra in aethere suspensum. Ibid., p. 398 B: Cum ibi (in antro in quo recedebat ad orandum) moratus esset per longum tempus cogitavit laudatus Eustratius quare esset tanta mora. Surgens igitur cum prope speluncam inspecturus advenisset, videt sanctum in oratione non super terram stantem sed suspensum a terra in aere quasi duobus cubitis totum illuminatum et supra solem splendentem.*
[2] *A.S.*, vol. ii of Feb., p. 83 C.
[3] *Ibid.*, p. 85 CD: *Illa namque ipsis oculis contueri desiderans, quidnam filius inter secreta noctis silentia operis faceret, profundo jam vespere, sociis aliis foeminis, prope accidit : tum apte captans latebras, ut videret quidem ipsa a nullo autem penitus conspici posset ; magnum illud visuque pariter atque auditu tremendum cernit, uti iterum ipsa mater jurejurando vidisse affirmavit his, qui illa modo essent enarraturi. Erat orationi intentus totaque mentis attentione Deo assistebat. Pedes autem ne quid minimum terram tangebant, velutque in Deum toto corpore attollebatur. Hoc mater cum non semel sed iterum tertioque oculis percepisset, finem dubitandi fecit, nec ultra periculum facere quaesiit*

37

LEVITATION

had it from an eye-witness, Epiphanius, who became afterwards
Patriarch of Constantinople.[1]

The belief in levitation still prevails in the modern Russian
Church, as it appears from the following story which I pick out of
an article by M. Pierre Iswolsky on Seraphinus of Sarov.   Seraphinus lived in the first half of the nineteenth century. He was
proclaimed saint in 1903 by Nicholas II.
   " St Seraphinus, while he prayed, was raised off the earth as if the
law of gravitation did not exist for him.   A paralytic was once taken
into his cell lying on a bed.   St Seraphinus exhorted him to con-
centrate all his thoughts into one fervent prayer for recovery, without looking towards him, and then knelt down praying before an
image of the Holy Virgin.   Complying with the saint's order, the
invalid did not turn his eyes for some time towards him, but feeling
curious, he looked round; he saw St Seraphinus in the attitude of
prayer, lifted up in the air, and could not help crying out for surprise.
St Seraphinus told him sternly: ' The Lord will cure you, but keep
this in your mind: do not believe that Seraphinus is a saint, and till
I am dead, never tell anybody what you have seen.'   The invalid
rose, restored to health, and came back to the inn of the monastery.
He did not answer the questions that were put to him on the way he
had been cured, and only disclosed the mystery after the death of
the saint."[2]

[1] For further details cf. A.S., vol. vi of May, pp. 15-16, Corollarium ad
xxviii maii: *Accumbente igitur Andrea, quemadmodum supra meminimus,
in oenopolio cum venerabilibus illis adolescentibus mensae ; forte auribus meis
praetereuntis illac, hominum infimi, allapsa vox ejus est ; et declinans tantisper
a via, contuli me ad vestibulum, clam, quid ageretur speculaturus.   Igitur cum
adolescentes salutato Andrea viam suam prosequerentur, accidit etiam cauponem,
qui Christianus erat, cujusdam rei causa officina egredi, et Andream intus
manere solum : qui huc atque illuc circumspiciens, ubi neminem deprehendit,
extensis in cœlum manibus precari pro tribus memoratis adolescentibus coepit, et
(testis mihi Deus est, qui perdit loquentes mendacio), levatus a terra in aerem
sublimis pependit.*
   [2] *Un Saint russe au dix-neuvième siècle*, in *Les Lettres*, Oct. 1, 1921,
pp. 493-494.

SECTION II
CATHOLIC TRADITIONS

CHAPTER I

ANCIENT TRADITIONS (FROM THE ORIGIN TO THE THIRTEENTH CENTURY)

St Dunstan (918-†988).—St Stephen of Hungary (977-†1038).—St Ladislaus of Hungary (1041-†1095).—St Bernard (1091-†1153).—St Dominic (1170-†1221).—St Christina the Admirable (†1224).—St Francis of Assisi (1186-†1226).—Blessed Philippinus (*contemporary of St Francis*). —Peter of Monticello (*do.*).—St Jutta (†1226).—St Elisabeth of Hungary (1207-†1231).—Blessed Bentivoglio de Bonis (†1232).—Blessed Gherardesca (†1240).—St Edmund (†1242).—St Hedwig (†1243).— St Lutgard (1182-†1246).—Blessed Agnes of Assisi (1198-†1253).— Blessed Giles of Santarem (1190-†1267).—St Margaret of Hungary (1242-†1271).—St Douceline (1214-†1274).—St Bonaventure (1221-†1274).—St Thomas Aquinas (1226-†1274).—St Agnes of Bohemia (1203-†1282).—St Ambrose of Siena (1220-†1286).—Blessed Franco (†1291).—St Albert (1212-†1292).—Blessed Benvenuta Bojano (†1292). —St Margaret of Cortona (1247-†1297).—Blessed Helena of Hungary (1235-†1298).

S‌T DUNSTAN, Archbishop of Canterbury, is so well known for the part he played in the religious and political life of England that I need not give here even an outline of his biography. Let us only say that, according to one of his biographers, he was seen uplifted to the ceiling of the cathedral, in the presence of many witnesses, on Ascension Day, three days before his death, May 17, 988.[1]   A former biography, whose anonymous author gives

[1] *A.S.*, vol. iv of May, p. 374 D: *Post prandium vero, vel magis ultimam coenam, denuo cum Fratribus ecclesiam Christi ingreditur, signatoque sepulcri sui loco, omnibus ad altare Christi ascendentibus conspicuo, coenaculum pro modo aestivi temporis requieturus ascendit.   Circumdat pausantem luctifica Ecclesiae familia : quae sive metu sui, seu morte illius turbata, horrendos lacrymando quaestus insonuit.   Quos illo sanctissimis ut semper rationibus fovente atque ad spem futuri seculi diligentibus informante, conspiciunt virum invisibili quadam Dei virtute e terra moveri, motum ad suprema domus festigia tolli.   Hi autem, qui paulo ante propinquiores astiterant, miraculi insolentia territi, relictis*

39

LEVITATION

himself as a contemporary and ocular witness, does not refer to the event.[1]

St Stephen, King of Hungary, died on August 15, 1038. The Pope Benedict IX canonised him a few years later. He is said to have experienced levitation during his prayers. No concrete details are available.[2]

The Life of one of Stephen's successors on the throne of Hungary, St Ladislaus, contains a similar fact, reported with more details. One night Ladislaus had remained a long time praying in the monastery of Warasdin. His servant, who waited for him outside, growing impatient, entered the chapel. There he saw his master in contemplation lifted above the floor.[3]

Of St Bernard, Abbot of Clairvaux and Doctor of the Church, Görres reports a case of levitation while he was preaching.[4] I was unable to trace this fact to any original source.

One year before his death (1220), St Dominic, the founder of the Preaching Friars, was spending some time in Castres as a

---

sedibus devolant omnes. Stant tamen innixi parietibus et maceriarum liminibus, de longe sursum aspicientes, exitum rei videre cupientes. Existimabant namque, aut alio quovis et insolito modo ab eis tollendum. Sed mox ea qua subvectus fuerat suavitate depositus, convocat omnes qui fugam inierant, tali eos allocutione demulcens. (Vita auctore Osberno Praecentore Cantuariensi, Ex MS. Antuerpiense et Bonifontis.)

[1] *Ibid., Vita auctore B. Presbytero coaevo, et teste oculato, p. 245 et seq.*

[2] *A.S.*, vol. i of Sept., p. 541 BC: *Deinde eo ardentius pro explorata divinae clementiae gratia, in Dei charitate permansit : quem in partiendo tempore, tali usum instituto fuisse ferunt, interdiu dicendo juri, ac regalibus officiis et negociis ducere, in divina contemplatione versari, cum assiduis lacrymis pro publica et privata salute supplicare, piis precibus aequiora Numina reddere, in divinam quandoque contemplationem usque adeo rapi, ut homo subtractus, in aëre pendere videretur : nam quum in remotam quandam basilicam secessisset . . . Numinis exorandi causa, distentis circum tentoriis noctem transegit; qua quidem intempesta, quum in tabernaculo ad contemplandum suscitaretur, usque adeo in Divinitatis contemplatione correptus est, ut corpus evectam in aëra mentem subsequeretur.*

[3] *Ibid., vol. vii of June, p. 286: Quadam nocte Waradinense monasterium ingressus est, ut oraret. Factum est autem, dum prolixius oraret, quidam cubicularius ejus, qui foris eum solus expectabat, praenimia mora taedio affectus, surrexit et introspexit ; viditque Dominum suum, glorificato corpore, sursum in aere mirabiliter elevatum.*

[4] *La mystique*, vol. ii, ch. xxi, p. 284.

40

guest of the Benedictine monastery of the town. One day, as he had retired to the chapel and was late for dinner, the Prior, Friar Matthew, sent for him. The messenger found the saint praying before the altar, lifted up a cubit above the floor. He reported the fact to the Prior, who went himself to the chapel, where he beheld Dominic still raised above the earth.[1] He is also said to have been levitated on the day when he brought miraculously to life the nephew of Cardinal Orsini, who had fallen from his horse. These are the words of Sister Caecilia, who is said to have been an eye-witness of the event: " But when he came to the elevation of our Lord's body and held it on high between his hands, he himself was raised a cubit above the ground, all beholding the same, and being filled with great wonder at the sight."[2] This took place at St Sixtus' Church in Rome.

St Christina the Admirable was born about 1150 at Saint-Trond, in the diocese of Liège. Her Life was written eight years after her death by Thomas of Cantimpré, who says he questioned many eye-witnesses, among them Thomas, the parish priest of Saint-Trond, then Abbot of the abbey of the same name. This biography was published in the Acta (vol. v of July). One reads in it that after being considered dead, Christina, in the course of her funeral, was raised up to the vault of the church, where she remained suspended. Everybody fled at the sight, except her elder sister and the priest.[3] From that day Christina's life was a long series of torments on behalf of her relatives, who considered her

---

[1] A.S., vol. i of Aug., p. 405: . . . Hujus tunc Prioris tempore beatus Dominicus more suo remansit ante altare in ecclesia orans. Cum autem jam ascendisset dies, et prandium paratum esset, et mensa posita, misit Prior unum de clericis, qui ad prandium vocaret sanctum ; qui cum intrasset ecclesiam, vidit beatum virum Dominicum totaliter separatum a terra, et quasi per unum cubitum in aere elevatum. Tremens ac stupens nuntiat hoc domino suo, qui aliquandiu expectans tandem ivit, quasi per unum cubitum elevatum vidit et tanto tempore expectavit, quousque a celesti habitatione revertens ad incolatum corporeum ante altare prostratus jacuit.

[2] Ibid., p. 575 E: Cum vero corpus Domini Jesu tenens purissimis manibus, elevasset in altum, cunctis qui adfuerunt, videntibus et stupentibus, ipse pariter a terra in altitudinem unius cubiti elevatus est. Cf. p. 458 D.

[3] A.S., vol. v of July, p. 651, n. 4 and 5: Memorabilis Christi virgo Christina ex oppido S. Trudonis in Hasbania honestis parentibus oriunda fuit . . . Ex interno contemplationis exercitio virtute corporis infirmata, vita excederet. . . . Mane ergo facto, ad ecclesiam deportatur. Cumque, pro depositione ejus missarum oblatio fieret, subito commotum corpus exsurrexit in feretro, statimque instar avis evecta, templi trabes ascendit. . . . A presbytero ecclesiae sacramento constricta est coacta descendere.

41

as possessed. She avoided company, took shelter in wild places, on trees, up towers or on churches.[1] She could remain suspended from tiny branches like a bird.[2] Sometimes she was to be found poised on the top of a pole, singing the Psalms.[3]

Of St Francis of Assisi's life nothing needs to be said. Everybody knows something about it. The levitations recorded in his biography by St Bonaventure or in the *Actus* (Fioretti) are as follows: At the end of his life, when he had retired to La Verna, his ecstasies grew more frequent. Brother Leo, his favourite disciple, had been entrusted with taking bread and water to him twice a day, to the cave where he sheltered himself on the side of the mountain. Now, it happened that Brother Leo found the saint in ecstasy outside the cave, and his body was floating in mid-air, so high that he could only reach his feet. Sometimes he found him lifted half-way up the tall beech-trees that grew there; or again he was raised so high as nearly to vanish from view.[4] Sometimes a bright halo surrounded his entranced body.[5]

Some writers say that one day St Francis carried off Brother Masseo in a levitation along with him. This seems to originate from a strained interpretation of the text of the *Actus*, where the saint is simply said to have taken hold of Brother Masseo in a fit of ecstatic rapture and have raised him above the ground. The text does not suggest that Francis himself remained suspended.[6]

[1] *Ibid.*, p. 652 B: . . . *cum Christina hominum praesentias miro horrore fugeret in desertis, in arboribus, in summitatibus turrium vel templorum, vel quarumlibet rerum sublimium, putantes eam plenam daemonibus.* . . .

[2] *Ibid.*, p. 653 A: *Instar passeris in subtilissimis arborum ramusculis dependeret.*

[3] *Ibid.*: *Super palos etiam sepium frequenter stabat erecta et ibi Psalmorum decantabat cursum.*

[4] *Actus*, c. 9, 32-35: *Et aliquando inveniebat eum extra cellam elevatum in aere per tantum spatium quod poterat tangere pedes ejus. Et tunc amplexabatur pedes ejus et deosculabatur cum lacrymis, dicens: " Deus, propitius esto mihi peccatori, et per merita hujus sanctissimi viri fac me tuam misericordiam invenire." Aliquando vero invenit eum usque ad medios fagos elevatum a terra. Erant autem ibi de dictis arboribus procerae altitudinis valde. Aliquando vero invenit eum in tanta altitudine aeris elevatum a terra quod vix eum videre valebat. Et tunc frater Leo genuflectebat et totum se extendebat in terram, in loco scilicet unde sanctus pater orando erat assumptus in altum. Cf. ibid.,* c. 39, 5-7, pp. 128-129, and *A.S.*, vol. ii of Oct., p. 858 B.

[5] *A.S.*, vol. ii of Oct., p. 769 F: . . . *visus est nocte orans, manibus ad modum crucis protensis, tot corpore sublevatus a terra, et nubecula quadam fulgente circumdatus.* . . .

[6] *Actus*, c. 13, 14-19, pp. 47-48: *Et quum pervenissent ad quamdam ecclesiam, intrantes in eam, sanctus Franciscus abscondit se post altare ad orandum.*

Of other two companions of St Francis—whom I place here as contemporaries, though I do not know the exact dates of their births and deaths—Blessed Philippinus and Peter of Monticello, levitations are also recorded. The first, in his ecstasies, would fly over the tops of the highest oaks, as Bonaventura de Podio and another Friar testified.[1]

Peter of Monticello also had a levitation witnessed by Servadeo of Urbino, the guardian of the convent of Ancona. Peter was in contemplation before a crucifix, suspended five or six cubits above the floor of the church.[2]

One reads, too, in the *Actus* that a certain tyrant was converted because he saw another Franciscan, whose name is not recorded, suspended in the air as he was praying with tears for this man's conversion.[3]

Et ibi recepit divinae visionis tam excessivum fervorem animam ejus ad paupertatis concupiscentiam totaliter inflammantem, quod videbatur ex facie et oris hiatu quasi flammas amoris emittere. Et egrediens ad socium sic ignitus ore vehementer dicebat: "A! a! a! a! frater Massee, praebe mihi teipsum." Et hoc fecit ter. Frater Masseus stupens de tam vehementi fervore, quum tertia vice sanctus Franciscus dixisset: "Praebe mihi teipsum," misit se totum infra brachia sancti patris. Tunc sanctus Franciscus, cum hiatu magno et Spiritus sancti fervore ac clamore valido reboando a! a! a! a! levavit fratrem Masseum cum ipso flatu in aere et impulit illum ante se quantum posset esse unius longae hastae mensura. However, M. P. Sabatier, the learned editor of the *Actus*, has mentioned the passage in his index under the head *levitation* (*elevatio a terra*, p. 242). The same mistake is to be found in Dr. Imbert-Gourbeyre's *La stigmatisation* (vol. ii, p. 268). The latter is likely to have borrowed it from Görres, for he disfigures in a similar way the name of Brother Masseo, whom he calls Maffi. Now, Görres writes: "As everybody knows, St Francis one day carried Brother Maffei up in his flight" (*La mystique*, vol. ii, ch. xxii, p. 310). *Cf.* also Farges (Eng. tr., p. 537): "Several of these ecstatics displayed wonderful strength at the time. St Francis of Assisi in his aerial flight carried with him Brother Maffi."

[1] *A.S.*, vol. iii of April, p. 408: *Divinis gratiis adauctus ad consortia rapiebatur Angelorum, supra altissimas quasque arbores elevatus. Viderunt eum aliquando Fr. Bonaventura de Podio et socius ejus, qui ex alio Conventu eum visum venerant, junctis manibus, facie in coelum erecta, immobiliter in aere haerentem super ilices proceras.*

[2] *Actus*, c. 53, 6, p. 161: *Frater Petrus de Monticulo qui visus fuit in aere levatus a fratre Servadeo de Urbino, tunc guardiano suo, in loco antiquo Anconae, usque ad pedes crucifixi in altum positum, forte per quinque vel sex cubitos a terra, id est a pavimento ecclesiae.*

[3] *Ibid.*, c. 60, 25-26, p. 182: *Et ecce in ipsa oratione elevatus est in aere usque ad culmen palatii, et ibi in aere fecit tam magnum lamentum et fletum pro anima dicti domini, indulgentiam postulando, quod vix unquam fuit visus homo qui caros suos consanguineos seu amicos defunctos tam cordialiter fleret, sicut iste*

LEVITATION

St Jutta lived as an anchoress not far from Kulm (Prussia) in the thirteenth century. She had taken shelter in a deserted house. Her ecstasies, says her biographer, occurred twice a day, and were accompanied with levitations which were witnessed by the people in the neighbourhood.[1]

What is reported about a levitation of St Elisabeth of Hungary recalls that of St Dominic at Castres. A Sister, going to fetch her in the choir, saw her prostrate before an image of the Virgin and then rising a foot above the ground.[2] Elisabeth was the daughter of Andrew II of Hungary, who married her to Louis, the son of the Landgrave of Thuringia and Hesse. At the death of this prince Elisabeth became a Franciscan tertiary. She was canonised by Gregory IX four years after her death (1235).

Blessed Bentivoglio de Bonis, born at San Severino, companion and compatriot of Brother Masseo, St Francis's friend, died at Christmas, 1232. Brother Masseo is reported to have beheld him " lifted up in the air, very high above the ground, while praying in a wood." Masseo was at this time a parish priest. Struck by this sight, he left his presbytery and became a Franciscan friar.[3]

Blessed Gherardesca of Pisa belonged to the Camaldolese Order. One day, on St John's feast, a lady from Pisa saw her in the church of

---

frater pro peccatis illius. Et fuit in illa nocte ter elevatus in aere semper cum lamento pio et lacrymis compassionis. Et ille dominus latenter observans omnia praedicta audiebat caritativum lamentum et compassionis singultus lacrymarum.

[1] *A.S.*, vol. vii of May, p. 597 D: *Elegit autem ad habitandum locum in Culmensi Episcopatu, tribus milliaribus Thorunio distantem, medio vero a Culmza, sub aedificio quodam tunc desolato, nunc etiam diruto et solis ruderum vestigiis inveniendo, secus stagnum grande quod Bielcznae vocatur. Ibi viventem solitarie observaverunt accolae, bis die quolibet solitam elevari in aere, ministerioque angelorum sic sustineri, donec a colloquio Domini, instar Moysis vultu coruscante, reverteretur.*

[2] *Ibid.*, vol. ii of May, p. 125, n. 13: *Die autem quadam accidit ut ex senioribus una Elisabetham quaereret, negotii alicujus cum ea communicandi causa ; qua non inventa in monasterio, abiit ad chorum, ibique sororem quamdam humi jacentem reperit ante imaginem B. Mariae Virginis : quam dum agnoscens considerat (erat autem ipsa Elisabetha) vidit eamdem cubito uno elevari a terra.*

[3] *Actus*, c. 53, 3, pp. 160-161: *Frater etiam Bentevoglia de Sancto Severino, qui fuit visus in aere levatus per magnum spatium a terra, quum oraret in silva, a fratre Masseo de eadem terra, qui propter illud miraculum dimisit plebendatum. Et factus est frater Minor tam sanctae vitae quod multa fecit miracula et requiescit Mori.*

44

ANCIENT TRADITIONS

St James of Podium, suspended six cubits above the floor. She was much frightened by the sight, but the sweet singing of the ecstatic removed her fears.[1]

St Edmund, then Archbishop of Canterbury, was seen levitated by his friend and chancellor, St Richard of Chichester, in the following circumstances:
" One day, when the saint had invited several persons of great quality to dine with him at his palace, he made them wait a long while before he came out to them. When dinner had been ready some time, St Richard, who was his chancellor, went to call him, and found him in the chapel, raised a considerable height above the ground in prayer."[2]

St Hedwig, at the death of her husband, Henry, the Duke of Poland, in 1238, entered the abbey she had founded at Trebnitz. She is said in her biography (by Surius) to have been seen one day surrounded with light and lifted above the earth.[3] No further details are given.

At the age of twenty, St Lutgard, a contemporary of Christina Mirabilis, entered a convent of Cistercian Sisters, of which she became the Prioress in 1315. Her Life was written—like Christina's—by Thomas of Cantimpré. It contains but one allusion to a fact of levitation: one Whitsunday, as Lutgard was singing the *Veni Creator Spiritus* with the other nuns, she was seen raised two cubits above the ground.[4]

[1] *A.S.*, vol. vii of May, p. 164 C: *In festo B. Joannis Evangelistae erat quaedam Domina,Theodesca nomine, civis Pisana, in ecclesia Jacobi de Podio, quae est extra civitatem Pisanam, cum B. Gerardesca. Et cum sancta oraret, stabat in aere ferme decem cubitis elevata. Tum mulier illa tremabunda surgens, cum videret Sanctam sublevatam suavi cantu angelorum more concinere, coepit grandi laetitia intra se dicere : vere hodie cum sancta ero in Paradiso, particeps regni Dei.*
[2] Alban Butler, *Lives of the Fathers, Martyrs,* etc., vol. iv, part ii, pp. 681-682.
[3] *A.S.*, vol. viii of Oct., p. 235 B: . . . *dum corpus ejus luce clara circumdatum videretur in aere sublevatum, secundum quod aliqui notaverunt.*
[4] *A.S.*, vol. iv of June, p. 192 F–193 A: *In sancto die Pentecostes cum in choro a monialibus, Veni Creator Spiritus, cantaretur ; ab his quae in choro erant manifestissime visum est, Lutgardem ad duos cubitos a terra in aere sublimari.*

45

LEVITATION

Blessed Agnes of Assisi, a Franciscan, the sister of St Clare, is said by Görres to have experienced levitations. This author gives neither his sources nor any details of the phenomenon.[1]

Giles of Santarem, the son of a Governor of Coimbra (Portugal), came to Paris to study medicine and practised witchcraft. Then he changed his life and entered the Dominican Order, of which he organised a monastery later on in Santarem. He died in 1267. His biographer, Andrew of Resende, reports his levitation in curious circumstances. Giles was passing through Lerena (between Coimbra and Scallabis) and lodged with a lady called Pichena. Having retired to his room, which he shared with another Dominican of Scallabis, he began meditating, sitting on the side of his bed.

Some moments after his companion found that he was rapt and lifted above his couch. Very surprised, Brother Andrew called the lady of the house with other persons to show them the strange sight. He even endeavoured to move the ecstatic about, but he was unable to shift him from his place. The news got abroad, and people soon crowded in from all the neighbourhood. They were so eager to see Giles that some who could not enter the house climbed up the roof and broke through it to look into the room. When Giles came to himself again and heard of what had happened, he left the house about the middle of the night.[2]

Blessed Margaret of Hungary, when twelve years old, was received as a member of the Dominican convent of the island called

---

[1] Vol. ii, ch. xxi, p. 284.

[2] *A.S.*, vol. iii of May, pp. 409, 15: *Quodam tempore cum pergens Conimbrigam, devenisset Lerenam, quod oppidum aequis fere spatiis Scallabi distat et Conimbriga, divertit apud nobilem et religiosam matronam Pichenam nomine. Cumque ad solis occasum cubiculum ingressus, in sponda lecti sedens aliquantulum meditaretur ; ecce derepente tam vehementer absorptus est, ut terra elevatus, nullo sustentato, penderet immobilis. Quod cernens socius ejus Frater Andreas Petreius Scallabitanus harum insolens rerum, accita matrona et familiaribus domus, aliquot frustra impulsionibus et attractionibus illum nitebatur deponere: non enim modo moveri de loco non potuit, sed nec etiam vel leviter inclinari. Quod ubi innotuit viciniae, tanta subito occurrit multitudo, ut cum neque cubiculum neque januae turbam ceperent, tectum ipsum effractum detectumque sit a tam mirae rei videndae studiosis. Atque eo sic ad multum jam noctis perdurante, qui spectatum advenerant, partim exorati, partim irrepente, jam somno admoniti domum quisque suam se receperunt. Postea vero quam illa evigilans a socio rescivit quid sibi contigisset, ingenuo magis quam necessario pudore, multum doluit se a vulgo deprehensum; et cavens ne vel minima subreperet humanae laudis dulcedo, si exorta die videndi sui copiam faceret, statim de tertia vigilia, nocte adhuc concubia, discessit.*

46

from that time *Margit Sziget* (Margaret Island), near Budapest. She practised great austerities, and died at the age of twenty-eight (January 18, 1271). Her biographer, Garini, says that she was seen several times raised off the ground. These levitations always took place on certain feasts. Her body was lifted more than one cubit above the earth.[1]

St Douceline, a Provençal beguine, the sister of the famous Hugues of Digne, who was Provincial of the Franciscan Order in Provence, experienced frequent ecstasies, during which she rose above the earth. " One day she was ravished in God in the church, and a noble knight, whose name was Jacques Vivaud, Lord of Cuges Castle, was there with his son. It was in the evening of a feast and the sermon was over. The knight heard from his wife, a noble and godly lady, called Madame Sancie, that the holy Mother had been rapt from the morning, and that she had herself accompanied her to a chapel of the friars, where she had on that day received Communion. Accordingly, hearing of all this, he went very devoutly to visit her. And he saw her in the air, suspended by the marvellous power of attraction that drew her towards God, suspended without any support, without touching anywhere, lifted up so high that the said knight and his son, both kneeling down in great reverence and taking off their hats, kissed the soles of her feet very devoutly."[2] Another man from Marseilles, Raimon du Puy, saw her in the same condition; " she had been rapt in the friars' church before the altar where she had communicated, raised off the ground and in the same position in which Jacques Vivaud had seen her. Now this citizen knelt down quite devoutly, and he measured with his hand how high she was lifted from the ground, and he found she was raised a good palm high. With great faith he placed his head, in which he had a pain, under her revered feet, and kissed them piously."[3] Another time " it happened on Easter Day that she was in ecstasy in her oratory, lifted up in the air and suspended by the power of her marvellous rapture, so that a lady could measure with her hand the space between her feet and the floor, and she found that she was

---

[1] *A.S.*, vol. iii of Jan., p. 516: . . . *et visa est pluries inter coelum et terram plusquam per unum cubitum elevata, nullis corporis sensibus utens. Ibid.*, p. 519: . . . *pluries in die Sancto Parasceves, et omnium Sanctorum, ac Assumptionis Beatae Virginis, vigiliis et solennitatibus, visum est corpus ejus inter coelum et terram plusquam unum cubitum elevatum.*
[2] *Vie de sainte Douceline*, translated from the Provençal by R. Gout, pp. 109-110.
[3] *Ibid.*, pp. 110-111.

raised a good palm and was not supported by anything."[1]   She was also seen, one Assumption Day, moving through the choir in mid-air, as if she followed an imaginary procession.[2]

Sometimes the ecstatic was but slightly lifted up; she kept touch with the ground with her great toes.[3]   Or, again, she was seen suspended " with one of her feet raised a palm above the floor, the other touching the ground only by the tip of the great toe; and she remained in that position from the time she had communicated to the evening, about the time of Compline."[4]

In 1260 St Bonaventure, coming from Narbonne, where he had held a general chapter, went to the monastery of La Verna in the valley of the Casentino to collect material for his Life of St Francis. One day, as he was working at his book in his cell, St Thomas Aquinas came to visit him.   He found him in ecstatic levitation. He withdrew, saying: " Let us leave alone this saint working for a saint."[5]

St Thomas Aquinas himself is not very often mentioned among the saints who are said to have experienced the phenomenon.   Still his biographer, William of Tocco, who was his contemporary and familiar, says that he was seen several times raised from the earth in his ecstasies. The first time it was in the convent of the Dominicans at Salerno: the saint was meditating before the high altar after Matins; Brother James and another saw him lifted two cubits from the floor.   Another time, in a convent at Naples, he was seen in the same condition by Brother Dominic. The latter, having noticed that Thomas used to go down to church before Matins, followed him twice there.   He saw him in ecstasy in St Nicholas's chapel; his body stood about two cubits above the ground.[6]

---

[1] *Ibid.*, p. 142.   *Cf.* pp. 124, 128, 140, 141, 150.
[2] *Ibid.*, p. 151.   [3] *Ibid.*, p. 109.   [4] *Ibid.*, p. 113.
[5] *A.S.*, vol. iii of July, p. 791 E: *Rursus cum intenso affectu studeret, contemplando et adnotando Vitam beati Francisci, gloriosus sanctus Thomas de Aquino, qui eadem tempestate meritis claruit, et Bonaventurae magna caritate conjunc us fuit, accedens ad illius cubiculum, per foramen ostii introspexit, viditque illum in contemplatione raptum, et a terra mirifice sublevatum, tum retrocedens ad suos : Sinamus, inquit, Sanctum qui laborat pro Sancto.*
[6] *A.S.*, vol. i of March, p. 669 A: *Nam cum esset Salerni in conventu Fratrum, visus est praedictus Doctor, ante majus altare in oratione existens, post matutinas a fratribus Iacobo et praedicto socio suo, qui ipsum exempli gratia observabant, duobus cubitis elevatus a terra, velut si fas est dicere, futurum agilitatis vel aliquod simile participium accepisset, quo sine pondere, quasi in sua levitate maneret.   Ibid.*, p. 669 AB: *Simile sed magis stupendum vidit*

48

St Agnes, the daughter of Primislaus Ottokar, King of Bohemia, refused to marry the Emperor Frederick II and entered the order of the Poor Clares, of whom she became the General-Superior. Her biographer says that she used to be lifted up in the air during contemplation. One Ascension Day, as she was walking in the garden of the convent with Sisters Benigna and Prisca, she was raised off the earth and vanished from their view. She reappeared only an hour later. Questioned about her mysterious absence, she would not give any answer.[1]

Brother Vincent of Arezzo, in his Life of Ambrose of Siena, reports that this Dominican twice levitated while he was preaching.[2] Ambrose seems to have been reluctant to admit the reality of the fact. It was, he said, a divine favour granted to those who attended his sermons, to reward their devotion, to have shown them such marvel.[3]

Blessed Franco of Grotti, near Siena, after a profligate youth, was converted to the religious life. After a series of pilgrimages he took the Carmelite habit. Görres has the following anecdote about him, which he has drawn from the *Speculum Carmelitanum*: One day Franco had a vision of the Virgin in his cell. In his rapture his body began to irradiate such effulgent light that his fellow-religious came up, thinking there was a fire. When they entered the cell, they found Franco in rapture and raised off the earth.[4]

---

in conventu Neapolitano de praedicto Doctore Frater Dominicus de Caserta Sacrista, vir oratione devotus, actione solicitus et virtute probatus, qui alias habuit visiones mirabiles: qui advertens Fr. Thomam semper de camera sui studii ad ecclesiam ante Matutinas descendere, et ne videretur ab aliis ad suam cameram festinus redire, semel ipsum curiosius observavit. Et accedens retro in capella S. Nicolai, ubi fixus in oratione manebat, vidit ipsum quasi duobus cubitis elevatum in aëre.

[1] *A.S.*, vol. i of March, p. 510 DE: *Inter ostenta, licet prope quotidiana, singulare fuit illud quod sacra alia virgo subinde vidit, cum caussa, qua nescio, sacrum odoeum pro sua confidentia sub horam orationis audacter introivit. Haerebat Agnes inter preces sublimis omnino a terra atque tres amplius aut quatuor dodrantes ab humo elata, in aera ferebatur, neque jam pro more sola facies coruscabat, sed ipsum insuper conclave plenum numine ex circumfusa nube fulgida habebatur. Eo die quo Ascensum Domini in coelos Ecclesia solemnem agit, cum in horto inter Benignam et Priscam virgines psalleret, rapta ex medio illarum, vix in hora illis reddita fuit, nihilque de absentia requisita, praeter decorum et blandum risum significavit.*

[2] *A.S.*, vol. iii of March, p. 191 D: *Testatus est etiam praefatus F. Vincentius quod quamplures alii religiosi et seculares (dixerint) dum beatus vir, populo cum magno spiritu fervore praedicaret, bis in aera elevatum se vidisse*

[3] *Ibid.*   [4] *La mystique*, vol. ii, part ii, ch. 21

Brought up with the Carmelites of Mount Trapano (Sicily), Albert Adalbati was receivèd himself into the order of which he became Provincial. After giving himself up to preaching and the supervision of the monasteries of his province, Albert retired into a wilderness near Messina, and died there in 1292. He used to say the Psalms with the greatest devotion, and would then be raised three cubits above the ground. After contemplation he was gently brought down to the earth again.[1]

Benvenuta Bojano was a Dominican tertiary. She is known for her austerities. Imbert-Gourbeyre has mentioned her among levitated saints without details or reference to any source.[2]

St Margaret of Cortona, a Franciscan tertiary, expiated by twenty-three years' cruel mortification her former disorderly life. Father de Chérancé gives, in his biography, the following description of her first ecstasy: " Margaret was busy looking after a young mother, related to Dona Diabella, in the house of the latter. Availing herself of a moment's liberty, she retired into a corner of the room to bewail her sins. When she was praying with the greatest fervour, the Spirit of the Lord seized upon her and drew her up to him with the irresistibility of an eagle pouncing upon its prey, and carried her up away into the air. The saint's body was raised several cubits above the earth. . . . Two eye-witnesses, Dona Mechtild (the confined lady) and a workman with whom the devoted tertiary often shared her alms, testified to the truth of the fact."[3]

Blessed Helena was the daughter of Bela IV, King of Hungary. She married Boleslaus V, Duke of Poland. After the latter's death the took the habit of the Poor Clares. She is mentioned as a levitated saint by Imbert-Gourbeyre.[4]

[1] *A.S.*, vol. vii of Aug., p. 236 CD: *Relatum fuit a suis coevis Fratribus, quod quilibet sacerdos dicere tenetur, dictus Pater omni nocte totum Psalterium legebat ante Crucifixi imaginem nudis ac flexis genibus, cum tanta devotione, quod a terra per spatium trium cubitorum levabatur ; et postea, oratione finita, ad terram suaviter demittebatur.*
[2] *La stigmatisation*, vol. ii, p. 239, n. 1.
[3] De Chérancé, *Sainte Marguerite de Cortone*, p. 57 (after *Acta Canonizationis* and Bevegnati, c. ii, 1).
[4] *La stigmatisation*, vol. ii, p. 239, n. 1.

CHAPTER II

ANCIENT TRADITIONS (Continued) (FOURTEENTH AND FIFTEENTH CENTURIES)

Blessed Bartholus (†1300).—Blessed Peter Armengol (1238–†1304).—
Blessed Joan of Orvieto (†1306).—St Agnes of Monte-Pulciano (1277–
†1317).—Blessed Margaret of Castello (†1320).—Blessed Robert of
Salentum (1273–†1341) —Blessed Dalmatius Monner of Gerona (1291–
†1341).—Blessed Venturino of Bergamo (1304–†1346).—Catherine
Colombini (†1367).—St Catherine of Siena (1347–†1380).—Nicholas
of Ravenna (†1398).—St Vincent Ferrer (1350–†1419). St Colette
of Corbie (1381–†1447).—Blessed Peter of Palermo (1381–†1451).—
St Peter Regalati (1391–†1456).—St Antoninus of Florence (1389–
†1459). — St Diego (†1463). — Blessed James of Illyria (†1485).—
Savonarola (1452–†1498).—Antony of Santa Regina (XVth century).

BLESSED BARTHOLUS, of the Order of the Servants of
Mary, was given permission to live as an anchoret in a cave
near the village of Bascio-Caro (duchy of Urbino). There
he was sometimes seen in contemplation, insentient and suspended
in mid-air.[1]

Peter Armengol, of the family of the Counts of Urgel, related
to the Kings of Castile, led at first quite an unedifying life, and even
became the head of a gang of robbers. Stung with remorse he asked
for admission into the Order of Mercy, whose habit he took in 1258.
He gave himself up to the severest austerities, and was employed
in redeeming Christian slaves from the Saracens. Hanged at
Bougie, he escaped death by a miracle, for he is said to have remained
six days hanging from the gallows unhurt. Witnesses declared on
oath they had seen him raised from earth as he prayed.[2]

---

[1] *A.S.*, vol. iii of June, p. 486 F: *Cupiens solitariam et eremiticam vitam
ducere, speluncam, ne longe a vico Bascio-Caro per dimidium milliare, Superi-
orum nostrorum permissu, sibi pro domicilio delegerat. Ea quidem in crypta
usque adeo orationi et contemplationi deditus erat, ut nonnulli viderent ipsum
aliquando in aere suspensum, ea quae coeli sunt ab omni sensu alienatum contemplari.*

[2] *A.S.*, vol. i of Sept., p. 334 B: *Testati sunt autem praedicti Commenda-
tores Sanctae Mariae de Pratis et Sanctae Mariae Montis Albi, se illum
pluries vidisse, cum oraret, extra se factum in extasi, et in aere elevatum. (Acta
ex oculatis et juratis testibus.)*

LEVITATION

At fourteen Joan of Orvieto entered the Third Order of St Dominic. Görres reports that the other Sisters on St Peter's feast saw her rise in the air, head downwards, with outstretched arms. On Ascension Day she experienced an aerial rapture in which she was lifted up from the ground in a normal attitude.[1]

Agnes of Monte-Pulciano when very young became the Abbess of the Dominicans of Proceno (duchy of Urbino). The Sisters saw her several times levitated. One day she was lifted up high enough into the air to embrace a crucifix hanging far above the ground. Then she came gently down again.[2]

Blessed Margaret, of the Dominican Third Order, was born blind and spent her life in the convent of Citta del Castello, in Umbria. A Sister, Venturella, is reported to have seen her, with several others, lifted a cubit over the ground.[3]

One day Robert of Salentum, a Celestine Father, was lifted more than a cubit above the floor of the church, when meditating. A fellow-religious, wondering at the sight, could not help taking hold of him, and exclaimed, " Father, how is that ?" which at once recalled the ecstatic to his senses.[4]

Dalmatius of Gerona (Catalonia) was a Dominican. He first professed theology, but after twenty years he went to live as an

[1] Görres, vol. ii, ch. xx (quoting Steill, July 23).
[2] *A.S.*, vol. ii of April, p. 792: *. . . a terra per spatium unius cubiti et sine aliquo corporali sustentaculo in aera elevari, et factori suo subjungi (cerneretur). Et licet hoc quam pluries ageretur, videntibus quibusdam sororibus, quae propter admirationem et exemplum facta ejus curiosius observabant, unum tamen visum est semel per dictas Sorores, quod stuporem audientibus ingerit pariter et amorem. Dum enim quadam vice, puella Deo devota coram imagine Crucifixi devotius oraret ; in tantum eam arripuit amor Sponsi sui, quod relicta terra tam alte fuit corpus suum purissimum sublevatum in aere, quod ipsi imagini altare in eminenti loco positae se pari situ conjunxit . . . postquam suae ferventis caritatis affectui per actus exteriores, quantum ei licuit, satisfecit, ea levitate, qua in altum ascenderat, descendit ad ima.*
[3] *A.S.*, vol. i of April, p. 192: *Visa est ipsa (Soror Venturella) atque ab omnibus praesentibus plus quam cubitum unum elevata ab humo.*
[4] *A.S.*, vol. iv of July, p. 503: *Acciderunt autem et alia relatione digna. Nam cum solus in ecclesia sanctae Crucis staret ad persolvendum divina, tanto coepit a terrenis divinarum elevari amore, quod tunc versus coelum coepit elevari et corpore: nam super se raptus et in extasi positus, fuit amplius quam per cubitum, videntibus qui aderant, elevatus a terra. Quod videns discipulus ejus, ipsum incaute apprehendens, vocavit eum dicens: quid est hoc Pater ? Qui illico ad se reversus, dixi : Fili male fecisti; quia mente ferebar in Deum.*

52

anchoret at the Sainte-Baume in Provence. The following account of one of his levitations is to be found in Marchese: " Dalmatius often went to pray in a solitary vale called Camota. One day, as he was not present at dinner-time, Brother Benedetto of Aquanotti went to fetch him. Arrived in the vale he could not see anybody. At last he saw him suspended in the air, level with the top of a high tree. Then the ecstatic sank gradually down to the ground where he remained some time prostrate in prayer.[1]

Venturino of Bergamo was raised above the ground at Mass when saying the *Sanctus*, and his face was radiant with light. A lady of Bologna, having heard of the marvel, came one day to attend his Mass in order to behold it.[2]

Catherine Colombini, cousin of St John Colombini, the founder of the Jesuates, has no biography of her own in the *Acta*; but one reads in the Life of the latter that one Christmas night she was raised about two ells over the pavement of the church and remained two hours suspended in mid-air, surrounded with brightness.[3]

St Catherine of Siena experienced ecstasies from a child. She was only six years old when she was enraptured with a feeling of levitation. This occurred in a cave, near Siena, where she had retired, she fancied, to lead the life of an anchoress. I borrow from Johannes Jörgensen—who writes it after the best two biographies of the saint—the relation of this ecstasy: " She had taken a loaf along with her, and so provided for, undertook to live in solitude. She began to pray, and found herself in the strange condition where everything vanished around her, and she felt as if she was soaring in a world of effulgent light. She was sensible of being lifted up gradually above the ground, higher and higher, till eventually her head knocked against the vault of the cave, which woke her up. . . . She realised she must have remained long in the cave; the sun was low, the cicadas were chirping in the fig‑trees, and up there, at San Domenico, they were ringing the bells for Vespers."[4] Later on,

---

[1] Marchese, September 24, quoted by Görres, vol. ii, ch. xxii.

[2] Görres, *La mystique*, vol. ii, ch. xxii, p. 312.

[3] *A.S.*, vol. vii of July, p. 363 F: *Nocte igitur solemnissima ad recolenda Christi Natalitia instituta, dum orationi cum reliquis sororibus insisteret, extra se rapta attolli coepit in altum ac duabus circiter ulnis a pavimento per horas binas haesit immobilis, luce mirabili undique vallata.*

[4] Jörgensen, *Sainte Catherine de Sienne*, p. 25 (after the *Legenda major* of Raymond of Capua, confessor and friend of the saint, and the *Leggenda minore* of Brother Tommaso Nacci Caffarini, who has summed up the first one, adding personal recollections to it. *Cf. A.S.*, vol. iii of April, pp. 870-871).

LEVITATION

the famous Dominican Sister had levitations before eye-witnesses:
on August 18, 1370, after receiving Communion, she gained her cell
and lay down on her couch in ecstatic trance. After remaining a
long time motionless, her body was lifted up into the air, as three
persons present testified.[1] Caffarini reports that she was seen,
lifted several feet above the ground, by the Dominican Niccolo di
Bindo da Cassina, who had come especially from Pisa to examine
her ecstasies;[2] and Stefano Maconi asserted in the process of Venice
that he had himself witnessed the levitations of Catherine.[3]

The Dominican, Nicholas of Ravenna, often rose from the earth
while saying Mass. He was also levitated when preaching. According to Marchese, he once rose a palm above the ground. This
occurred on St Francis's feast.[4]

Father Fages, so lavish of miracles in his biography of St Vincent
Ferrer, does not refer to any levitation of his. One may read
though in the Bollandists that the saint was seen one night in his
cell suspended in the air, his body radiant with light. This was
reported by one of the followers of the celebrated itinerant preacher,
who said he had seen the fact through the door of his cell.[5]

[1] *A.S.*, vol. iii of April, p. 910 A: *Sed anno eodem, die xviii mensis
Augusti, facta est super eam manus Domini, dum ejusdem diei mane sacram
Communionem sumpsisset. Nam primo sacerdote tenente Sacramentum in
manu sua, et jubente ut diceret, Domine non sum digna ut intres in me; tunc
sumpto Sacramento, videbatur ei, quod sicut piscis intrat aquam, et aqua in
ipsum sic anima sua intraret in Deum, et Deus in eam: et sic sensit se totam
tractam a Deo, vixque poterat redire ad cellulam suam, ubi super stratulo ligneo
suo, de quo supra mentio facta est, se ponens permansit diu immobilis. Sed
post longam moram elevatum est corpus ejus in aera, stabatque suspensum absque
corporeo fulcimento, sicut tres infra scriptae testes testificatae sunt se vidisse :
tandem descendit ad lectum praedictum, et coepit loqui silenter verba vitae, super
mel et favum dulcia pariter et profunda, quae omnes socias audientes commove-
bant ad fletum.*
[2] Jörgensen, *ibid.*, p. 99.
[3] *Epistola Domni Stephani de gestis et virtutibus S. Catharinae, A.S.*,
vol. iii of April, p. 272 A: *Circa quem extaticum statum ejus unum valde
mirabile non est omittendum, sed cum debita veneratione recolendum: quia
praecipue quando in quibusdam arduis ejus anima ferventius in oratione semetip-
sam exercitabat, et cum impetu majori satagebat ascendere, gravedinem quoque
corporis a terra sublevabat: unde multotiens a quampluribus in oratione visa
fuit a terra suspensa et elevata, quorum ego sum unus, de quo vehementer
admirabar.* This *Epistola* is the text of the deposition of Maconi.
[4] *Diario Domenicano*, vol. vi, p. 24.
[5] *A.S.*, vol. i of April, p. 495: *Solebat quoque narrare vir quidam, nomine
Leonardus Gayanus, qui eum multo tempore una cum aliis secutus fuerat, quod*

54

The Life of Colette of Corbie, who reformed the Order of the Poor Clares, a contemporary and friend of Vincent Ferrer, abounds with marvels; but levitation is hardly referred to in it. At least, this kind of fact is recorded with a scarcity of details which is surprising when one considers the prodigious character ascribed to it. Some Sisters are said, indeed, to have seen her several times soaring in the air and being lifted up so high as to be out of sight.[1]

Peter Jeremias of Palermo belonged to the Dominican Order. He employed himself on the reformation of the monasteries of his Order in Sicily, and died at Palermo in 1451. His life has been written by one of his fellow-religious of St Zita's monastery. One may read in it that he often rose above the ground during his meditation. His body then became radiant with light. One day his Superior, seeing this brightness through cracks in the door of his cell, thought there was a fire in it. He had the door broken through, and only found the saint in contemplation.[2]

Peter Regalati (of Regalada), a Spanish Franciscan friar, also emitted a bright light when he was in ecstasy; he rose into the air, and remained suspended several hours in this position.[3]

Similar facts are reported about Antonino Pierrozi, called Antoninus of Florence, a Dominican whom Eugenius IV appointed Archbishop of this town. During contemplation his body became effulgent and used to soar in mid-air. Sometimes he was raised

---

quadam nocte nonnulli aspicientes per rimas quasdam portae cellulae, ubi quiescebat, viderunt cellam ipsam mirabili claritate resplendentem, et in medio virum Dei a terra penitus elevatum, oculos ad coelum ac manus junctas tenentem, et devotione vehementissima orantem.

[1] *A.S.*, vol. i of March, p. 558: . . . *pluries visa fuit a praedictis Religiosis corporaliter elevata sic in altum in aera, quod ipsarum penitus frustrabatur intuitu, ab earum oculis evanescens.*

[2] *A.S.*, vol. i of March, p. 295 A: *Inter orandum saepius a terra sublimior visus, splendorem e januae rimis egredientem Superior noctu cum vidisset, cellam comburi ratus, eam perfregit, Petrumque precibus instantem invenit, qui tamquam e somno excitatus, nec quid loqueretur habuit, nec de illata januae vi quaestus est.*

[3] *A.S.*, vol. iii of March, p. 857 E: *Nec raro accidit ut in oratione positum viderint alii sublatum in aera, tantoque splendore circumfusum, ut qui eminus hunc intuebantur, ardere Abroxanum conventum crederent, accurrerentque, reprimendo incendio manus operamque commodaturi.*

up to a crucifix, which he embraced. Eye-witnesses testified the facts at his process of beatification.[1]

St Diego was a lay-brother of the Franciscan Order. The levitations which he is said to have experienced inspired Murillo to paint a famous picture which is to be seen in the Louvre: *La cuisine des anges* or *Le miracle de San Diego*. A little on the left of the picture the saint is seen floating in mid-air, kneeling, with his hands clasped and his eyes lifted to heaven. Further on the left stand three personages, two noblemen and a religious, whose attitude expresses great surprise. On the right several angels who have taken the place of the ecstatic are busy performing different cooking operations in the kitchen. I have been unable to find an account of this scene in the Life of the saint. Indeed, his biography in the *Auréole séraphique* does not mention any levitation at all.

James of Illyria, a Franciscan lay-brother, according to Imbert-Gourbeyre, used to experience frequent raptures with levitation.[2] The author does not give any reference.

Many miracles are ascribed to Jerome Savonarola, the celebrated Dominican who died at the stake in 1498. Among others, he is said to have been seen lifted up into the air and radiant with light in the time he was a prisoner. One adds that his gaoler was converted by the sight of this marvel.[3]

Brother Antony of Santa Regina was gardener in the Franciscan monastery of Santo Benedetto di Marco. When he was praying,

---

[1] *A.S.*, vol. i of May, p. 339 F: *Elevatio Antonii per nonnulla brachia dum oraret, et cum splendore nimio circumfuso in camera ejus, et quod pluries visus et deprehensus fuerit taliter orans sic corporaliter elevatus, et aliquando etiam in elevatione applicatus cuidam Cruci cum imagine Crucifixi, et cum eo ardentissime ac devotissime loqui. Probarunt hoc Nicolaus Primerani annorum LXXV, cui Primeranus pater hoc ipsum retulit, qui eumdem sic vidit elevatum et orantem. Dominicus de Boninsegnis ann. XLII, qui audivit a Bartholomaeo, domestico famulo Antonii, qui eum viderat nocte in oratione sic elevatum. Nobilis Hieronymus Stupha ann. LXVI de auditu ab alio servitore Antonii, qui eum elevatum invenerat. Fr. Julianus Dominici de Florentia ann. LXVI qui similiter audivit ab alio domestico, Gregorio Imolensi, qui vidit eumdem elevatum et Cruci applicatum cum splendore. Hieronymus de Butis, Florentinus civis ann. LXX, qui a Guilielmo domestico Antonii, qui eumdem sic in oratione elevatum per quatuor brachia a terra deprehenderat.*
[2] *La stigmatisation*, vol. ii, pp. 265-266.
[3] *Jérome Savonarole*, by F. T. Perrens, p. 287.

reports Wadding, the well-known annalist of the Friars Minor, he soared as high as the biggest trees. Some people of Grosseta saw him thus, on the road to Batignano, suspended in mid-air before a tree on which a cross was hanging.[1]

[1] Wadding, *Annales ord. Min.* (quoted by Görres, vol. ii, ch. xxii, p. 301).

57

CHAPTER III

MODERN TRADITIONS (SIXTEENTH CENTURY)

Blessed Osanna (1449–†1505).—Blessed Ladislaus of Gielniow (†1506).—
Blessed Giovanni Angelo Porro (1450–†1506).—St Francis of Paula
(1416–†1507).—St Bartholomew of Anglario (†1510).—Blessed Clara
Bugni (1471–†1514).—Blessed Colomba of Rieti (1467–†1521).—
Blessed Conradini of Brescia (†1529).—St Andrew of Spoleto (†1532).
—St Angela of Brescia (1474–†1540).—Christine of Aquila (1480–
†1543).—St Francis Xavier (1506–†1552).—Domenica del Paradiso
(1473–†1553).—St Thomas of Villanova (1488–†1555).—St Ignatius
of Loyola (1491–†1556).—St Peter of Alcantara (1499–†1562).—
Blessed John Marinoni (1490–†1562).—Blessed Salvador of Orta
(1520–†1567).—St Louis Bertrand (1526–†1580).—St Teresa of Avila
(1515–†1582).—Frances of Saint-Dominic (†1583).—St Catherine of
Ricci (1522–†1589).—St John of the Cross (1542–†1591).—St Paschal
Baylon (1540–†1592).—St Philip Neri (1515–†1595).—Luke of Medina
del Campo (sixteenth century).—Giovanni Battista Piscator (second
half of the sixteenth century).

BLESSED OSANNA of Mantua belonged to the Third
Order of St Dominic. She was beatified by Leo X. Her
biographer, Francis Silvester of Ferrara, a Dominican friar,
who was her familiar, says that when a child she was seen by her servants, who were accompanying her to church, gliding along without
treading on the ground, as if buoyed up in the air.[1] Later on she was
seen lifted about two cubits from the earth while she was praying.[2]

[1] *A.S.*, vol. iv of June, p. 583 C: *Eam agens aetatem qua ceteri nondum
spiritualia capiunt movimenta, usque adeo divinis rebus animum intenderat, ut
quidquid rerum gereret, Christum semper alloqueretur, mente inquio et cogita-
tione : sed et Christo familiariter adeo (utebatur) ut suis omnibus optatibus
praesto esset. Igitur ruri cum matre ea tempestate morata, cum die quadam
domesticae mulieres ad quampiam ecclesiam, mille et quingentis passibus ab sua
domo distantem, accedere vellent ; puellam Osannam comitem assumunt. Inter
eundem autem, admotus lateri Christus : eam comitabatur, qui cum dulcia
agens et secreta colloquia (erat enim ab aliis paululum segregata) terram pedibus
haud contingebat, sed paulum elevata per aera incessit.*

[2] *A.S., ibid.*, p. 584 D: *Accidit itaque semel ut flagrantissimo animo
Mantuae incolumitatem, salutemque nonnullis privatis civibus rogaret : tanta
autem caritate id egit, ut spiritus secum in aera corpus extolleret : nam duobus
ferme cubitis aliquantulum temporis humo extitit elatum. Quam rem cum depre-
hendisset, vehementer admirata, num aliquis eam vidisset circumspexit: noluisset
enim ab quoquam id inspectari. Quod cum astare neminem cerneret, summo
Creatori quas potuit gratias egit.*

Blessed Ladislaus of Gielniow took the Franciscan habit while very young. After undertaking a mission among the Tartars, he came back to Poland, became guardian of the Franciscan monastery of Warsaw and Provincial of his Order. He is a patron saint of the Poles and Lithuanians. Ladislaus was preaching on the Passion, in the cathedral of Warsaw, on Good Friday, in the year 1505. Having come to the account of the Flagellation, he fell into an ecstatic trance and, lifted from the ground, remained some time suspended over the pulpit, to the great wonder of the congregation.[1] Then he was gently brought down to earth again.[2] He came home quite exhausted, was laid up, and died a month later (May 4). His biographer says he had other levitations, but does not give any details about them.[3]

Details are also lacking concerning the levitations of Giovanni Angelo Porro, who is only reported to have been raised nearly six feet from the ground.[4] The blessed one belonged to a noble family of Milanese. He entered the Order of the Servants of Mary, and lived on Mount Senario, the cradle of his Order. He died at Milan in 1506 (October 24).

The ecstasies of St Francis of Paula are recorded with fuller circumstances, and they are said to have been experienced in presence of witnesses of note. As the Calabrian thaumaturge was on his journey to the Court of France, where he had been ordered to go by

[1] A.S., vol. i of May, p. 590 EF: *Tunc jam ardentis ignis, divini amoris in camino cordis sui succensi, flamma vehemens, contineri intus non valens; tamquam e fornace, septuplum plusquam ante ardente, subito in tantum erupit ad extra ; ut ipsum visibiliter, coram illat ota congregata multitudine, omnibus clara spectantibus, viris et mulieribus, senibus et juvenibus, peccatoribus et justis, devotis et indevotis, in altum tolleret ; ita ut, cunctis videntibus, et prae novitate rei aliis inauditae stupentibus, aliis alte exclamantibus Jesus, Jesus, Jesus ! aliis in terram cadentibus, aliis prae stupore, timore, et rei novitate a sensibus quasi alienatis ; supra suggestum elevatus in aere pendulus appareret. Stabat sublimis inter coelum et terram, nullo homini auxilii adminiculo subnixus, per extasim sursum sublatus (aere ipso, loco solidi corporis, ad ejus sustentandum corpus ministerium praebente) quasi in coelum vellet abire clare visus. Mansit sic justo temporis spatio, nec fari amplius potuit in languore positus, totusque in Deo immersus.*
[2] *Ibid.: Igitur lento motu ab aere descendens, sensit se vehementi debilitati affectum, languore correptus . . . lecto decumbit.*
[3] *Ibid., p. 589 B: Frequentissime solebat experiri hunc suavem enthusiasmum : persaepe a terra in sublime elevabatur.*
[4] A.S., vol. x of Oct., p. 887 B: *Addit Cardius eum (tum) visum esse supra terram elevatum, quanto est statura unius hominis.*

Sixtus IV, he was lodged in Naples at Ferdinand I's palace. The latter is reported to have seen the saint in his room enraptured, with radiant body suspended in mid-air.[1] The same phenomenon was observed in France at Le Plessis, near Tours, where the ecstatic happened to be raised in the church five or six cubits from the floor. Among the eye-witnesses of the marvel, Anne de Beaujeu, Louis XI's daughter, is mentioned.[2]

Bartholomew of Anglario (Tuscany) was a Franciscan Observant. His Life was written by his contemporary, Francis Redi, who says that he sometimes experienced levitation in his ecstasies. He was seen thus in the forest of Castiglione (between Arezzo and Cortona), lifted two feet from the earth in a kneeling posture. He also levitated in the church of La Verna, where he rose as high as a crucifix hanging in the choir.[3]

Clara Bugni, a Franciscan tertiary, is simply mentioned as having experienced levitation in the list of Imbert-Gourbeyre.[4] She is said in the *Palmier séraphique* (vol. ix, pp. 301-302) to have been lifted up to a high crucifix the very day when she received stigmata.

Colomba of Rieti (or of Perugia) became a Dominican tertiary in 1486, and left Rieti to live in Perugia, where she gained a great renown of sanctity. After her death she was revered as a saint, but never canonised. Her cult was even forbidden by a decree of Urban VIII (1625). Sebastian of Perugia, her confessor, reports that she sometimes levitated, but does not give any particulars about

---

[1] S. Martin, *Vie des Saints*, vol. ii, col. 51.

[2] *A.S.*, vol. i of April, p. 118 AB: *Inventus est aliquando bonus Pater Plessiaci prope Turonas in ecclesia, quinque vel sex cubitis elevatus a terra. . . . Atque hoc testata est Anna, Domina Borbonii, filia Ludovici et soror Caroli Regum.* Francis died in 1507 and was canonised twelve years later. Anne of Beaujeu died in 1522.

[3] *A.S.*, vol. ii of March, p. 664 D: *Frequens ac fervens in oratione ac divinarum rerum contemplatione fuit, in qua coelestes dulcedines aliquando gustavit: saepius etiam inspectus sublimis ab humo rapi intentus ad aethera, quod in Castilionis sylva accidit, ubi eum genibus flexis vir quidam intuitus fuit duobus amplius pedibus a solo distantem: qui index ad Fratres accedens, testis extitit veritatis. Saepius vero in majori Alverniae montis templo, coram imagini Servatoris in Cruce fixi supra chori locum posita qui tunc medius erat, gestum est idipsum, et plures admirati sunt elevatum.*

[4] *La stigmatisation*, vol. ii, p. 239, n. 1.

the circumstances of the phenomenon. He is content with saying that her body was gently raised towards God.[1]

Blessed Conradino of Brescia was Superior of the Dominican monastery of Brescia, then of Bologna. The inhabitants of this town having rebelled against the Holy See, the Pope pronounced an interdict against them. Conradino excited their anger by publishing the sentence. He was thrown into prison. There, according to Görres, he was seen rising above the ground in ecstasy.[2]

Andrew of Spoleto (or of Cassia) became a Franciscan after a disorderly youth. He went over to Fez to evangelise the Saracens. To prove the truth of the Christian religion he accepted to stand on a burning stake. Not only was he spared by the flames, but he was seen levitated in the midst of them, rapt in ecstasy. The Moors stoned him as a sorcerer.[3]

Imbert-Gourbeyre mentions one " Angèle de Brixen " as having experienced levitation.[4] I suppose he means St Angela Merici of Brescia (*Brixiensis*), who founded the congregation of the Ursulines and was beatified in 1768.

Father Simplicien Saint-Martin, who wrote a history of the chief personages of the Augustinian Order, reports in it that Christina of Aquila once rose five feet from the ground on the feast of the Holy Sacrament. Another time she is said to have remained suspended twenty-four hours in mid-air during an ecstasy.[5]

Father Bouhours, in his Life of St Francis Xavier, says that this saint would sometimes retire in the middle of a conversation in order to pray. Afterwards, " when looked for, he used to be found before the Holy Sacrament, or in some secluded place, deep in contemplation, suspended above the earth, his face radiant with light."[6] Several witnesses testified to the facts. " Some said that in the beginning they saw the saint motionless in a kneeling posture; then they observed him gradually rise from the ground, while his face grew so

[1] *A.S.*, vol. v of May, p. 189 F: *Aliquando in aere elevato corpore toto suaviter ferebatur in Deum.*
[2] Vol. ii, ch. xxii, p. 284.
[3] *Cf. France franciscaine* (1924), a biographical sketch by Father Delorme.
[4] *Les stigmatisées*, vol. ii, p. 234, n. 1.
[5] Imbert-Gourbeyre, *La stigmatisation*, vol. i, p. 141.
[6] Bouhours, *La vie de S. François-Xavier*, vol. ii, bk. vi, p. 211.

bright that they were dazzled by it. Some declare that when he spoke to them about godly things, they noticed that his body was raised by itself from the earth."[1] These raptures took place sometimes when he was saying Mass, immediately after the Consecration. " He was seen thus raised in Malacca and at Meliapor, and also in Goa when giving Communion. And what is remarkable, as he was in the habit of giving Communion with bent knees he seemed to be lifted from the ground in this posture."[2]

These traditions have been officially recorded. One reads, indeed, in his office[3] that he was seen lifted above the earth by the people attending his Mass.

Domenica del Paradiso, a Dominican, is simply mentioned as a levitated saint by Imbert-Gourbeyre (*Les stigmatisées*, vol. ii, p. 234, n. 1), who does not give any details on the circumstances of the risings of this mystic. His source is the Life of Domenica written by Ignazio del Nente (Firenze, 1625).

One levitation is mentioned in the Life of Thomas of Villanova, but it is—with that of Christina of Aquila—the longest on record. One Ascension Day, after the *Acta Canonizationis*, Thomas, then Archbishop of Valencia, was reading the antiphon *et videntibus illis elevatus est* when he was rapt and raised from the floor. He remained thus suspended in mid-air without moving for twelve hours, in view of all the servants in his palace and of different inhabitants of the town.[4] Thomas was born in Castile in 1488, and had taken the Augustinian habit about the time when Luther had thrown it off. He had accepted the archbishopric of Valencia to obey Charles V's order.

Ignatius of Loyola, when he came to live in Barcelona as a student —he was then thirty-three years of age—lodged at one Doña Agnes Pasqual's, whose son, John, has reported some details about the

---

[1] *Ibid.*   [2] *Ibid.*, p. 212.

[3] Die iii Decembris, lectio iv: *Ipso magistro (Sancto Ignatio) eo brevi devenit, ut in rerum divinarum contemplatione defixus, a terra aliquando sublimis elevaretur : quod illi sacrificanti coram populi multitudine aliquoties evenit.*

[4] *A.S.*, vol. v of Sept., p. 832 F: *Semel enim die Ascensionis Domini in ambulatione secreta palatii archiepiscopalis, recitans Horas canonicas ad antiphonam nonae (Et videntibus illis elevatus est) Thomas in ecstasim raptus, et elevatus a terra, prorsus immobilis mansit ab hora quinta matutina ad quintam vespertinam : scilicet duodecim horarum intervallo, nedum a domesticis sed etiam ab innumeris civitatis incolis visus.*

saint's life. He had seen him praying in his room, and is said to
have seen him rapt with bent knees and outstretched arms four or
five palms above the floor, while the whole place was filled with a
dazzling light.[1] The Jeronymite nuns of Barcelona gave testimony
of similar raptures in the process of canonisation, saying they had
seen him lifted above the earth after praying several hours before
the altar of St Matthew.[2]

St Peter of Alcantara, of the Franciscan Order, founder of the
Friars Minor of the Strict Observance, was a contemporary of St
Teresa, who regarded him as a master of the mystical life. This
mystic during his contemplation was sometimes suspended as high
as the wainscot of the choir. He was also often seen in the garden
of the monastery soaring up to the highest branches.[3] One of his
levitations is said to have lasted three hours.[4] Sometimes he was
carried away through the air by an impetuous ecstatic flight.[5] One
day, hearing from the garden somebody singing the first words of
the Gospel according to St John, *In principio erat Verbum*, he was
suddenly rapt and flew through the air to the church,where he alighted
at the foot of the high altar.[6] Often shepherds and passers-by could

[1] *A.S.*, vol. vii of July, p. 441 BD: *Et noctibus non paucis ipsum observabat,
ac videbat (Joannes Paschalis) cubiculum splendore plenum, ipsum vero in aera
sublatum, flexis genibus plorantem, suspirantem ac dicentem. . . . Cf. ibid.,*
p. 443 B: *Multoties Barchinonae in domo Agnetis Pasqual visus est in oratione raptus absque usu sensuum, solum respirans, et aliquoties faciem miraculose
splendentem habens. . . . Aliquoties etiam a terra in aere elevatus uno cubito
cum dimidio, haec verba proferens : O Domine, si homines te cognoscerent.*
[2] D. Bartoli, *Histoire de Saint Ignace de Loyola*, vol. i, p. 120.
[3] *A.S.*, vol. viii of Oct., p. 764 F: *. . . orans in choro et in Dei contemplatione absorptus, usque ad laquearia spiritus ardore ferretur. Saepe ad radices
arborum genuflexus, supremos ramos velut avis volando attingere videbatur. . . .*
[4] *A.S., ibid.,* p. 734 A: *Antequam ad sanctissimi corporis communionem
pervenisset, vehementi raptu per tres horas ultra cubitum a terra sublevatus. . . .*
[5] *A.S., ibid.,* p. 764 F: *aliquando ab horto ad ecclesiam subito per aera
ducebatur.*
[6] *A.S., ibid.,* p. 755 F and 756 A: *Quadam die duo religiosi sacris ordinibus
initiati, a sancto Viro praeceptum acceperant sese praeparandi, ut Missam
decantarent. Unus illorum, ut cantus experimentum faceret, in hortum se-
cesserat, ubi forte tunc S. Petrus contemplationi intendebat. Itaque cum a
praedicto religioso Evangelii verba : In principio erat Verbum, etc., intonari
audisset, accensus spiritu genua et caput inflectens, implexusque tamque rota
volatu celerrimo ad portam conventus, indeque per alias portas sine ulla laesione
ferebatur ultra cubitum a terra elevatus ; usquedum coram sanctissimo Sacramento in ecclesia in altissima extasi raptus substitisset. Aliqui religiosi, qui
Sanctum assequi non poterant cum ante aram majorem in illo statu deprae-
hendissent, aliquamdiu prius expectari, ut ad se rediret ; mox omni industria
experiri, an sensus retineret.*

see him in contemplation, suspended in the air before a calvary, at Pedrosa. During these levitations his body was sometimes luminous.[1]

Blessed John Marinoni, after studying at the University of Padua, became a secular priest. He was first attached to San Pantaleone's, then to St Mark's, as a canon, but he left his prebend to take the habit of the Theatines. He lived some years in Naples, where he had been entrusted with the spiritual direction of a convent. One Ascension Day, as he was preaching to the nuns, and as he quoted the passage in the Acts, " Ye men of Galilee, why stand ye looking into heaven ?" he was rapt, and his body was lifted from earth. The fact is mentioned in Görres, who does not give his source.[2]

Blessed Salvador of Orta (Catalonia) was a lay-brother of the Franciscan Order. He had been first a shepherd and afterwards apprenticed to a cobbler. He lived a long time in the monastery of Orta and gained the reputation of a great wonder-worker. He died in Sardinia in 1567 (March 13), aged forty-seven years. His biographer, Dimas Serpi, recounts that he experienced a levitation in the following circumstances: As Brother Salvador was collecting alms in Maella (Catalonia), he was asked to dinner by one Antony Vughet. Cutting a pomegranate, the sight of the purple grains tidily packed under the rind seemed to him so wonderful a symbol of divine order that he was thrown into ecstatic rapture, and rose above the floor, and remained thus suspended with outstretched arms. His host, greatly wondering at the sight, called his neighbours in at once to show them the prodigy.[3]

[1] A.S., ibid. p. 764 EF: Si quis de Deo sermonem coram ipso agebat dabat novis excessibus mentis occasionem ; saepe coram cruce lignea orans, brachiis in modum crucis extensis, multum supra terram evectus, omnium transeuntium et pastorum admirationem movebat. Super omnes autem raptus is singulari praerogativa notandus, quo obstupescentibus quibusdam religiosis Pedrosi existens, dum crucem in horto a se erectam devotis oculis respiceret, divini amoris fervore accensus sursum ferri, in aere coram ipsa cruce suspendi, lucidissimos ex oculi radios emittere et in crucem vibratos, ab ipsa miraculi reflexione in Sanctum redire, candidissima nube radios solis imitante caput ipsius circumdari, totamque splendore viciniam illustrari, resoluta tandem nubicula Vir Dei ad se reversus, modesta et hilari compositione in cellam suam se recipere visus est.
[2] Görres, vol. ii, ch. xxi, p. 284.
[3] A.S., vol. ii of March, p. 679 AB: Ipso praecedenti die, quo Maellae stipem petebat Salvator, ab Antonio Vughet fuit ad prandium invitatus. Placide hic annuit se venturum mendicatione finita : ibi autem inter alia fercula

The Spanish Dominican, Louis Bertrand, after evangelising the Caribbees, returned in 1569 to his own country, disgusted with the cruelty of the adventurers who had pounced upon South America. He had twelve more years to live. He used them in directing the monasteries of his Order and preaching. His Life was written by Bartholomew Avignoni, of the same Order, Postulator of his cause. There we read that Louis sometimes rose from the ground in his ecstasies. Here is the account of one of his levitations: The saint was one day returning from Moncada (some miles from Valencia) with a servant. Coming across a cornfield, then in the ear, he asked his companion to wait for him by the wayside, and retired into the field far enough to be lost sight of. A man of Moncada, Baptist Ferreri, who happened to pass that way, asked the servant whom he was waiting for on the road; puzzled at his answer, he ascended a mound and surveyed the neighbourhood. Then he beheld Louis Bertrand rapt in ecstasy, and his body floating above the ears of corn. Some Arabs, says the same author, witnessed a similar sight in Tubara, where they saw the saint lifted a cubit above the ground.[1]

Chronologically the levitations of Teresa of Avila should be placed here. As the traditions are more abundant in her case, and based on better detailed accounts, I devote the next chapter to them.

---

illata est lanx malorum granatorum plena, quorum unum accipiens et cultello dividens, O Deus, inquit, si tam pulchro ordine cunctas hujus tuae creaturae particulas disposuisti, quam ordinata erit coelestis tui palatii species, ubi Angeli spiritusque beati magis ardebunt faciem contemplantes tuam, quam grana haec pulcherrima serie distincta rubent. Quae cum dixisset, in crucis formam extendit brachia, raptusque in extasim alte sublatus a terra est : quod praedictus Antonius cum videret, exiliit a mensa, multosque accivit tanti prodigii spectatores futuros.

[1] *A.S.*, vol. v of Oct., p. 407 B: *Sic ille contemplabatur ut aliquoties non solum in ecstases reperetur, verum etiam ejusdem corpus elevaretur a terra ; uti factum est, dum e Moncada eodem, quo ibidem concionatus fuerat, die reversus est. Relicto enim retro se servo, qui ejusdem equum ducebat, ingressus est agrum, alto frumenti segete plenum, in quo a famulo non poterat videri. Ibi tam ferventer coepit contemplari, ut corpus ejus supra omnes spicas tolleretur in aerem. Interim illac transivit quidam incola Moncadae, Baptista Ferreri appellatus, qui a famulo petiit, quid ubi ageret. Respondit is, se expectare Bertrandum : quo audito, homo curiositate ductus voluit ipsum videre, et in locum eminentiorem in ora plateae insiliens, illum supra spicas segetis in aera sublatum vidit. Simile quid conspexerunt quidam Indi in Tubara, qui aediculam, in qua ipse hospitabatur, forte ingressi, spectarunt eumdem bene media ulna elevatum, quemadmodum supra dictum est.*

LEVITATION

Frances of Saint-Dominic, a Dominican, is mentioned without details in *La stigmatisation* (vol. ii, p. 239, n. 1) as a levitated mystic.

Catherine of Ricci is a well-known stigmatisée. She was fourteen years old when she took the habit of a Dominican tertiary at the convent of Prato (Tuscany), of which she became the Prioress later on. St Philip Neri thought very highly of her and exchanged spiritual letters with her. She was canonised by Benedict XIV, who had a summary of her life published. This summary mentions that when Catherine was rapt in ecstasy, her body rose into the air and remained thus suspended. Numerous witnesses are said to have observed the fact.[1]

St John of the Cross, the celebrated mystical Doctor, is said to have experienced a levitation in the course of a spiritual conversation with St Teresa. This will be found in the next chapter, devoted to Teresa. I am not aware of any other fact of the same kind being reported with details about St John.

After being a shepherd up to twenty years of age, Paschal Baylon left Aragon, his native country, to live in the kingdom of Valencia. There he continued to tend sheep, and was received as lay-brother in a Franciscan monastery. He died at Villareale, near Valencia, on May 17, 1592, aged fifty-two. His Life was written by one of his friends, John Ximenes. The latter says that Paschal, when rapt in ecstasy, was sometimes suspended in the air. Brother Andreas Rodriguez saw him one day in that position, and testified to the fact.[2]

Philip Neri, the well-known founder of the Congregation of the Oratory, was born in Florence in 1515. " Miracles," says Father F. W. Faber, " were going out from him almost like ordinary actions."[3] And among the marvels he worked, the same author mentions levitation: " . . . he in the secret of his room is floating

---

[1] *Aliquando etiam ipsum ejus corpus elevabat, ac diu in aere pendens, multis inspectantibus sustinebat* (quoted by Imbert-Gourbeyre, *Les stigmatisées*, vol. ii, p. 236).

[2] *A.S.*, vol. iv of May, p. 66: *Solebat orare cum tanta attentione et vehementia spiritus, ut absque sensu externarum rerum raptus in Deum, aliquando etiam conspiceretur ad cubitum unum elevatus a terra. Ita Jumillae in choro eum a se visum, cum illuc forte esset ingressus, deposuit Fr. Andreas Rodriguez, seque eo viso vehementer pavefactum.*

[3] F. W. Faber, *Notes on Doctrinal and Spiritual Subjects*, vol. i, p. 415.

MODERN TRADITIONS

in the air, waving to and fro like a branch in the summer wind, girdled with a golden light, hearing unutterable words and seeing unutterable things deep down in God."[1] Indeed, this ornate-looking description is based on historical information. Jerome Barnabei, in his Life of Philip, based on the documents of the process, says that the saint was frequently levitated. As a rule, it happened when he was saying Mass; he would then be lifted up between ten and fifteen feet above the ground. A girl who saw him in this situation thought he was a possessed person.[2] Cardinal Paul Sfondrati is mentioned among the witnesses of the facts. The latter said to Pope Paul V that he had seen Philip praying, lifted above the floor and nearly touching the ceiling.[3] Another time, when praying for the recovery of a sick person, he was seen raised to the ceiling, his body bathed in light.[4] Gregory Ozes saw him one day thus suspended and luminous while he prayed in the Basilica of the Vatican, before the sepulchre of the Apostles.[5] Father Anthony Gallonio, one of

[1] *Ibid.*, p. 416.
[2] *A.S.*, vol. vi of May, p. 584 EF: *Inter sacrificandum autem saepe illum in aera extolli, a pluribus observatum est: et in coenobio Turris Speculorum itidem dum Sacrum faceret, tres aut quatuor ulnas a terra sublimem conspexere plures ex religiosis illis Virginibus: id quod et in ecclesia sancti Hieronymi cum vidisset puella quaedam, ad matrem statim se vertit et dixit, Arreptium hominem istum opinor: viden' ut sese librat in aere? At illa, Tace, inquit, vir sanctus est, atque ecstasim patitur. Sulpitia quoque Sirleta, hoc idem non semel intuita, in hanc ipsam suspicionem inciderat; cum autem deinde venisset ad Sanctum conscientiam de more expositura, remque, ut erat, fateri erubesceret, Dixi, inquit, nec ultra prae pudore loqui poterat, Tum vero Philippus; age, stulta, nempe de me detraxisti, cumque illa annueret; Cedo, subjicit Pater, quid dixisti? At Sulpitia, cum pridie Sacrum faceres, atque in aere sublimem te viderem. Hic vero Dei famulus, manu silentium indicens, Quiesce, inquit. Illa tamen pergens, Tum ego mecum ipsa dixi, Certe vir iste arreptitius est. Hic vero Philippus gaudio exultans, atque subridens, Ita profecto, ita est: arreptitius sum.*
[3] *A.S., ibid.*, p. 584 DE: *Saepius quoque toto corpore in aera sublatus est: atque inter ceteros affirmavit Paulus Camillus Cardinalis Sfondratus, qui haud ita multo, ante quam ex hac vita discederet Paulo Quinto Pont. Max. narravit, sese olim orantem Dei Servum, plures ulnae a terra sublimem et prope ad ipsam cubiculi contignationem, suis oculis conspexisse.*
[4] *A.S., ibid.: Jo. Baptista . . . adeo periculoso morbo correptus est, ut nihil propius videretur, quam ut animam afflaret. Supervenit interea Philippus, eumque invisit; mox se in aliud cubiculum recipit, Deum pro illius salute exoraturus. Post mediam noctem nonnulli ex domesticis, ubinam sit Pater, inquirunt; eumque offendunt in aere sublatum, coelestique lumine circumfusum: quo viso obstupefacti exclamant: Properate, currite. His vocibus accurrunt omnes, Deique famulum ad lacunar usque elevatum, et coelesti luce radiantem conspiciunt.*
[5] *A.S., ibid.: Vidit illum pariter orantis specie in sublime elatum, et clarissimo splendore circumdatum, Gregorius Ozes Romanus, antequam ad Domi-*

67

the favourite disciples of the saint, has told us the feelings of the ecstatic during these raptures: " It seemed to him as if he had been caught hold of by someone and wonderfully lifted above the ground."[1] Philip had a marked dislike for these prodigies, and felt particularly uneasy when they occurred publicly. Therefore, every time he entered a church with somebody he was careful to be short with his devotions, so as not to exhibit his rapturous raisings.[2]   The same Gallonio says that on April 16, 1594, Philip, then very near his end, was lifted above his bed.[3]

I could not ascertain the dates of birth and death of the Franciscan Luke of Medina del Campo (south of Valladolid).   I only know he lived in the sixteenth century.   Arturus, in his *Martyrologium Franciscanum*, says that during his ecstasies his body grew bright with light and rose above the earth.[4]

Giovanni Battista Piscator was Master of the Novices of the noviciate of the Jesuits in Rome, in 1585, and had St Aloysius Gonzaga among his pupils.   Virgilio Cepari, in his Life of this saint, says that Giovanni Battista was sometimes seen, in contemplation, raised several palms over the floor.[5]

---

nicanam familiam se reciperet, quemadmodum ipsemet testatum reliquit. Praeterea in locis etiam publicis atque in ipsis ecclesiis, invitus interdum hujusmodi ecstases et raptus patiebatur ; quamobrem, cum aliquando oraret in Vaticana Basilica ad Sepulcrum Apostolorum visus est repente in sublime levari toto corpore, vestibusque ita obvolutis, quasi genibus flexis terram contingeret ; mox in locum suum reponi: veritus autem ne forte id astantes observassent, se illinc statim proripuit.
    [1] *A.S., ibid.,* p. 465 F: *Quo tempore salutarem Hostiam de more attollebat, ita ejus mens rapiebatur in Deum, ut manus sublime erectas deponere non posset.   Retulit ille postea, videri sibi se ab aliquo apprehendi; atque alte a terra per vim mirabiliter sustolli.*
    [2] *A.S.,* p. 584 DE: *Quapropter cum saepe illi hoc accideret, ubi templum aliquod cum suis adibat, salutato numine Deique Matre, per Orationem Dominicam atque Angelicam salutationem, statim surgebat ne scilicet orando diutius, in Deum raperetur.*
    [3] *Vita,* by A. Gallonio, p. 227, Italian edition (quoted by L. Ponnelle, *Saint Philippe Néri,* p. 68, n. 2).
    [4] Quoted by Imbert-Gourbeyre, *La stigmatisation,* vol. ii, p. 285.
    [5] *Vita B. Aloysii Gonzagae, S.J., A.S.,* vol. v of June, p. 845 C: . . . *in tironum exedra repertus sit orationi intentus, cum e terra aliquot palmorum intervallo divina vi sublatus, penderet in aere.*

68

CHAPTER IV

ST TERESA (SIXTEENTH CENTURY—Continued)

WITH St Teresa of Avila, the famous reformer of the Carmelite Order, we have for the first time a personal direct testimony about levitation. Explaining the difference between Union and Rapture, the saint writes as follows:[1]
" During rapture, the soul does not seem to animate the body. . . . A rapture is absolutely irresistible, whilst Union, inasmuch as we are still as on our own ground, may be hindered, though that resistance be painful and violent; it is, however, almost always impossible. But rapture, for the most part, is irresistible. It comes, in general, as a shock, quick and sharp, before you can collect your thoughts or help yourself in any way, and you see and feel it as a cloud or a strong eagle rising upwards and carrying you away on its wings.

" I repeat it; you feel and see yourself carried away, you know not whither. For though we feel how delicious it is, yet the weakness of our nature makes us afraid at first, and we require a much more resolute and courageous spirit than in the previous states, in order to risk everything, come what may, and to abandon ourselves into the hands of God, and to go willingly whither we are carried, seeing that we must be carried away, however painful it may be. And so trying is it, that I would very often resist and exert all my strength, particularly at those times when the rapture was coming upon me in public. I did so, too, very often when I was alone, because I was afraid of delusions. Occasionally I was able, by great efforts, to make a slight resistance; but afterwards I was worn out, like a person who had been contending with a strong giant; at other times it was impossible to resist at all: my soul was carried away, and almost always my head with it,—and now and then the whole body as well, so that it was lifted up from the ground.

" This has not happened to me often: once, however, it took place when we were all together in Choir, and I, on my knees, on the point of communicating. It was a very sore distress to me; for I thought it a most extraordinary thing, and was afraid it would occasion much talk; so I commanded the nuns—for it happened

[1] *Life of St Teresa*, trans. by David Lewis, 5th ed., ch. xx, pp. 160 *ff*.

69

after I was made Prioress—never to speak of it. But at other times, the moment that I felt that our Lord was about to repeat the act, and once, in particular, during a sermon—it was the feast of our house, some great ladies being present—I threw myself on the ground; then the nuns came around to hold me; but still the rapture was observed.

" I made many supplications to our Lord, that he would be pleased to give me no more of those graces that were outwardly visible; for I was weary of living under such great restraint, and because his Majesty could not bestow such graces on me without their becoming known. It seems that, in his goodness, he has been pleased to hear my prayer; for I have never been enraptured since. It is true that it was not long ago.

" It seemed to me, when I tried to make some resistance, as if a great force beneath my feet lifted me up. I know of nothing with which to compare it; . . . for it is a great struggle, and of little use, whenever our Lord so wills it. There is no power against his power. . . .

" I confess that it threw me into great fear, very great indeed at first; for when I saw my body lifted up from the earth, how could I help it ? Though the spirit draws it upwards after itself, and that with great sweetness, if unresisted, the senses are not lost; at least, I was so much myself as to be able to see that I was being lifted up."[1]

Bishop Yepes, a contemporary of the saint, and one who knew her personally, has given in his *Vida* of Teresa further details about the rapture into which she was thrown on the point of receiving communion. Don Alvaro of Mendoza, Bishop of Avila, was giving communion to the nuns at the aperture in the wall of the choir called *comulgatorio*, when the saint, rapt in ecstasy, was lifted up from the ground, raised above the height of the aperture and unable to receive the Host.[2]

Returning to Rapture and its effects, the saint says again:

" When the rapture was over, my body seemed frequently to be buoyant, as if all weight had departed from it; so much so that now and then I scarcely knew that my feet touched the ground."[3]

Once, immediately after communion, the saint, feeling herself caught up from the earth by the ecstasy, grasped at the bars of the grille, imploring God to deprive her of favours likely to make her

[1] *Ibid.*, p. 163.
[2] Yepes, *Vida, Virtudes y Milagros*, i, ch. xv (quoted by H. Thurston, " Some Physical Phenomena of Mysticism," *Month*, April-May, 1919, p. 274).
[3] *St Teresa's Life*, ch. xx, p. 169.

pass for a holy woman. Another time as a rapture was coming on her in choir, she clutched at the mats on the floor and was carried up into the air, still holding them in her hands.[1]

Maria of San Jose, a contemporary and friend of Teresa, declares in manuscript notes, still unpublished, that Mother Maria Baptista saw her Superior suspended in mid-air on two different occasions.[2]

One of the most famous levitations of the saint is that which she experienced during a conversation with St John of the Cross, who had come to the convent of the Incarnation to visit her. Teresa was listening to John, speaking about the Trinity, through the grate of the parlour, when he was rapt in ecstasy and rose from the floor, lifting up his seat along with him into the air. St Teresa, who was kneeling, was also lifted up above the ground. Sister Beatrice of Jesus, daughter of Francis Alvarez, a first cousin of the saint, happened to enter the parlour, and witnessed the strange sight.[3] The scene was commemorated by a picture representing it, which was placed in the parlour with an inscription recalling the event.[4]

The first official depositions on these facts began in 1595, thirteen years after the saint's death, thirty years after the writing of her autobiography. A few eye-witnesses were still living. This is, for instance, the deposition made under oath by Sister Anne of the Incarnation at the inquiry of Segovia:

[1] Yepes, bk. i, ch. xv (quoted by H. Thurston, p. 277).
[2] Mir, *Vida de Santa Teresa* (Madrid, 1912) (quoted by H. Thurston, p. 277).
[3] *A.S.*, vol. vii of Oct., p. 239 BC: *Cum quadam die in locutorio monasterii Incarnationis altissimos ac pro more suo fervidissimos de Sanctissimae Trinitatis mysterio sermones miscere coepissent, et Johannem sublime loquentem Teresia in genua prevoluta per cancellos auscultaret ; adeo utriusque animus divino igne incaluit, ut primum quidem Joannes una cum sede in qua requiescebat, tanquam cum suo curru Elias, mox vero etiam Teresia, genibus ut erat flexis, rapti fuerint sursum versus. Testem hujus rei habemus Beatricem a Jesu (filiam Francisci Alvarez, patruelis S. Teresiae), tunc ad Incarnationis monacham, sed postea ad Excalceatas cum aliis pluribus transgressam ; quae ipso ecstaseos tempore locutorium ingressa fuerat ad nuntium aliquod sanctae ferendum, atque ex ea postmodum tam miri spectaculi causam et occasionem didicerat. Idem non semel contigisse censendum est, tum ex fide historicorum, tum maxime ex eo quod ferunt S. Matrem dictitare solitam, caute de Deo colloquendum esse cum P. Joanne a Cruce ; quippe qui non solum raperetur ipse, verum efficeret ut alii quoque raptus paterentur.*
[4] *Siendo priora deste convento de la Encarnacion nuestra Santa Madre, y vicario de dicho convento S. Juan de la Cruz, estando en este locutorio hablando en el misterio de la Santissima Trinidad, se arrobaron entrambos, y el Santo subio elevando tras si la silla, como se ve en la pintura.*

71

" On another occasion, between one and two o'clock in the day-time, I was in the choir waiting for the bell to ring, when our Holy Mother entered and knelt down for perhaps the half of a quarter of an hour. As I was looking on, she was raised about half a yard from the ground without her feet touching it. At this I was terrified, and she, for her part, was trembling all over. So I moved to where she was, and I put my hands under her feet, over which I remained weeping for something like half an hour while the ecstasy lasted. Then suddenly she sank down and rested on her feet, and turning her head round to me, she asked me who I was, and whether I had been there all the while. I said yes, and then she ordered me under obedience to say nothing of what I had seen, and I have, in fact, said nothing until the present moment."[1]

The levitations of St Teresa are mentioned in the *Acta authentica canonizationis*, where it is recalled that the facts have been testified to by a number of witnesses.[2]

Now and then the phenomenon would be accompanied with an emission of light.[3]

[1] M. Mir, *Vida de Santa Teresa*, i, p. 286. *Cf. Obras*, vol. vi, pp. 212 and 283, n. 71 (quoted by H. Thurston, p. 277).

[2] *A.S.*, *ibid.*, p. 399 CD: *Saepissime enim in oratione positam extra se raptam fuisse constat ; et aliquod aliquando adeo vehementibus spiritus eleva-tionibus rapiebatur ut corpus etiam ipsius a terra in altum levaretur: ut deponunt in remissoriali Abulensi vigesimus super 15 ; et in 2 part. Salmantini quadra-gesimus septimus testis super decimo, et quadragesimus nonus super tertio, et centesimus et centesimus secundus testis super eodem ; et in 2 part. primus testis super 74, et vigesimus testis super 2, et trigesimus super 70 ; et in 3 p. primus testis et secundus super 2 et alii plures. Inter quos in specie de raptibus et elevationibus corporis a terra deponunt de visu in remissoriali Abulensi quadra-gesimus nonus testis super 15, etc.*

[3] *A.S.*, *ibid.*, p. 399 E.

CHAPTER V

MODERN TRADITIONS (Continued) (SEVENTEENTH CENTURY)

Margaret Agullona (1536–†1600).—Mary Raggi (1552–†1600).—Alphonsus Rubius of Valencia (†1601).—Blessed Andrew Hibernon (†1502).— St Mary Magdalen of Pazzi (1566–†1607).—St Francis Solano (1549–†1610).—Blessed Juan de Ribera (1532–†1611).—St Joseph of Leonessa (1556–†1612).—Damiano of Vicari (1569–†1613).—St Camillus of Lellis (1550–†1614).—Blessed Passitea Crogi (1564–†1615).—Blessed Bernardino Realino (1530–†1616).—St Alphonso Rodriguez (1531–†1617).—Francis Suarez (1548–†1617).—Ursula Benincasa (1547–†1618).—Blessed Mary of the Incarnation (1566–†1618).—John Leonardo of Lettere (1569–†1621).—Frances Dorothy of Villada (1558–†1623).—St Michael of the Saints (1589–†1625).—Dominic of Jesus - Mary (1559–†1630).—Jaquette de Bachelier (1550–†1635).— Onofrio of Fiamenga (†1639).—Blessed John Massias (1585–†1645).— St Marianne of Jesus of Paredes (1618–†1645).—Margaret of the Blessed Sacrament (1619–†1648).—Joan (Rodriguez) of Jesus-Mary (1584–†1650).—Christine Mary of the Cross (1585–†1650).—St Peter Claver (1589–†1654).—St Joseph of Copertino (1603–†1663).—Mary of Jesus of Agreda (1602–†1665).—St Bernard of Corleone (1605–†1667).— Mary Villani (1584–†1670).—Blessed Charles of Sezze (1613–†1670).— Teresa of the Cross (†1673).—Joan Mary of the Cross (1603–†1673).— Mary Paret (1636–†1674).—St Francis of Saint-Nicholas (1608–†1678). —Biagio of Caltanisetta (†1684).

MARGARET AGULLONA is known as an ecstatic and stigmatisée. One reads in the Franciscan Martyrology of Arturus, on December 9, that one Sunday in the octave of the Ascension, when Vespers were being sung for the feast of the Crown of Thorns, Margaret, at the sight of a painting of the Crowning of our Lord with thorns, was rapt into ecstasy and lifted from the ground. Her body remained suspended in mid-air, and could be seen moving lightly to and fro in the gentle draught that blew from the door. Many people of Valencia are said to have witnessed the scene together with the Franciscan nuns.[1]

Mary Raggi, a Dominican tertiary, also a stigmatisée, according to Imbert-Gourbeyre, often rose, in her raptures, three or four feet above the earth. Her body became radiant.[2]

[1] *La stigmatisation*, vol. i, pp. 184-185.   [2] *Ibid.*, vol. i, p. 182.

73

LEVITATION

We read in the *Palmier séraphique*, a collection of Franciscan biographies, that Alphonsus Rubius of Valencia, a lay-brother who died in 1601, was sometimes raised from the ground in his ecstasies. He was once raised high enough for his fellow-religious to be able to pass beneath his feet without touching him.[1]

Blessed Andrew Hibernon of Murcia became a Franciscan lay-brother in 1557. He was beatified in 1791 by Pius VI. His aerial upliftings are recorded in the *Summario* of his process.[2]

Mary Magdalen of the celebrated Florentine family of the Pazzi is a well-known stigmatisée. She took the habit of the Carmelites in 1583, at the age of fifteen years, and led a life of cruel mortification. Her biography was written by her confessor, Virgilio Cepari, an esteemed hagiographer and spiritual director. The latter recounts that on May 3, 1592, feast of the Invention of the Cross, the saint was lifted about fifty-five feet from the ground, to reach a crucifix she wanted to embrace. When she went up or down the stairs, she did not seem to tread the steps, but rather to fly over them.[3]

St Francis Solano, a Friar Minor, is mentioned by Imbert-Gourbeyre as having experienced frequent levitation.[4] Francis spent the last twenty years of his life in evangelising Peru, where he died in 1610. He was canonised by Benedict XIII in 1726.

Levitation is referred to in the Life of Blessed Juan de Ribera, by Castrillo (p. 92). I take his name from Father Thurston's list.

Joseph of Leonessa (States of the Church), a Franciscan missionary and preacher, had his name inscribed in the Roman Martyrology by Benedict XIV in 1746. In the summary of his life that the latter ordered to be published, we read that the saint remained sometimes

---

[1] Vol. vi, p. 317.
[2] Pp. 324, 325, 331 (quoted by H. Thurston, p. 335).
[3] *A.S.*, vol. vi of May, p. 261 CD: *Ascendebat et descendebat per scalas, agilitate tanta, ut volare potius quam pedibus terram contingere videretur : et secura inferebat sese in loca periculosa. Sicut in festo repertae Crucis die iii Maji MDXCII, quanto discurrens per chorum, absque scalis alioque humano subsidio, ascendit super coronidem ecclesiae, altam ulnis quindecim et latam solum tertia partae ulnae : ubi omnino intrepida consistens, Crucifixum sumpsit, clavisque extractis depositum recepit gremio, et adstrinxit pectori. . . .*
[4] *La stigmatisation*, vol. ii, p. 266.

several hours meditating before a crucifix. During these raptures he was lifted from the earth and his body grew very bright.[1]

The lay-brother Damiano of Vicari was also a Franciscan. The Menology of his Order states that one night he was seen soaring in the air in the church of Bivona (Sicily), all radiant with light.[2] The *Palmier séraphique* says that he ascended to the vault of the church.[3]

St Camillus of Lellis was born in 1550 at Bacchianico (Abruzzi). After being a soldier, he took the habit of the Franciscans, and later on founded the Congregation of the Regular Clerks for the service of the sick. Philip Neri was for a time his spiritual director. He died in 1614, and was canonised by Benedict XIV in 1746. In the summary of his life published by the latter it is said that the saint experienced raptures and was sometimes levitated.[4]

Blessed Passitea Crogi, a Capuchin nun, better known under the name of Passitea of Siena, had her Life written by her compatriot Father Venturi. Mary of Medici had her biography translated into French. Passitea is there said to have experienced ecstatic raptures when she was quite a child: " Après que cette enfant fut délivrée de ses langes et qu'on lui eust vestu une robbe, son confesseur a rapporté que les anges commencèrent de lui apparaître et de converser avec elle. A cela il adjoustait que fort souvent ces bienheureux esprits la souslevant par fois en l'air, luy faisaient ressentir des contentements en l'âme qui ne se peuvent exprimer."[5] Another biographer, L. Maracci, mentions similar facts with more details:
" According to the violence of the ecstasy she rose more or less from the ground. Sister Felice deposed that she had seen her raised three metres; Sister Maria Francesca, more than four metres, and at

---

[1] *Hinc ante sanctissimam Christi Domini de Cruce pendentis imaginem lures horas consistere visus est, aliquando brachiis extensis atque sublatis, aliquando vero in sublime raptus a terra, radiosque ex vultu emittere lucidissimos* (*Compendium vitae*, quoted by Imbert-Gourbeyre, *Les stigmatisées*, ii, pp. 235-236).
[2] Quoted by Görres, vol. ii, ch. xxii, p. 313.
[3] Vol. ix, p. 95.
[4] *Quin etiam in aera quandoque elevatus atque suspensus, mirabiles extases patiebatur* (*Compendium vitae*, quoted by Imbert-Gourbeyre, *Les stigmatisées*, t. ii, p. 236 [n. 1 of p. 235]).
[5] Venturi, *La vie incomparable de la Bienheureuse Mère Passidée* (quoted by Imbert-Gourbeyre, *La stigmatisation*, vol. ii, p. 275).

the same time that she was completely surrounded with an immense effulgence of light. This lasted for two or three hours. On one occasion at Santa Fiora in the house of the Duchess Sforza, when she was present with a crowd of other people, Passitea was surprised by a rapture, under the influence of which she was raised a man's height from the ground. The Duchess, who was a witness of the occurrence, caused an attestation of the fact to be drawn up, which was signed by all present."[1]

Sometimes she was seen to be transported from place to place without moving her feet and without touching the ground. " Thus in an expedition she undertook with Suor Diodata on a muddy day, when the latter was covered with mire, Passitea reached her journey's end without a speck."[2]

Blessed Bernardino Realino, a Jesuit, died in 1616 at Lecce (south of Brindisi). In the inquiry held at Naples, in 1621, for his beatification, one Signor Tobias da Ponte deposed on oath that he had seen Bernardino levitated. In 1608 he had come to Lecce in order to get spiritual advice from Father Bernardino. One Saturday in April, after Easter, waiting for the Father, he sat in a lobby into which opened the door of his room. After a moment, he noticed that this door was not completely shut, and that through the aperture rays of light were streaming. Quite puzzled by the sight, and wondering whether there was not a fire within, he drew near, pushed the door a little further open and peeped into the room.

" Thereupon," writes Father H. Thurston, from whom I am quoting, " he perceived Father Bernardino in a kneeling attitude before his prie-dieu, his face turned towards heaven, his eyes closed, and his whole body lifted a good two and a half feet above the floor (*in aria sollevato da quattro buoni palmi sopra*), while, rapt in ecstasy as he was, he kept repeating these words: ' *Gesu Maria state in mia compagnia.*'

" The witness," adds the same author, " then described the feelings of reverence mingled with fear which led him, after gazing for a while at this spectacle, to slink away home like a culprit, though he had time to notice again the radiance which streamed from the room through the partly opened doorway."[3]

[1] L. Maracci, *Vita della V.M. Passitea Crogi Senese*, p. 148 (quoted by H. Thurston, p. 334).
[2] *Ibid.*
[3] *Beatificationis et Canonizationis V.S.D. Bernardini Realini, S.J. Summarium super dubio an constet de virtutibus . . .*, pp. 200-202 (quoted by H. Thurston, pp. 326-327).

This is the very text of the deposition:
" Being asked to take good heed and bethink himself whether
all that he had described was not rather an hallucination or fancy
of his brain, and whether the radiance and light he had seen was
not a reflexion of the sun's rays or an ocular deception or some other
natural effect, he answered: ' The thing was so clear, unmistakable
and real, that not only do I seem to see it still, but I am as certain
of it as I am of speaking now, or of seeing the things around me. . . .
I noticed the light coming through the doorway not only once, but
twice, thrice and four times, before the shadow of any such idea
occurred to me. And so I began to debate with myself how there
could be any fire in the room, since the rays which issued from it
could only be caused by a great fire, just as when the blacksmiths
at their forge are hammering the red-hot iron on the anvil; and so I
stood up on purpose, and pushing open the door, I saw with my own
eyes Father Bernardino raised from the ground as unmistakably as
I now see your Illustrious Lordship. . . .'
" And being again admonished and bidden to be careful not to
be led by any mistaken sense of devotion to exaggerate or to represent
the facts otherwise than as they really were, because the saints
had no need of such perverse championship, but on the contrary are
displeased thereby, and being asked again whether any part of his
statement needed modification, he replied: ' What I have deposed
is the whole pure and unvarnished truth, without fiction or exaggeration, and it seems to me a small matter in comparison with the
sanctity, virtue and miracles of Father Bernardino.' "[1]
Further questioned as to the whereabouts of the scene he had
witnessed, Signor Tobias seems to have furnished the inquirer with
precise and satisfactory details.[2] Moreover, it is to be mentioned
that another witness, Father Antony Beatillo, gave exactly the same
account of the facts, after the version he had heard several years before
from Tobias da Ponte, his friend and countryman, of whose character
he spoke very highly.[3] Other witnesses testified to the light they
had seen at several times radiate from Father Bernardino's body,
but did not mention any uplifting over the ground.[4]

St Alphonso Rodriguez was born at Segovia in 1531. He
was first a married man. When his wife died, with his two sons he
entered the Society of Jesus as a lay-brother. He was employed
forty years as porter at the College of Palma (Mallorca Island). He

[1] Ibid., p. 328. [2] Ibid.
[3] Ibid., p. 329. [4] Ibid.

77

was beatified in 1825 by Leo XII. Imbert-Gourbeyre mentions him among the saints who experienced levitation, but without any reference to a source.[1]

Quite a circumstantial story of levitation is to be found in the Life of Father Francis Suarez, the famous theologian, also of the Society of Jesus. The document is a declaration by Brother Jerome da Silva, porter of the College of Coïmbra, written on the order of Father Antony de Morales, confessor of Suarez and of the said Brother. The paper was enclosed in an envelope with this inscription: " Confession matter; not to be opened before the death of Father Francis Suarez." This is the text itself:

" I, Brother Jerome da Silva, S.J., hereby certify that I have written this document by order of my confessor, Father Antony de Morales, and that the same Father has commanded me to give it to no one, nor to let it be read, but to keep it closed in an envelope with an endorsement absolutely forbidding anyone to open it until after the death of Father Francis Suarez. And so did I, as the said Father had asked me, deeming that the holiness of Father Suarez, whose works have brought such enlightenment to the Church of God, should not remain hidden, and adding that God might take me from this world should the disease I suffer from come to a crisis. Therefore, he ordered me to write the present paper and testify upon oath to the truth thereof.

" First of all, as I was porter of our College in Coïmbra, and Don Pedro of Aragon, then Rector of the University of Salamanca, was lodged at our house, I called for Father Suarez on his behalf. But arrived at the latter's chambers, I found that he had placed a stick across his door; and thinking he was taking rest, and might keep our guest waiting, I took the stick off, stepped into the room, called the Father by his name, and made a noise several times with my feet, without receiving any answer. The shutters of the outer room were closed; I entered the inner room; I did the same things as before, and as there was more light there, one of the shutters being ajar, I could plainly see Father Suarez in a kneeling posture, lifting up his hands, bareheaded, before his crucifix. As he did not move, I drew nearer and pulled him three times by the sleeve of his cassock; but he neither moved nor answered, which nearly threw me out of my senses for a quarter of an hour. I came out, looking for Brother Aguilar, his companion, and as I could not find him, I waited till the Father had finished. The latter came to himself from this deep

[1] *La stigmatisation*, vol. ii, p. 239, n. 1.

meditation about half an hour or three-quarters of an hour later, and I delivered my message without telling him that I had entered his chambers.

" Another day, at the same hour—it was about two in the afternoon—Don Pedro of Aragon ordered me to ask Father Suarez to be kind enough to go with him to Santa Cruz to visit the monastery. As the Father had bidden me fetch him whenever this gentleman wanted him, I went up at once. I found, across the door, the stick that the Father used to place there at this time of the day. As the Father himself had requested me to call him, and as his companion was not to be found, I removed the stick and entered. The outer room was in darkness. I called the Father, but he made no answer. And as the curtain which shut off his study was drawn, through the space left between this curtain and the jambs of the door I could see a great brightness. I lifted the curtain and entered the study. Then I saw a bright light radiating from the crucifix; it was a dazzling light and was like the reflexion of the sun from window-panes. The light was emitted by the crucifix, and I could not look at it without being dazzled. It streamed from the crucifix on to the face and breast of the Father, and, in this brightness, I could see him kneeling bareheaded before his crucifix, with his hands clasped, and his body in mid-air, raised five palms from the floor, on a level with the table where the crucifix stood. On seeing this, I withdrew, but before I left the room, stopping bewildered and as beside myself, I leaned against the door-post and remained there the time of three *Credos*. Then I went out, my hair standing on end, and I waited at the outer door quite wonder-struck. A good quarter of an hour later, I heard some noise within, and the Father, coming to remove his stick, noticed I was there. I told him then the gentleman was waiting for him. He asked me why I had not let him know. I answered that I had entered his study and had called him, but that he had not replied. When the Father heard that I had come into the study, he seized me by the arm, led me back into the inner room; then clasping his hands and with his eyes full of tears, he prayed me not to say anything of what I had seen, at least as long as he lived. I asked leave to consult my confessor about the matter. He consented the more readily to it as we had both the same confessor. My confessor advised me to write down this account in the form above explained, and I have put my signature to it, as everything therein is true. And if it should please God that I die before Father Francis Suarez, those who read this may believe it as if they had seen everything themselves; but if it should please our Lord that the Father

79

die first, I shall be able to make sworn affirmation of the whole report so far as may be necessary. JERONIMO DA SILVA.[1]

Blessed Ursula Benincasa was born at Naples in 1547. She first lived as a hermit near a Carthusian monastery. Later she founded the Congregation of the Theatines. St Philip Neri thought very highly of her. She is said to have experienced ecstatic raptures during which she was lifted from the earth. This happened in church in presence of the congregation.[2] Suspected of possession, she was exorcised. She was levitated in the course of an exorcism at the Cardinal of San Severino's.[3]

Blessed Mary of the Incarnation, better known by the name of Madame Acarie, established in France the Carmelites of St Teresa, took a share in the foundation of the Ursulines and the reformation of Benedictine Abbeys. She was a married woman and had six children, of whom three daughters became Carmelites. She herself took the habit of this Order when she had lost her husband, in 1613. She died at Pontoise, near Paris, April 18, 1618. She was beatified in 1791 by Pius VI. Her Life was written by André Du Val, Professor of Theology at the Sorbonne, who knew her well and was at various times her spiritual director. He published her biography three years after her death. He refers therein to a levitation that Mary experienced at Cardinal de Bérulle's mother's house:

" Father de Bérulle, the Superior of the Congregation of the Oratory, saw her once so deeply rapt in ecstasy that her body was lifted up two or three feet above the floor, and remained a long time suspended in mid-air; after which she found herself quite worn out."[4]

A later biographer states that this rapture lasted three hours. Chancellor Séguier's mother had the fact from Father de Bérulle himself.[5]

Leonardo of Lettere, a Dominican, spent his life in Naples, in the monastery of *Santa Maria della Sanita*. Marchese, in his *Diario*

[1] R. de Scoraille, *François Suarez*, vol. ii, ch. i, pp. 298-302.
[2] Imbert-Gourbeyre, *La stigmatisation*, vol. i, p. 214 (after Diego Garzia, *Vita della vener. madre Orsola Benincasa*).
[3] *Ibid.*, p. 216. *Cf.* p. 217.
[4] A. Du Val, *Vie admirable*, etc., p. 509.
[5] J. B. A. Boucher, *Histoire de la bienheureuse Marie de l'Incarnation*, vol. i, pp. 403-404. For biographical details on Madame Acarie (without reference to levitations), see H. Bremond's brilliant pages in *Histoire littéraire du sentiment religieux en France*, vol. ii, pp. 193 ff.

Domenicano, records on February 12 that this friar was one day raised from the ground while praying in a kneeling position in front of a crucifix.[1]

Frances Dorothy of Villada, a Spanish Dominican nun, founded in Seville the convent of which she became Mother Prioress. One of her Sisters deposed at the process of beatification that she had seen Frances raised from the earth during her meditation: " On Assumption Eve," she says, " Mother Dorothy remained in choir after Matins. I offered to stay and keep her company, but she dismissed me. I went out of the church, but soon after I stole into it again, doing my best not to make any noise. About one o'clock in the morning I could see Mother Dorothy rising in the air, a cubit and a half from the floor; her face was glowing and her whole body surrounded with an effulgence of light. The rapture lasted about two hours. When it was over our Mother gave a rap on the bench as if to call me. Thinking she did not know I was present, I did not move; but she called me by name. I drew near and knelt down at her feet. Then she put her hand to my head and said: ' Mind that I order you on God's behalf not to say anything of what you have seen as long as I live; our Lord would be displeased with it. I warn you against talking, for I know you have a mind to do it; but as God trusts you with his secrets, you should be able to keep them faithfully.' "[2]

One may read in the Breviary, on July 5, that St Michael of the Saints was often rapt in ecstasy and then rose from the earth. It occurred especially at Mass, when he was consecrating, or simply at times in the course of conversing on spiritual matters.[3] Michael belonged to the Trinitarian Order. He died in 1625 at Valladolid, aged thirty-six, in the monastery of which he was Superior. He was beatified in 1779 by Pius VI, and canonised in 1862 by Pius IX.

Dominic Ruzzola, known in religion by the name of Dominic of Jesus-Mary, was born in 1559 in Catalayud (Aragon), and took

---

[1] Quoted in *La stigmatisation,* vol. i, p. 223.
[2] *Année Dominicaine,* March 13, quoted in *La stigmatisation,* vol. ii, pp. 228-229.
[3] Die v Julii, *Nam crebris et mirificis rapiebatur extasibus, quibus vel in sublime toto assurgebat corpore, vel coelum ascendere videbatur, cum aut de Dei bonitate loqueretur, aut sacris operans calicem elevaret. Cf. Vita . . .,* by V. della Vergine, pp. 45-49, 56 (quoted by H. Thurston, p. 335).

the habit of the barefooted White Friars in early youth. He became Father-General of the Order. He is said to have foretold
the defeat of the Invincible Armada, and thereby to have become
for a time rather unpopular. His Life was written by J. Caramuel
of Lobkovicz, twenty-five years after his death (1655). This biographer records that in the year 1593, some time after Ascension
Day, Dominic rose high enough for his fellow-religious to be hardly
able then to touch the soles of his feet.[1] Quite averse to these
manifestations, he would sometimes throw himself down on the
ground when he felt he was going to be lifted up. It is said that
one day in Valencia, when he was being raised off the floor in front
of the Blessed Sacrament, a bystander seized him by the feet.
Feeling himself carried up into the air, he was frightened, let go
his hold, and had a severe fall on the ground.[2]

Dominic experienced a rapture in Madrid in the presence of
Philip II, his wife, and some courtiers. It is reported that during
this ecstasy he remained suspended in the air, and the King could
make his body wave about by blowing on him as easily as if it had
been a feather (. . . *poiche stando cosi elevato in aria, con il soffio lo
facevano facilmente movere, come una penna*).[3] This took place in
December, 1601.

Jaquette de Bachelier, of Béziers, entered the Franciscan Order
in 1559. She was twenty-five. Her Life was written by a Capuchin,
Father Casimir. The latter says that one day, Jaquette having
remained at night in the Capuchins' church, when the religious came
to sing Matins they beheld a great brightness in the church, and
" they saw Sister Jaquette rising in the air with outspread arms,
rapt, and surrounded with the very brightness that had filled the
church."[4]

[1] *Crebro raptus in ecstasim a terra elevabatur ; et ad altitudinem tantam
interdum, ut Religiosi vix potuerint ejus in aere pendentis corporis plantas
manibus tangere.* (Ch. v, p. 138, col. 1.)
[2] *Vita*, by M. H. R. P. F., bk. i, ch. xv, p. 149 : *Mentre che una notte se ne
stava in contemplatione avanti il Santissimo Sacramento, fù elevato dalla forza
dello spirito in aria, un certo suo Emolo vi trovò presente per essersi nascoto
avanti, non sò, se con intentione d' insidiarlo, quando lo vidde elevato in aria,
con gran temeritá corse, e li prese i piedi, e vedendosi ancor lui alzar de terra si
pentì della sua audacia, e lasciati i piedi cadde in terra; e pagò la pena del suo
ardire.*
[3] *Ibid.*, bk. iii, ch. xv, pp. 241-242.
[4] Casimir de Tolose, *La vanité combattue*, etc., p. 156.

82

Onofrio of Fiammenga, a Franciscan lay-brother, according to Mazzara, used to be lifted up in his raptures and become phosphorescent. Onofrio died in 1639, in the Monastery of Trevi.[1]

After being a shepherd, John Massias was a lay-brother with the Dominicans of Lima. He used to pray in the church at night, rapt in ecstasy; " a novice entering in the dark was frightened to death by coming into contact with the Brother's leg and feet as he hung suspended in the air."[2] Blessed John Massias died in 1645. He was beatified in 1837 by Gregory XVI.

Marianne of Jesus of Paredes (Ecuador), surnamed the Lily of Quito, was beatified in 1853. She did not enter any religious Order, but practised severe austerities. She died on May 26, 1645. Her office says that many people saw her rapt, with radiant face, lifted from the ground.[3]

Margaret of the Blessed Sacrament, a Carmelite nun of Beaune —where she was born and died (†1648)—experienced, according to her biographer, Father Amelote, many levitations. Sometimes the phenomenon was rather akin to a sudden transport, as when Sister Margaret, unable from weakness to go back to the infirmary after her meditation in choir, was " carried away by angels with extreme rapidity."[4] But on the day of her profession she had a levitation proper:
" Sister Margaret, in order to prepare herself for the taking of her vows, which was to take place on the feast of the Presentation of the Blessed Virgin, retired the day before into a hermitage dedicated to this divine Mother; and as she was meditating there she was suddenly rapt in ecstasy and lifted up from the ground level with the altar."[5]
A later biographer, recording the same fact, adds that one of the Sisters, seeing Margaret raised in this way, " was careful to pass her hand under the knees of the maiden to ascertain that they did not touch the altar."[6]

---

[1] Imbert-Gourbeyre, *La stigmatisation*, vol. i, p. 256.
[2] *Vita del B. Giovanni Massias*, p. 139; quoted by H. Thurston, p. 330.
[3] May 26: *Nec defuerunt qui eam sublimem a terra, animo a sensibus advocato et vultu coelesti luce radiante, a se visam, confirmarent.*
[4] Amelote, *Vie de sœur Marguerite*, p. 53. *Cf.* p. 51.
[5] *Ibid.*, p. 130.
[6] Deberre, *Histoire de la vénérable Marguerite* . . ., p. 78.

Father Amelote refers also to various other facts of the same kind. For instance, he recounts that Sister Margaret was one day raised above her bed and remained " suspended between her couch and the canopy without being able to withstand the invisible force."[1] Two more instances are to be found in a third biographer, L. de Cissey: One day as Sister Margaret had gone to the garden to gather grapes for a sick person, the other Sisters saw her lifted from the ground up to a bunch that she could not have reached otherwise.[2] Which, indeed, does not mean that she was raised very high, for her growth had been stunted at twelve years of age.

Lastly, on Good Friday of the year preceding her death (that is, in 1647), she had been meditating several hours in front of a crucifix, when she was lifted into the air, her body upright, with outspread arms, and her head a little bent on the left side. She remained in that position about an hour, in the presence of the other Sisters.[3]

Joan (Rodriguez) of Jesus-Mary took the habit of the Poor Clares at Burgos, after being married forty-five years. She was sixty years old. She is known as an ecstatic and stigmatisée. Every week, for several years, during her raptures she went through the different scenes of the Passion. She would stretch upon a large cross, and the other Sisters said they had seen her lifted up with that cross from the floor.[4] One day, as she was walking along, supported through her weakness by Alphonso and Francis Ruiz, she heard at some distance the strains of some religious music. Suddenly she was impetuously borne away to the convent of the Augustinian Sisters, about eight stone's-throws off, whence a procession was just issuing. Her two guides, whom she had not let go, did not understand how they had been transported along with her.[5]

Christine Mary of the Cross was born in Milan in 1585. She took the habit of the Franciscan Third Order when she was twenty. She was an ecstatic, and, according to Mazzara, would sometimes be raised into the air during her raptures.[6] She died in Pavia on July 24, 1650.

The Spanish Jesuit, Peter Claver, is known as the apostle of the negro slaves of Bolivia, whom he evangelised forty-four years

[1] Amelote, *ibid.*, p. 208.   [2] De Cissey, *Vie* . . ., p. 222.
[3] *Ibid.*, pp. 220-221.
[4] Imbert-Gourbeyre, *La stigmatisation*, vol. i, p. 283.
[5] Görres, *La mystique*, vol. ii, ch. xxii, p. 310.
[6] Mazzara, Feb. 28, quoted in *La stigmatisation*, vol. i, p. 277.

of his life, endeavouring at the same time to abolish the slave-trade. He died in 1654 and was canonised by Leo XIII. He was often rapt in ecstasies, during which his body became radiant and rose from the earth. His servant said he had seen him in that position, holding a crucifix in his hand. In the course of his last illness he experienced a levitation. He was then so weak that the friar who looked after him—and was witness to the fact—had to put him to bed again when he came to himself.[1]

Here chronologically the facts regarding Joseph of Copertino should be recorded; but as this saint occupies quite a prominent place in the history of levitation, I thought it better to give him, like St Teresa, a special chapter to himself.

Mary of Jesus of Agreda (Old Castile), who was Mother Superior of the Franciscan convent of the Immaculate Conception of this town, is chiefly known for her visions. Her process of beatification was interrupted in 1771 by order of Clement XIV because of the too imaginative character of her revelations. This is what her biographer, Father J. Ximenes Samaniego, who knew her personally, says of her raptures and levitations:

" The raptures of the Servant of God were in this form: her body was deprived of the use of the senses as if it had been dead, and completely insensible to any bad treatment; it rose a little from the ground, and was as light as if it had had no natural weight, so that it might be moved to and fro to a certain extent by a slight breath, like a light feather. . . . She would remain in this situation two or three hours. These raptures occurred when she heard some spiritual reading, or if she was talked to about the greatness and the beauty of God or other divine mysteries, or, again, if she heard religious music; but as a rule it happened immediately after Communion."[2]

The other nuns, in order to edify people, used to exhibit Mary in this state.[3] The latter, having heard of it, locked herself up before making her thanksgiving; but the Sisters managed to remove a board of the partition, and took her before the grille of the choir. When carried, she did not weigh more than a feather.[4]

Görres describes as follows an ecstatic flight of Blessed Bernard of Corleone (near Palermo):

[1] B. G. Fleuriau, *La vie du vénérable Père Claver*, vol. ii, pp. 92-94.
[2] Samaniego, *Vie de la vénérable Mère Marie de Jésus*, pp. 86-87.
[3] *Ibid.*, pp. 126-127.　　　　[4] *Ibid.*, p. 129.

LEVITATION

" One Corpus Christi Day, St Bernard of Corleone was kneeling with his fellow-religious in the choir of the church, before the procession, and looking towards the Blessed Sacrament on the high altar, when his soul became so glowing with divine love that it carried away his body in its flight towards God, so that flying through the air before all the congregation, he remained suspended in front of the object of his love and adoration. Everyone came up in wonder to behold the prodigy, to kiss the feet of the friar or at least touch his garment; but this crowding around made him come to himself. and he gently sank down to earth again."[1] After being a soldier, Bernard had been received as lay-brother in the Capuchin monastery of Caltanisetta. He lived there thirty-five years in the practice of severe austerities. He was beatified in 1767 by Clement XIII.

Sister Mary Villani, a Dominican nun, who founded a convent of her Order in Naples,[2] has herself described her levitations. This is what she says about the matter in a letter to her director:

" On one occasion, when I was in my cell, I was conscious of a new experience. I felt myself seized and ravished out of my senses, and that so powerfully that I found myself lifted up completely by the very soles of my feet, just as the magnet draws up a fragment of iron, but with a gentleness that was marvellous and most delightful. At first I felt much fear, but afterwards I remained in the greatest possible contentment and joy of spirit. Though I was quite beside myself (*benche stavo fuora di me*), still, in spite of that, I knew that I was raised some distance above the earth, my whole body being suspended for a considerable time. Down to last Christmas Eve (1618), this happened to me on five different occasions."[3]

Sister Mary informed her confessor that she had obtained from God that these favours should not become known to others. So she happened to be the only witness thereto.

Mary Villani died on March 26, 1670. She is known as a stigmatisée.

The Franciscan Charles of Sezze is mentioned as having experienced levitation by Imbert-Gourbeyre, who does not give any reference.[4] Charles died in Rome in 1678. He was beatified in 1881 by Leo XIII.

[1] Görres, vol. ii, ch. xxii, p. 301.
[2] The convent *di Santa Maria del divino Amore.*
[3] D. M. Marchese, *Vita della V. Serva di Dio Suor Maria Villani* (quoted by H. Thurston, p. 322).
[4] *La stigmatisation*, vol. ii, p. 239, n. 1.

The Dominican lay-sister, Teresa of the Cross, was rapt in ecstasy when she heard talk of the things of God, or even if certain sacred names were pronounced in her presence. " Wherever she happened to be, in choir, in her room, in the refectory, or walking the cloisters, her body lost its natural weight, and she was raised into the air without letting go what she held in her hands. Sometimes she would remain thus suspended in mid-air, out of her senses, five or six hours running."[1]

It all ended in Teresa's being transferred to another convent, considered as a witch, and lastly sent back into the world. Later on, the convent of Liège where she had been admitted first received her again. She died there in 1673.

Mary Paret, born in Clermont, January 5, 1636, died in the same place, July 16, 1674, in the odour of sanctity. She belonged to the Third Order of St Dominic. Her biography was written by Richard Guillouzou of the same Order, and published four years after her death. The tertiary experienced, according to her biographer, frequent raptures, when her body became luminous and was lifted from the ground. One day she was seen coming downstairs without treading on the steps. She was usually rapt in ecstasy after Communion.[2]

Joan Mary of the Cross of Roveredo, a Franciscan tertiary, began to experience ecstasies when thirteen years of age. She would at times rise from the ground and remain suspended a foot high for about a quarter of an hour. This happened chiefly at church after Communion, and puzzled the congregation very much. When the death of her father left her free, Joan Mary took the habit of the Poor Clares and founded a convent of which she became Mother Superior. This ecstatic was also a stigmatisée. She died in 1673, aged seventy.[3]

Francis of Saint-Nicholas, a Franciscan, was often rapt in ecstasy while saying Mass. These raptures were sometimes accompanied with levitation. This happened when he said Mass at the Chapel of the Escorial. He is said to have been raised, one day, as high as the vault of the church.[4]

---

[1] Imbert-Gourbeyre, *ibid.*, vol. i, p. 333.
[2] R. Guillouzou, *Vie de la sœur Marie Paret* (quoted by Imbert-Gourbeyre, *La stigmatisation*, vol. i, p. 335).
[3] *La stigmatisation*, vol. i, p. 325.
[4] Guérin, *Palmier séraphique*, vol. iv, p. 16.

Another Franciscan friar, Biagio of Caltanisetta, offered, when enraptured and levitated, a number of curious symptoms which have been described as follows by Dr. Imbert-Gourbeyre:

" His heart was palpitating in his breast as if it had been filled with boiling water. His breast was actually swelling. He shivered from head to foot as if in a fit of fever, and cried out while he was being raised into the air before a crowd of bystanders who could see his swelling breast and heard a sound—as of two stones knocking against each other—proceeding from it."[1]

[1] Imbert-Gourbeyre, *ibid.*, vol. ii, p. 247.

CHAPTER VI

ST JOSEPH OF ·COPERTINO[1] *(SEVENTEENTH CENTURY—Continued)*

JOSEPH MARY DESA deserves a niche of his own in this gallery of levitated saints. Indeed, the acts of his process of canonisation admitted more than seventy cases of raptures with levitation for the one town of Copertino and the neighbourhood.[2] Besides, not only levitations proper are recorded of him, but ecstatic flights—that is, aerial upliftings with transport from one place to another. No saint, observes the Bull of canonisation, can be compared to him in this respect.[3]

Joseph was born in Copertino, a little town of the province of Otranto, kingdom of Naples, on June 17, 1603. After being apprenticed to a cobbler, he was admitted as a novice by the Capuchins in the monastery of Martina in August, 1620. But he proved so helplessly incapable that, after a trial of eight months, he was dismissed from the noviciate and deprived of the habit. Then, with the assistance of his uncle, Father Francis Desa, he obtained his admission as tertiary into the Order of the Conventuals, in the monastery of Grotella, near Copertino, and on June, 1625, he was received as a cleric. In spite of the little progress he had made in learning, his piety and extreme good-will were so manifest that he was admitted to solemn vows, and eventually to the priesthood on March 28, 1628. He soon became famous in the province for his holiness. This fame caused him to be accused by the Inquisition of Naples of deceiving the crowd by false miracles. Summoned to Naples before this tribunal, he was not found guilty, and dismissed some weeks after; though he seems to have still been regarded with a certain amount of suspicion, for he was not sent back to Grotella, but to Rome, with a message for the Father-General of the

[1] This form should be preferred to Cupertino, derived from the Latin Cupertinum.
[2] *A.S.*, vol. v of Sept., pp. 1002 ED, 1021 D.
[3] *Ejusmodi autem cum volatu extases ita crebrae et mirabiles in eo fuere, ut patrum et majorum nostrorum memoria nemo fortasse facile inveniatur, qui earumdem vel frequentia vel magnitudine Josephum aequiparet* (quoted by Bernino, *Vie*, in Appendix).

LEVITATION

Order. The latter, by order of Pope Urban VIII, sent Joseph to
the monastery of Assisi, where he arrived the last day of April, 1639.
He remained fourteen years in the Sacro Convento, but as his
reputation of holiness had spread about the province, as it had done
before, and brought to Assisi a great concourse of people, he was
transferred to the monastery of the Capuchins at Pietrarubbia
(duchy of Urbino). But there he became more widely known than
he had ever been; people crowded into the church from Monte
Feltro, Fossombrone, Fano, Pesaro, Aricio and Cesena, to assist
at his Mass. Joseph stayed only three months at Pietrarubbia; the
Archbishop of Urbino sent him by order of Rome to the Capuchin
monastery of Fossombrone. Three years after, a Papal brief ordered
Joseph to be restored to the Conventual Order, and on July 10, 1657,
the saint arrived at the monastery of the Conventuals at Osimo,
an old city in the Marches. He was to die there six years later, on
September 18, 1663.

I will recount hereafter the principal levitations or ecstatic flights
mentioned in the life of St Joseph. I shall, as a rule, follow the
chronological order, without binding myself to it whenever it would
prevent me from grouping facts of similar character.

Once, on Christmas Eve, as he heard a tune played on the bagpipes
by some shepherds he had invited to celebrate the Nativity, Joseph
began to dance in a fit of ecstatic jubilation, then with a loud cry
flew through the air from the middle of the church to the high altar,
a distance of about forty feet.[1] In his biography Bernino gives the
deposition of one of the shepherds, as recorded in the acts of the
process:

" I was tending my sheep near Grotella. On Christmas Eve,
Brother Joseph came to me and the other shepherds of the plain,
and said to us: ' Will you not come, tonight, and play on your
bagpipes in the church at Grotella, to celebrate the birth of Jesus
Christ?' Thus invited, I came with many other shepherds, with
our bagpipes and flutes. Brother Joseph, who looked very pleased,

[1] *A.S.*, *ibid.*, p. 1021 AB: *Ac primo quidem Cupertini in nocte vigiliae
Natalis Domini, Josephus, auditis tibiis et fistulis quorumdam pastorum, quos
ad celebrandam caelestis Pueri nativitatem invitaverat, coepit primum prae
vehementi laetitia tripudiare, deinde emisso suspirio cum magno ejulatu, velut
avis per aera volavit a medio ecclesiae usque supra altare majus, plus quam
quinque perticis inde dissitum, ibique tabernaculum Sanctissimi Sacramenti
complexus, quarta circiter parte horae suaviter haesit, nec tamen ullum e cereis
ardentibus, quorum altare plenum erat, interim dejecit, nec ulla ipsius vesti-
menti pars igne contacta est. Stupebant ultra modum pastores illi. . . .*

90

came to meet us. We entered the church together with Brother Joseph at our head. It was about ten or eleven o'clock in the evening, and we were a great many shepherds playing on our bagpipes and flutes in the nave of the church. Then we could see Brother Joseph begin to dance, in his excessive joy, to our tunes. But suddenly he gave a sob, then a great cry, and at the same time he was raised into the air, flying from the middle of the church, like a bird, to the high altar, where he embraced the tabernacle. Now, from the middle of the church to the high altar the distance was about forty feet.[1] A most wonderful thing is that the altar being covered with lighted candles, Brother Joseph flew and alighted among these candles and threw down neither a candle nor a candlestick. He remained thus about a quarter of an hour on the altar, kneeling and embracing the tabernacle, and then came down without being helped by anybody and did not disturb anything. He left us with tears running down his cheeks, saying: 'My brethren, that will do. Be blessed for God's sake.' We were struck with awe and wonder. I thought to myself: ' It is certainly a miracle.' "[2]

Another time, on the occasion of a procession for the feast of St Francis, Joseph, dressed in a cope, was lifted up to the edge of the pulpit, about fifteen palms from the ground, and remained suspended there enraptured, with outspread arms, in a kneeling position.[3] This took place at Copertino before the other religious and the people of the town.

During the night of Holy Thursday, as he was praying with some fellow-religious in front of the sepulchre erected on the high altar, amidst many lamps, Joseph sprang into the air towards the chalice without disturbing the decorations, and came back to his place through the air when ordered to do so by his Superior. He was seen to fly in the same manner to the altar of St Francis, or to that of the Virgin at Grotella, while the Litany was being recited.[4]

[1] *Più de cinque canne.* More than five rods, says the Latin text of Pastrovicchi.
[2] D. Bernino, *Vie de S. Joseph de Copertino*, p. 68. (From process, Fo. 65, No. 12, B, par. 77.)
[3] *A.S., ibid.,* 1021 B: . . . *non minor fuit Religiosorum et incolarum Cupertini admiratio, dum B. Josephum, pluviali indutum, ut in sollemnitate S. Francisci supplicationi adsisteret, viderunt volantem supra pulpitum, quindecim palmis a terra elevatum, et in ejusdem ora expansis brachiis diu ecstaticum et genibus mirabiliter flexis.*
[4] *A.S., ibid.,* B: *Stupendus pariter fuit raptus quadam nocte feriae V hebdomadae Majoris, dum coram sacro sepulchro, quod in majori altari erectum*

LEVITATION

One day, seeing workmen who tried to erect a high and heavy cross for a calvary on a little hill between Copertino and Grotella, Joseph flew about eighty paces[1] from the portal of the monastery to the said cross, lifted it as easily as if it were a straw, and put it into the hole dug for that purpose. Later on he was often seen flying through the air towards this calvary from a distance of ten or twelve paces, and rising to one of the arms or to the top of the central cross.[2]

As a fellow-religious was speaking to him about the descent of the Holy Ghost on the Apostles, a friar happened to pass with a lighted candle in his hand. At the sight, Joseph was rapt in ecstasy; he uttered a cry and flew fourteen paces into the air.[3]

Another time he flew up to an olive-tree, because a priest, Don Antonio Chiarello, had said to him, " Brother Joseph, what a beautiful heaven God has made !" And he remained on the tree half an hour, in kneeling posture, lightly poised on a branch that could be seen to wave to and fro as if a bird had been perched on it.[4]   When he

---

erat, illuminatisque nubibus, ac multis lampadibus exornatum, cum ceteris Religiosis oraret. Inopinato quippe recta volavit ad urnam divini sui thesauri amplexandum, intactis ornamentis omnibus ; et post aliquod temporis spatium, a superiore revocatus, simili volatu rediit, unde venerat. Pari modo interdum volavit supra altaria S. Francisci et B. Mariae Virginis Cryptellae inter recitandum Litanias. Cf. Bernino, p. 296, after Fo. 548, No. 40, A, par. 48, and ch. xxii, p. 316, after Fo. 32, No. 12, A, par. 26.

[1] Fifteen paces, according to Bernino, p. 291.

[2] *A.S., ibid.,* p. 1021 BC: *Prae ceteris tamen mirabilis simul ac visu gratus fuit ejusdem raptus amoris, cum in quodam exiguo colle, Cupertinum inter et conventum Cryptellae sito, volens exhibere montem Calvariae, erectisque ibidem jam duabus crucibus, vidensque decem homines conjunctis viribus ob grave pondus frustra conatos crucem tertiam, reliquis majorem et quinquaginta quatuor palmos altam, in destinato loco erigere, interno igne suo motus Beatus, a porta conventus per spatium passuum circiter octoginta versus eamdem crucem volavit, arreptamque ipse solus velut levissimam paleam sustulit, et in parata scrobe collocavit. Ad hasce cruces deinde orare solebat, crebroque contingit, ut modo per decem modo per duodecim passus, nunc supra clavum mediae crucis, nunc supra ejusdem apicem, volaret, raptus ab amore suo crucifixo.*

[3] *A.S., ibid.,* 1021 C: *Volavit praeterea quatuordecim passibus per aera, Spiritus sancti igne abreptus, quando de illius ad Apostolos adventu loquens, Religiosum quemdam, lucernam accensam manu gestantem, transeuntem conspexit.*

[4] *A.S., ibid.,* 1021 C: *Volavit pariter supra oleam, cum a quodam sacerdote sibi dici audisset: " Frater Joseph, quam pulchrum caelum fecit Deus !" Eoque supra eamdem spatio mediae horae flexis genibus permanente, stupenda res erat, ramum illum, cui insistebat, videre leviter motum non secus ac si avis in eo consedisset.*

92

came to himself, he could not come down, and required a ladder to do it.[1]

On July 10, 1657, as he was going to the monastery of Osimo where he was transferred by order of the Pope, Joseph was shown by a priest the cupola of the church of Loreto, which is about six miles from Osimo. On looking, the saint had a rapture, and exclaimed: " Do you not see the angels ascending and descending from heaven to that Sanctuary ?" And uttering his cry, he flew through the air about twelve palms high to an almond-tree about thirty yards away.[2]

Another time, at Fossombrone, he was borne in a rapture over the highest trees of the garden. It was on the second Sunday after Easter, on which the Gospel of the Good Shepherd is read. The sight of a lamb in the garden reminded Joseph of the Gospel words; he was rapt in ecstasy and flew very high up into the air. This is how Bernino reports the fact: " It was on the Sunday when the Gospel *Ego sum Pastor bonus* is read; in the evening, after supper, Joseph, going into the garden with the other friars, came across a lamb, and stopped to look at it. As he seemed to want to take hold of the animal, a young friar took it up and placed it in his arms. Joseph lovingly pressed the lamb to his breast, then took it by the legs and put it on his shoulders. By insensible degrees, the saint grew more and more excited. He began to walk at a quicker pace, and then to run through the garden. The religious and some lay visitors followed him, wondering what was going to happen. Presently they saw the lamb and Joseph himself in mid-air. The lamb had been hurled with wonderful strength by the saint, who, almost at the same time, had flown after it, and was now suspended in the air at the height of the trees of the garden. He remained thus in the

---

[1] Bernino, p. 295.
[2] *A.S., ibid.,* 1040 DE: *Interea dum Beatus in rusticam pergulam ascendisset, oculosque per viciniam versaret, Religiosus quidam sacerdos tholum famosae ecclesiae sacrae Domus Lauretanae a longe indigitavit, in quam Josephus obtutum figens, " An vides, attonitus inquit, angelos e coelo et sacra Domo euntes et redeuntes ?" Haecque dicens ac saepius repetens, emisso solito clamore, deorsum raptus, versus amygdalam spatio sex perticarum in longitudinem, in altitudinem vero palmorum duodecim volavit. Erat tum dies decima Julii anni MDCLVII cujus vespere B. Josephus in S. Francisci conventum sui ordinis Minorum conventualium Auximi advenit.* The almond-tree of St Joseph is still an object of veneration.

93

air, kneeling, for more than two hours—that is, half an hour after sunset."[1]

Several times Joseph managed to lift somebody up into the air in his flight. This occurred the first time in the church of St Clare at Copertino on the occasion of the clothing of some nuns. Joseph was at the ceremony in a corner of the church, where he was kneeling. As soon as he heard the antiphon " Come, thou bride of Christ," intoned by the choir, he was seized with ecstatic jubilation, rushed towards the confessor of the convent—a member of the Order of the Reformation—grasped him by the hand, snatched him off the floor, and began whirling round with him in mid-air.[2]

The same thing happened to the Father Custos of the Sacro Convento at Assisi, Raffaelle Palma. As solemn Vespers had been sung in honour of the Immaculate Conception in the chapel of the noviciate, Joseph begged him to repeat with him the words *Pulchra est Maria*; took him by the side, and rose with him into the air, while he kept exclaiming: " Beautiful Mary ! Beautiful Mary !"[3]

---

[1] Bernino, ch. xiv, p. 212. *Cf. A.S., ibid.*, 1038 EF (*Ex proc. ord. Auxim.* a fol. 1344 *et seq.*, Summ. pag. 168, par. 299): *Secunda ecstasis accidit in eodem horto, vespere Dominice, in qua legitur Evangelium: Ego sum Pastor bonus. Josephus, viso ibidem agnello, pro more suo a rebus creatis ad supernaturalium ac coelestium contemplationem excitari se sensit. " Ecce, ait exsultabundus, oviculam ";, cumque eam arripere vellet, Religiosus quidam eamdem cepit, et in ipsius brachiis deposuit. Ipse vero postquam ei aliquantulum blanditus esset, arreptam cruribus suo collo imposuit, et hac ratione divinum Pastorem contemplatus, per hortum versus patrem guardianum, qui aderat, cucurrit, laetabundus exclamans: " Pater guardiane, ecce bonum Pastorem, qui ovem reportat." Post haec agnello in altum vibrato, ipse retro illum per aera supra arbores volavit, ibidemque flexis genibus, et brachiis apertis ultra duas horas in ecstasi mansit, Religiosis, qui aderant, supra modum stupentibus.*

[2] *A.S., ibid.*, 1021 CD: *Majorem tamen, quam usquam alibi Josephus stuporem movit circumstantibus in ecclesia S. Clarae Cupertini, ubi, cum ipse quoque adesset, dum aliquot sacrae virgines religioso habitu induerentur, et musici ea verba canerent : Veni Sponsa Christi, visus fuit e suo angulo, in quo genibus flexis orabat, velociter currere ad quemdam patrem Minorem Reformatum, ejusdem monasterii confessarium, manuque apprehensum, vi humana majori, sublevare e terra, et cum laetissimo raptu et violento tripudio secum per aera circumducere. . . . Cf.* Bernino, p. 153.

[3] *A.S., ibid.*, 1022 C: *Multo tamen magis admiratus est et stupuit pater Custos, quando post Vesperas in honorem immaculatae conceptionis in sacello tirocinii Assisiatis solemniter cantatas, rogatus a Josepho, ut secum repeteret : " Pulchra Maria " vidit se ab eo apprehensum constrictumque ad latera, et ab ipso et cum ipso saepius exclamante, " Pulchra Maria, Pulchra Maria !" in aera sublatum. Cf.* Bernino, pp. 150-151, after Fo. 571, No. 40, D, par. 64.

He also lifted into the air a lunatic who had been brought to the monastery of Assisi for Joseph to cure him. This lunatic was a noble citizen of Assisi named Balthasar Rossi. He was led to the saint bound to a chair, for he was dangerous and used to assault people, saying they were mad. Joseph ordered the man to be set free, made him kneel down in his oratory, and, laying his hand on his head, said: " Do not fear, Chevalier Baltasar; commend yourself to God and his Holy Mother." With these words, he clutched the lunatic by the hair, uttered his usual cry, and was raised off the floor with Baltasar, whom he held for a time in mid-air to the amazement of the bystanders. Then, after a quarter of an hour,[1] he sank to earth again and dismissed the nobleman with these words, " Now, cheer up, Chevalier ! "[2]

During a short stay at Nardo, after leaving Copertino, Joseph was seen to be lifted up in ecstasy in the church of St Francis to the awe of all present. He was also levitated at the same time in the house of a sick person whom he was visiting. On hearing a song, he uttered his usual cry, was raised off the floor and lifted in kneeling posture on to the edge of a table.[3] The same thing occurred on May, 1649, at Assisi, when he was at the bedside of Father Gabriel of Caravaggio, then dying. At the moment of Extreme Unction, Joseph rose in ecstasy into the air and was lifted over the bed.[3]

Passing through Monopoli, on his way to Naples, where he was summoned by the Holy Office, Joseph was led by his fellow-religious

[1] Bernino, *ibid.*

[2] *A.S., ibid.*, 1022 CD: *Prae ceteris tamen plurimis raptibus quos brevitatis ergo praetermittimus, ille admirabilis simul et utilis fuit, quem quidam vir nobilis, amens et furiosus, expertus fuit. Hic ligatus in sedili ad Josephum delatus est, ut pro ejusdem incolumitate Deum precaretur. Tum vinculis soluto, et in sacello genuflectere vi coacto, erexit sese in pedes suos Servus Dei, manuque capiti ejus imposita, ait : " Domine Baltazar, ne metue ; commenda te Deo, ejusque sanctissimae Matri." Haec dicens apprehendit capillos ejus, et in consuetum clamorem Ah ! prorumpens, sustulit se e terra, et ipsum per capillos secum elevatum, brevi tempore in aere sic detinuit, non sine ingenti circumstantium stupore. . . . Cf.* Bernino, p. 152.

[3] *A.S., ibid.*, 1021 E: *Egressus itaque Cupertino, Neriti paulisper moratus est; ubi cum sacro omnium adstantium horrore visus est in ecclesia S. Francisci in ecstasim raptus ; et nunc in quadam domo, quam aegri sanandi gratia adierat, ad conspectum imaginis, quae Ecce Homo exhibebat, instar statuae haerere immobilis ; nunc in alia aede, audita quadam rustica cantilena, dare solitum clamorem, et sublatus e terra, in ora tabellae genu flectere. Cf.* Bernino, pp. 300 and 302, ch. xxii, after Fo. 556, No. 40, C, par. 3.

to the monastery church to see a new statue of St Antony of Padua. As soon as he beheld the image, his feet were swept off the ground, and he flew through the air to the altar where the statue was set— a distance of about fifteen palms—and returned to his former place in the same way.[1]

At Naples, in the church of St Gregory of Armenia, where he had said Mass, he suddenly rose with a cry from the corner of the chapel where he was praying, flew up to the altar among the flowers and burning candles, with outspread arms, to the great amazement and terror of the nuns of St Ligorio, who cried out, " He will catch fire !" But with a new cry, he flew back to the middle of the nave, alighted on the floor, and began whirling about on his knees, exclaiming, " O most Blessed Virgin ! O most Blessed Virgin !"[2]

A sacred image or song, a blade of grass, the leaf of a cherry-tree the texture of which he admired, anything was for Joseph an occasion of rapture.[3] The Acts of his process refer to fifteen levitations which he experienced in front of images of the Holy Virgin,[4] and the height of one of these upliftings reaches about seventy feet.[5]

Brother Giunipero of Palermo said he had seen Joseph rise, kneeling, from the floor in his cell, as he heard a canticle sung by his novices. Father Francesco Antonio Terralavore dell' Aquila, seeing that the frock of the ecstatic was still touching the ground,

[1] *A.S., ibid.,* 1021 E: *Post haec dum Neapolim pergens, Monopolim transiret, a Religiosis fratribus suis in ecclesiam suam ductus, ut novam pulchramque S. Antonii Patavini statuam videret, ad ejusdem conspectum subito elevatus a terra, per quindecim palmorum spatium volavit versus dicti Sancti imaginem, super altare collocatum ; unde deinde simili volatu per eamdem viam ad priorem locum reversus est. Vix cessaverat primus raptus, quin ingruente secundo, denuo inter recitandum litanias volaverit ad altare Virginis sine labe conceptae, a quo pari modo per aerem rediit ad locum, unde fuerat sublatus.* Cf. Bernino, p. 92.

[2] *A.S.,* 1021 F: *Neapolitana quoque civitas prodigiosos ejus raptus admirata est ; ubi ipse ab inquisitore jussus (ut supra diximus), Missam celebrare in ecclesia S. Gregori Armeni, quae monialium S. Ligorii est, ibidem in ejusdem ecclesiae angulo intentus precibus, cum ingenti clamore subito sublevatus volavit, et erectus in pedes, super altare stetit, expansis in modum crucis brachiis, membrisque inter flores et ardentes cereos ita insertis, ut moniales altis vocibus exclamarent : " Aduritur, aduritur !" verum ille edito denuo clamore, simili volatu ad medium ecclesiae illaesus reversus est, ubi, positis humi genibus, exsiliens, seque, velocissime circumagens, " Ah beata Virgo, ah beata Virgo !" cantabat.* Cf. Bernino, p. 96.

[3] Bernino, ch. xix, pp. 267-268.
[4] *Ibid.,* ch. xxii, p. 313.   [5] *Ibid.*

passed his hand beneath his knees, to ascertain if he was actually off the floor.[1] So did also one of the three children who sang under the direction of Antonio Cassandri, of Brescia, chapel-master at the Sacro Convento of Assisi, when he saw Joseph lifted over the floor of his cell, on hearing a sacred song.[2]

His raptures in saying Mass were of daily occurrence, and they were often accompanied with levitation.[3] Sometimes, though, he was not lifted off the floor, but simply raised a little over it, standing on the ends of his great-toes. He came to take up that position when consecrating at Mass, and kept it till after Communion.[4]

The levitations or ecstatic flights of Joseph took place several times in presence of notable witnesses. The Father-General of his Order, having brought him to Pope Urban VIII, the saint was rapt in ecstasy and lifted into the air before the Pontiff, and remained thus suspended till his Father-General's order brought him back to his senses. Urban VIII marvelled much at the sight, and declared

[1] R. Nuti, *Vita*, pp. 472-473: *Fra Giunipero da Palermo raccontò al P. Abbate, che un Mercordì essendo andato il P. Maestro con li Novitij in camera del P. Giuseppe, mentre erano nell' oratorio il servo di Dio con li Novitij cantarono alcune canzonette spirituali, composte da lui in lode della Beatissima Vergine, e replicatele tre, ò quattro volte, egli andò in estasi, restando come soleva inginocchioni, e stando a lui più vicino d' ogn' altro, il Padre M. Francesco Antonio Terralavore dell' Aquila, dalla positura dell' habito dubito, che non stesse inginocchioni in terra ; e però pose sotto le sue mani, e si accorse benissimo, che non toccava la terra con i ginocchi; e avvisatone il Padre Maestro, egli con tutti li Novitij si chiarirono di questa verità, e per maggior certezza, doppo esser stato così un quarto d'hora, lo sentirono cader in terra con le ginocchia, restando tanto maggiormente certificati, e confermati nella credenza, ch' egli stasse in aria ; e poco doppo hebbe un' altr' estasi pure in aria, come raccontò il Padre Maestro sudetto.*
[2] *Ibid.*, pp. 467-468: *Si ritrovava Maestro di cappella in questo sacro Convento [d'Assisi] il Padre Antonio Cossandri da Brescia, e haveva sotto la sua disciplina tre figliolini, che cantavano come tre Angeli, mà quello, che più importa havevano il timor di Dio, e le buone creanze ; haveva messo in musica un Dialogo trà alcune anime del Purgatorio, che quei figliolini cantavano sù l'Arciliuto ; li mandò una sera accompagnati dal P. Antonio Ottaviani di Assisi à cantarlo nella camera del P. Giuseppe, quale in sentirlo se n' andò subito in estasi inginocchioni, mà uno di quei figliuoli mettendogli le mani sotto le ginocchia, trovò che stavano sollevate da terra in aria ; ne avvisò il Padre Antonio sudetto, quale facendo esquisita diligenza, trovò verissimo quanto gli haveva detto quel figliulo, perchè il corpo del Padre Giuseppe non toccava in nessun luogo in terra.*
[3] *A.S.*, *ibid.*, 1021 D; Bernino, p. 303.
[4] Bernino, ch. xxii, p. 296.

that if Joseph were to die in the course of his pontificate, he would not fail to bear witness to the fact.[1]

Among the most remarkable flights Joseph performed during the thirteen years he lived at the Sacro Convento, the one witnessed by the High Admiral of Castile should be mentioned. This personage was Spanish Ambassador to the Papal Court, and passed through Assisi in 1645 with his wife, on purpose to visit the famous saint. He entertained him in his cell, and returned to the church, where his wife was waiting for him. " I have seen and spoken with another St Francis," he said to the latter, who also expressed her desire to meet Joseph. At her request the Father Custos ordered the saint to go into the church and speak with the lady. " I will comply," answered Joseph, " but I do not know whether I shall be able to speak." Scarcely had he entered the church, when he flew to a statue of the Immaculate Conception, twelve paces off, over the heads of the bystanders, alighted on the foot of the statue, prayed some moments there, and flew back, with his great cry, to his former place, whence he returned instantly to his cell. The Admiral, his wife, and their retinue were quite amazed. " Stupefied " would be more suitable as far as the lady is concerned, for, according to the Acts of the process, she actually fainted, and required plenty of smelling-salts to recover her senses.[2]

[1] *A.S.*, *ibid.*, p. 1021 F: *Quia vero decreverat Deus ipsum etiam coram primae dignitatis personis admirabilem exhibere, fecit, ut, dum Romae moraretur, eum pater Generalis ad osculandos summi Pontificis Urbani VIII pedes secum duceret : quod dum ageret, Jesum Christum in suo Vicario contemplatus, in ectasim raptus et elevatus a terra haesit, donec a Generali suo revocaretur : ad quem conversus multumque admirans Pontifex ait : "Si Josephus Pontificatus sui tempore moriturus esset, sese de facto testimonium dicturum."* Cf. Bernino, p. 105.

[2] *A.S.*, *ibid.*, 1022 AB: *Nec facile dictu est, quot ejusmodi raptus fuerint, quibus ipsum Deus annis tredecim, quos Assisii exegit, honorare dignatus est : sed inter celebriores . . . primo loco recensetur, quem subdo. Postquam magnus archithalassus regni Castellae, Hispaniarum legatus apud Sedem Apostolicam, dum anno MDCXLV transiret Assisium, in cubiculo cum Josepho collocutus fuisset, imperavit ei pater custos sacri conventus ut e cubiculo ad ecclesiam descenderet, ubi archithalassi conjux magno ipsum videndi, et cum eo loquendi desiderio expectabat. Respondit Josephus : " Obediam ; sed non scio, an futurum sit, ut cum ipsa loqui possim." Revera vix in ecclesiam ingressus, oculos in statuam S. Mariae sine labe conceptae, quae in altari stabat, conjecerat, quin ad ejus pedes amplexandos spatio duodecim passuum super omnium adstantium capita provolaverit; postquam autem Reginam Coeli aliquantulum adorasset, super eadem cum solito stridore revolavit, et extemplo ad cellam suam repedavit, stupente cum uxore sua archithalasso, sancteque concussis, qui in eorum comitatu*

Still more striking is the levitation witnessed by John Frederick, Duke of Brunswick,[1] which caused this nobleman to abjure his Lutheran faith and become a Catholic. John Frederick, who was then twenty-five, was visiting the different Courts of Europe in 1649. As he was in Rome, he came to Assisi on purpose to visit Joseph. On his arrival at the Sacro Convento, he was lodged in the rooms reserved for persons of rank, and, as he wished to speak with the saint and then continue his journey, he was led, with his two chamberlains, next morning to the door of the chapel where Joseph was saying Mass. From there the visitors could see Joseph, a little before Communion, with his loud cry in kneeling posture, fly five paces from the altar and return there with the same cry in like manner. On the next morning the Duke wished again to assist at the Mass said by Joseph, and this time he could see him raised a palm off the floor and remain thus suspended about a quarter of an hour, elevating the Host. On seeing this, the Duke began weeping. As to one of the chamberlains who was a Lutheran like his master, he declared his dissatisfaction at having come to this place where such spectacles robbed him of his previous tranquillity of mind. The prince conversed with Joseph till midday; and returned to visit the saint in his cell after Vespers. Not only did he declare himself ready to become a Catholic, but after assisting at Compline and following the procession, he enlisted in the Archconfraternity of the Cord of St Francis. He then returned to Brunswick to arrange his affairs, and the following year he came back to Assisi, where he abjured Lutheranism in the presence of Joseph and Cardinals Facchinetti and Rappaccioli.[2]

---

magno numero aderant. (In a note, 1023 A: *Ex testibus de visu ex proc. apost. Assis.,* fol. 227, etc.) *Cf.* Bernino, pp. 169-170, after Fo. 123, No. 13, B, par. 41.; Fo. 563, No. 40, D, par. 23; Fo. 576, No. 40, D, par. 83.

[1] The son of George of Brunswick and Wilhelmina Amelia, born in 1625. He married, in 1668, Benedictina Henrietta Philippina of Bavaria, who gave him four daughters. He died in 1689.

[2] *A.S., ibid.,* 1024, 43-44: *Non minus patuit efficacia orationi illius in adducendo ad fidem catholicam Johannem Fredericum principem Brunsvicensem ex haeresi Lutherana. Hic princeps aetatis vigenti quinque annorum, dum anno MDCLIX praecipuas Europae aulas viseret, curiositate sua ductus, Roma Assisium studiose divertit, Josephi videndi gratia, quem ex fama in Germania jam noverat. Ad sacrum conventum digressus, receptus et in parte aedium principibus destinata hospitatus fuit. Ibi suum cum Josepho colloquendi, ac mox deinde discendi desiderium exposuit; posteroque mane cum duobus comitibus e suo comitatu, uno Catholico, altero haeretico, ad portam ecclesiae deductus est. Celebrabat tum ibidem Missam Beatus; qui, etsi ea de re nihil sciret, sensit tamen, dum consecratam Hostiam rumpere vellet ; durissimam enim comperit ; eamque cum vi rumpere frustra tentasset, in patena reposuit, et oculis in sacro-*

LEVITATION

The Lutheran chamberlain, H. J. Blume, also became a Catholic in 1653.[1]

Among other witnesses of note who beheld similar facts, Mary, daughter of Charles Emmanuel of Savoy and Catherine of Austria, should be mentioned. This princess felt such affectionate reverence to Joseph that she settled for several months at Perugia in order to visit the saint frequently. She often witnessed his ecstatic flights during Mass, and saw him once in his private chapel lifted up three palms over the floor at the time of elevation. She also saw him

---

sanctam Hostiam fixis, primo in vehementem clamorem prorupit, deinde vero cum ingenti stridore per quinque passuum spatium retrorsum volavit flexis genibus par aera ; ac post similem vociferationem tandem ad aram reversus, sacram Hostiam, sed magno cum nisu, divisit. Rogatus proinde jussu principis a superiore causam sui planctus, respondit : " Popularis, hi, quos hoc matutino tempore ad Missam meam misisti, duri cordis sunt, quia non credunt omnia quae credit sancta mater Ecclesia; ideoque Agnus in manibus meis hodie mane obduruit, nec potui illum dividere." Perculsus ejusmodi facto responsoque princeps, de discessu suo nihil amplius sollicitus, desideravit post sumptum prandium cum Dei Servo colloqui, uti fecit usque ad tempus Completorii ; divina- que gratia ipsum interim magis excitante, voluit ejusdem Missae postridie denuo interesse; in qua Missa dum sacra Hostia elevaretur, ejusdem crux nigri coloris omnibus apparuit eodem tempore, quo celebrans cum solito clamore raptus in aera, uno palmo supra scabellum altaris cum Hostia et brachiis sic elevatis octava circiter horae parte permansit. Ad conspectum tanti prodigii coepit princeps vehementer flere: deinde vero unus e duobus comitibus, haereticus scilicet, indignatus ait: " Maledictus ego dum in has regiones veni: in patria mea securus eram; hic vero me agitant furiae et conscientiae scrupuli." Porro Josephus, qui omnia superiori lumine illustratus viderat, quemdam familiarem suum de futuro principis ad fidem accessu certiorem fecit : " Gaudeamus, inquiens, quia cerva sauciata est." Reipsa postquam cum principi usque ad horam prandii locutus fuisset, eumdem, dum post vesperos in cubiculum regrederetur, conspicatus occurrit ipsi obviam et proprio eum cingulo suo cinxit, magno cum fervore spiritus dicens: " Ego te vincio ad paradisum: Nunc vade, S. Franciscum venerare, assiste Completorio, processionem devote comitare, et fac, quidquid faciunt monachi." Haec omnia bonus princeps humiliter executus est, affirmans se catholicum esse ac praeterea manu propria se in albo sodalium cordigerorum S. Francisci inscripsit. Antequam tamen haeresim suam publice ejuraret, voluit in principatum suum redire, ut de ejusdem negotiis disponeret; unde anno subsecuto, ut promiserat, Assisium reversus, genibus ante Sanctissimum Sacra- mentum flexis, coram duobus cardinalibus Facchinetto et Rappacchiolo, pristinos errores suos abjuravit in manibus B. Josephi. . . . Cf. Bernino, pp. 172 ff., after Fo. 573, No. 4, D, par. 73; Fo. 567, No. 4, D, par. 42; Fo. 113, No. 13, A, par. 288; Fo. 88, No. 13, A, par. 131.

[1] Andreas Raess, *Die Convertiten seit der Reformation*, vol. vi, pp. 450-452, 558-571 (quoted by F. S. Laing, *Saint Joseph of Copertino*, p. 44).

fly upon the altar, after Mass, when he had laid aside his vestments, and remain there, rapt and kneeling.[1]

One of the last levitations of Joseph, which is also one of the most curious and best described—though very rarely mentioned—is the one he experienced in the course of a surgical operation. This is the deposition of the surgeon rancesco Pierpaoli, who witnessed the facts:

"During the last illness of Father Joseph, I had to cauterise his right leg by order of Dr. Giacinto Carosi. Father Joseph was sitting on a chair, with his leg laid on my knee. I had already begun cauterising, when I noticed that Father Joseph was rapt out of his senses; his arms were outspread, his eyes open and lifted to heaven. His mouth was wide open, his breathing had nearly stopped. I noticed that he was raised about a palm over the said chair, in the same position as before the rapture. I tried to lower his leg down, but I could not; it remained stretched out. A fly had alighted on the ball of his eye; in spite of my repeated efforts, I was unable to drive it away, as it kept flying back to the same place. In order to observe Father Joseph better, I knelt down. The above-mentioned doctor was examining him with me. Both of us ascertained undoubtedly that Father Joseph was rapt in ecstasy and actually suspended in mid-air, as I have already said. He had been a quarter of an hour in this situation, when Father Silvestro Evangelista of the monastery of Osimo came up. He observed the phenomenon for some time, and commanded Joseph under obedience to come to himself, and called him by name. Joseph then smiled and recovered his senses."[2]

The last levitation of St Joseph occurred on September 17, 1663, one day before his death. His upliftings and flights had begun immediately after his ordination (March 28, 1628). From that time—that is during thirty-five years—he was kept away by his Superiors from the exercises in choir, processions, and even common meals in the refectory, for the disturbance he would

[1] A.S., ibid., 1035 CD (Ex proc. ord. Assis., par. 235): Ut porro sacrificio ipsius saepe intererat, saepe etiam ejusdem ecstases et mirabiles raptus admirabundus spectavit. Vidit illum in privato suo sacello ad elevationem consecratae Hostiae tribus palmis a terra elevari. Cf. Laing, pp. 89-90.
[2] Bernino, ch. xvii, pp. 241-242, quoting Fo. 585, No. 40, F, par. 16, and Fo. 587.

cause by his levitations, which occurred sometimes in circumstances more comical than edifying.[1]

The Bull of canonisation of St Joseph, published on July 16, 1767, by Clement XIII, mentions the levitations and ecstatic flights of the saint,[2] but the legend inserted on his feast in the Breviary alludes to them but very vaguely.[3]

---

[1] For instance, he was seen one day in the refectory, raised off his seat, waving a sea-urchin about (Bernino, p. 71). Another time, while he was suspended in mid-air before the altar where the Blessed Sacrament was exposed, his sandals dropped on the floor (Bernino, ch. xxii, pp. 302-303, quoting Fo. 559, No. 40, D, par. 10).

[2] . . . *Hoc ille nempe quamdiu vicit, non tam verbis quam re ipsa pulcherrime docuit, quum terram veluti dedignatus, frequentes ac prope quotidianas extases patiens, sublimis in aera ferretur, ac modo exultabundus celerrimo impetu circumvolans, choreas veluti duceret, modo alios quoque secum sublime raperet.* . . .

[3] *Die xviii Septemb. In festo S. Josephi a Cupertino, Confess.*, lectio v: *Eluxit praecipue ardentissima ejus charitas in extasibus ad Deum suavissimis, stupendisque raptibus, quibus frequenter afficiebatur.*

CHAPTER VII

MODERN TRADITIONS (Continued) (EIGHTEENTH CENTURY)

Blessed Joseph Oriol (1650–†1702).—Marcelline Pauper (1663–†1708).— Blessed Bonaventure of Potenza (1651–†1711).—Blessed Francis of Posadas (1644–†1713).—John Baptist of Mastena (†1713).—Angiolo Paoli (†1720).—St Pacificus of San Severino (1653–†1721).—St Veronica Giuliani (1676–†1727).—Blessed Thomas of Cori (1655–†1729).— St John Joseph of the Cross (1654–†1734).—Blessed Angelo of Acri (1669–†1739).—Clara Isabella de Furnariis (†1744).—Geltrude Salandri (†1748).—Blessed Crispino of Viterbo (1668–†1750).—St Gerard Majella (1726–†1755).—St Paul of the Cross (1694–†1775).—St Benedict Joseph Labre (1748–†1783).—St Alphonsus Liguori (1696–†1787).—St Mary Frances of the Five Wounds (1715–†1791).

B LESSED JOSEPH ORIOL, says Abbé E. Daras, in his work on the Saints and Blessed of the eighteenth century, would sometimes be lifted from the ground in his raptures: " Very often he was seen, in the church of our Lady of the Pine in Barcelona, suspended with bent knees in mid-air without touching the ground at all. . . . He would remain whole hours raised from the earth. . . ."[1] One day, after confession, he was rapt into ecstasy while praying at the foot of the altar, and remained a long time in rapture, lifted about a foot and a half above the floor.[2] In 1698, as he was sailing from Marseilles to Barcelona, he experienced an ecstasy on board a Catalonian bark. His body was swiftly raised from the deck, to the great amazement of the sailors, who endeavoured to follow him in his uplifting by climbing up the shrouds. Raphael Baladas of Blanes, the skipper, had been so deeply moved by this scene that he could not help weeping whenever he described it.[3]

Joseph Oriol belonged to the secular clergy. He was canonised by Pius X in 1909.

Marcelline Pauper, born in 1663 at Saint-Saulze (Nivernais), was admitted at twenty-two into the congregation of the Sœurs de

[1] *Les saints et les bienheureux du XVIIIe siècle*, vol. i, p. 283 (after G. Masdeu).
[2] *Ibid.*, p. 275.
[3] *Ibid.*, p. 263.

103

la Charité of Nevers. Father de Lavergne, the founder of the congregation, was her confessor. By his order she wrote down the details of her mystic life. No levitation is mentioned in her autobiography, but in an appendix of which Marcelline is not the author, the following remark is to be read : "She (Marcelline) does not mention many divine favours she enjoyed ; among others the uplifting of her body two feet above her bed, which, in her humility, she ascribed to some nervous disorder. But one of her fellow-Sisters, Julitte Bernard, who was her inferior, at the house of Tulle declared to me she had witnessed these peculiar favours of hers.[1] Sister Marcelline died at Tulle, June 25, 1708, in the odour of sanctity.

Charles Lavagna of Potenza (Basilicata) obtained admission at the age of fifteen into the Order of the Cordeliers, and took the name of Bonaventure. He wished to remain a lay-brother, but his Superiors insisted on his being ordained. " When he said his first Mass," says Abbé Daras, " he melted into tears ; and his body was raised above the floor as if to draw nearer to God."[2] The same author refers to similar facts in another passage: " When he spoke about the sufferings of our Lord, of his love to men, his eyes seemed all ablaze, his feet were swept off the ground, the chair itself on which he was sitting was raised from the floor and lifted up together with him."[3] When he was contemplating the Host, after the consecration, " his eyes brightened up, perspiration ran all over his body, which was lifted from the floor, and remained suspended twenty minutes over the steps of the altar."[4]

One day (in 1711), as the parish priest Don Francesco, in giving him an apple, remarked how sweet the fruit smelt, the fragrance of it, says Abbé Daras, suggested to him the ineffable suavity of God; " he could not control his transports, he changed colour and lost the use of his senses, while his body was lifted eight or ten inches from the ground, and remained some time suspended in the air."[5]

It was in preaching or saying Mass that the Spanish Dominican Francis of Posadas was raised from the earth. " As soon as he began to speak . . . his face became radiant, his feet were raised, and several times they were seen to be off the ground."[6] One day, as he was saying Mass, " when lifting the Host, his body followed his

[1] M. Bouix, *Vie de Marcelline Pauper*, p. 156.
[2] E. Daras, *ibid.*, vol. i, p. 191.   [3] *Ibid.*, p. 207.
[4] *Ibid.*, p. 214.   [5] *Ibid.*, p. 226.
[6] *Ibid.*, vol. ii, p. 167 (after *Vita*, by J. del Pozo).

soul raised to God, and he remained suspended. When he came down again, many persons saw him surrounded with light."[1]

Francis did not realise what happened to him when he was levitated: " I do not know what is the matter with me," he said to his confessor, " whether the ground gives way beneath my feet, but I do not understand what it is."[2]

Similar facts are reported in the Life of the Beatus written by V. Sopena.[3]

John Baptist of Mastena, a Franciscan, after living six years in the Holy Land in monasteries of his Order, came back to his monastery of Como, where he died forty years after. On November 19, 1709, though rapt in ecstasy, he continued to sweep the floor, and he was seen to rise five feet above the ground, without letting go his broom. On another occasion, his confessor saw him lifted twenty feet from the floor and remain in this position. Another time he was found in his cell suspended above the floor at the height of a man.[4]

Angiolo Paoli, who died in 1720, is mentioned in the list of levitated saints of Father H. Thurston, who refers to his Life by T. Cacciari.[5] It is all I know of this holy man.

St Pacificus of San Severino became a Friar Minor of the Strict Observance in 1670. After being ordained (1678), he was employed as a preacher, but the state of his health interrupted this ministry. He retired to the monastery of St Francis of Forano (in the Marches).

During the inquiries for the cause of beatification, inhabitants of San Severino deposed that they had seen Pacificus rapt in ecstasy, while saying Mass, at the consecration; his face was luminous, his arms outspread, his body raised several palms above the steps of the altar.[6] Father Felix Pascal, Postulator of the Cause, reports that in September, 1714, as Pacificus was saying Mass in the chapel of the Crucifix at San Severino, he was lifted a palm above the steps of the altar, after the consecration; his body had become radiant. He remained thus suspended about five hours, without touching the floor. A lady of San Severino and her daughter were present. As Pacificus

[1] *Ibid.*, p. 178.   [2] *Ibid.*
[3] Pp. 43-44 (quoted by H. Thurston, p. 335).
[4] Imbert-Gourbeyre, *La stigmatisation*, vol. i, p. 373.
[5] *Vita*, p. 147.
[6] Daras, *ibid.*, vol. i, p. 89, after S. Melchiorri (*cf.* p. 73).

was rapt and could not finish his Mass, his assistant fetched his Father Superior, who ordered the ecstatic under obedience to recover his senses; which he did at once, and resumed his Mass.[1]

Ursula Giuliani, who took the name of Veronica, when she made her profession at the Capuchin convent of Città di Castello, experienced such strange mystical phenomena that she was suspected of imposture by ecclesiastical authority. Her office of Mistress of Novices was taken away from her, she was called a witch and threatened with the stake. She is said to have experienced very frequent raptures, and was often seen in the garden of the convent lifted over the tops of the trees.[2] St Veronica Giuliani was canonised by Gregory XVI on May 26, 1839.

One day, as Blessed Thomas of Cori was giving Communion in the church of Civitella (near Subiaco), he was rapt in ecstasy, and rose up to the vault with such swiftness that the bystanders were afraid his head would be broken. After floating some moments in the air, he sank gently down to the floor, still holding the ciborium in one hand and a Host in the other. He was also seen to be levitated while preaching from the steps of the altar at Civitella.[3] The day before his death—January 10, 1729—he was horizontally raised off his bed. The friar who looked after him said he had seen him in this position suspended about two feet in the air, surrounded with light.[4] These facts were mentioned by the Postulator of the Cause, Father Luca di Roma, in the biography he published in 1786 according to the documents of the process. Blessed Thomas belonged to the Order of Friars Minor of the Regular Observance. He had taken the Franciscan habit in his twenty-second year. He died aged seventy-four, January 11, 1729. Pius VI beatified him in 1786.

St John Joseph of the Cross is also said once to have been lifted up to the vault of a church. Usually he used to be raised only a few inches off the floor; at other times, five or six feet. On another occasion, in the year 1728, he was seen to follow a procession in ecstasy, carried through the air a distance of two miles, raised about half a foot above the ground. He also experienced upliftings while

[1] *Ibid.*, pp. 99-100.
[2] Imbert-Gourbeyre, *La stigmatisation*, vol. i, pp. 391 *ff.*, 401.
[3] Daras, *ibid.*, vol. i, p. 316, after Luca di Roma, *Vita* (*cf.* p. 31).
[4] *Ibid.*, p. 319; *cf.* Luca, pp. 123-126.

saying Mass.[1]   Charles Gaetano was born on August 15, 1654, in the island of Ischia (kingdom of Naples).   He had been admitted at sixteen years of age into the Alcantarine branch of the Franciscan Order.   He was beatified fifty-five years after his death by Pius VI, and canonised by Gregory XVI in 1839.

In 1722, Blessed Angelo of Acri, a Capuchin, was preaching a mission at Aprigliano, in the diocese of Cosenza.   Towards the end of the sermon he was rapt, holding out a crucifix.   His body was raised about a foot over the platform on which he was preaching. He remained thus suspended for a considerable time, and the congregation noticed with amazement that the crucifix remained also suspended in mid-air, though the ecstatic had entirely relaxed his hold on it.   In 1725, as he was preaching in Monteleone, he was lifted up more than five feet over the pulpit during a long rapture. On the last day of a mission he preached at Fiumefreddo, he flew from the pulpit to the foot of the altar where the Blessed Sacrament was exposed, a distance of about ten paces.   The same thing occurred at Belmonte.[2]

Father Charles of Cedraro, Custos of the monastery of the Friars Minor of the said place, declared in his deposition at the process that in April, 1724, he had seen Father Angelo levitated in the church of his monastery at Cosenza.   He had gone into the church to fetch the Father about midday; he found him rapt in the choir, lifted more than two palms above the floor.   He observed that the ecstatic was ghastly pale.[3]   Several transports from one place to another are also recorded in the Life of the blessed one.[4]   Angelo died on October 30, 1730.   He was beatified in 1825.

Clara Isabella de Furnariis is mentioned as a levitated mystic in Father H. Thurston's list.   He refers to the *Summario* of her process (p. 103).

Geltrude Salandri is also mentioned in the same place.   Her levitation is referred to in an anonymous Life (pp. 220-224), which Father Thurston calls admirable.[5]

[1] Guérin, *Petits Bollandistes*, vol. iii, p. 178.   Diodato dell' Assunta, *Vita*, pp. 13, 44, 46, 104 (quoted by Thurston, p. 330).
[2] Daras, *ibid.*, vol. ii, p. 110.
[3] *Ibid.*, pp. 103-104.   [4] *Ibid.*, pp. 98 ff.
[5] *Ibid.*, p. 335.

107

LEVITATION

Crispino of Viterbo, a Capuchin lay-brother, is simply named in *La stigmatisation* among levitated saints. No reference nor details are given (vol. ii, p. 319, note 1 of p. 318).

Gerard Majella, a Redemptorist lay-brother, was once rapt in ecstasy because he heard a blind beggar play on his flute a popular canticle:

Il tuo gusto e non il mio,
Voglio solo in te, mio Dio.

And in this ecstasy his body was raised above the ground.[1] This took place at Caposele, in the presence of the poor who had come to receive alms on that day, and of Dr. Santorelli. The blind man was called Philip of Falcone.[2]

On another occasion he is said to have flown through the air of his own accord. Here is the description of the scene as it is found in Father Tannoja:

" Gerard was coming from Deliceto with two young workmen employed at the house. On the side of the road from the village to the monastery stands a shrine dedicated to the Blessed Virgin. Gerard availed himself of the opportunity to speak of Mary's merciful kindness. Suddenly he stopped, took a pencil, jotted nervously down a few words on a bit of paper, and threw it up into the air as if he were sending a message to heaven. At the same time, the two young men saw him rise from the earth and fly through the air like a bird to the place called *il Francese*, above five hundred yards away. There he alighted and quietly walked to the house. The two witnesses of the strange scene died about 1804. They would repeat the details of it to anybody who wanted to hear them, and never were they found to vary in the account of the marvel they had beheld."[3]

[1] Dunoyer, *Vie de saint Gérard Majella*, pp. 375-376, after Summary of the apostolic processes, No. 17, par. 422.
[2] *Vie . . .*, by Un Père Rédemptoriste, pp. 394-395.
[3] *Ibid.*, pp. 113-114. *Cf.* A. M. Tannoja, *Vita del Servo di Dio Fratello Gerardo Majella*, ch. ix: *Ritornando un giorno da Iliceto con due giovanetti Villani, che necessitavano in Casa, come pervenne ad una Chiesa al di fuori del Paese dedicata a Maria SS., entrando nei misteri della Vergine, nell' instante con istupore di quelli si vide trasformato, prende il calamjo e scrivendo non so che sopra una carta, dando un salto, come lettera menolla in aria. Tanto fu far questo, quanto soffrire non un ratto ma un volo. Nell' istante i due Villani sel videro tolto dinanzi, ed egli andare a poggiare un mezzo miglio, e più in distanza da essi verso la nostra Casa ; vale a dire, dalla Chiesa ove ritrovavasi in un territorio che denominasi il Francese. I due vecchi Villani che ultimamente trapassarono, non cessavano, come mi attesta il Canonico Stramiello, raccontare con loro stupore ciò che veduto aveano.*

108

Another ecstatic flight performed in similar circumstances has been reported in the process by one Magdalen Flumeri, who had the story from her aunt Rosaria Bertucci, an eye-witness. One day the latter was going to the *Consolazione* for confession; she came across Gerard, who knew her well, and asked her to carry his cloak to the *Consolazione*, where he was going himself. Then he walked forward and got the start of her. She saw him enter a chapel that stood on the roadside; and when he came out of it he rose up in the air, and was thus borne, with outspread arms, from the chapel to the *Consolazione*—that is, more than half a mile.[1]

Gerard was seen again lifted up into the air on Good Friday, April 20, 1753, when after the traditional procession at Corato a painting showing the Crucifixion was brought back into the church of the Benedictine convent.[2]

Gerard died very young in 1755. He was canonised in 1904 by Pius X.

Paul Francis Danei, founder of the Passionists, known by the name of Paul of the Cross, was returning one winter day to Mount Argentaro, where he had his hermitage. He was feeling so tired out that he thought he was going to die; he lay down on the ground and prayed. Then he felt as if he were lifted from the ground, and in one moment he was carried near his monastery.[3] At Latera (diocese of

---

[1] Proc. Ordin. of Conza, Inter. 14, Fo. 1194 recto; Proc. Apost., n. 18, par. 128; Positio super Introductione Causae, *De Donis supernaturalibus*, pp. 432-433: *LXXVII. Testis Illustris Domina Magdalena Flumeri terrae Iliceti an.* 80, *juxta inter.* 14, Fo. 1194, *respondit: La stessa zia raccontavami ancora di cosa prodigiosa avvenuta sotto i suoi medesimi occhi, e per cui non poteva non annunziare il suo sommo stupore riferendole spesse volte a chiunque glieno chiedeva il seguente ratto del Servo di Dio. Menava ella fin dalla sua gioventù vita divata* (sic, *divota*), *e spesso recavasi alla Consolazione per confessarsi. Avvenne in una delle volte che ella colà recavasi che questo grand' amico di Dio ritornando d'Iliceto, ove era stato, alla Consolazione s'imbattè colla suddetta mia zia, la quale benissimo egli conoscendo, la pregò a recargli fino al Collegio ridetto il suo cappotto, che le consegnò, e come per modestia la precedette a breve distanza camminando a lei dinanzi, finchè giunse in una chiesetta in cui entro, ed uscendo si vide talmento elevato in aria colle brace, chia distese, che volò circa un miglio dalla Cappella suddetta fin presso la Consolazione. Mia zia che quella meraviglia degna di eterna memoria vedeva, stette immobile e stupefatta ad occhio fisso riguardò quel volo miracoloso dal principio al fine, nè finchè visse cessò mai dallo stupirsi per quel veramente stupendo avvenimento. Ecco como segnalava Iddio questo grande e virtuoso sùo Servo, che si fu grande per le virtù. . . .*

[2] Dunoyer, p. 289, after apost. process, No. 7, par. 375, 496.

[3] Daras, *ibid.*, vol. ii, p. 240, after *Vita*, by Pio del Nome di Maria.

LEVITATION

Montefiascone), while preaching to some priests in the sacristry, he was seen to rise into the air. In the island of Elba, during a sermon he was delivering there, carried away by his enthusiasm, he overstepped the edge of the platform from which he was talking, and remained suspended, treading the air above the heads of the congregation; then he returned in like manner to his former place.[1]

In the last years of his life he experienced a levitation in the following circumstances: he was having a conversation on some religious subject in the sacristy of the church of St John and Paul in Rome. At a certain moment his face began to brighten up and his body to shiver. Paul, seeing he was going to be rapt in ecstasy, propped himself up against the back of his seat, the arms of which he clutched at the same time, as if by way of resistance; but despite his efforts, he began to rise from the floor with his seat, the legs of which were lifted as high as the head of the person who bore witness to the fact. The latter adds that the saint remained rapt a long time, and then sank gently down to the ground again. When he came to himself he was slightly shaking.[2] According to Strambi, he also had levitations when saying Mass, and was once lifted two palms from the floor, before and after consecrating.[3]

As it happened to several other saints, the sight of the beauty of nature with the symbolic meaning it conveyed to him was enough to throw Paul into rapture. One day he was rapt in ecstasy in the presence of several inhabitants of Fabrica in the diocese of Orte, because he was looking at flowers and said they were " preaching " to him. " Do not preach any more !" he exclaimed, and he began commenting with extraordinary enthusiasm on the Greatness of the Creator. Then his body was raised from the ground, and he remained some time suspended in mid-air, with his arms lifted to heaven, while the lookers-on were weeping with emotion.[4]

Paul died on October 10, 1775. He was beatified by Pius IX in 1853 and canonised in 1867. His upliftings have been mentioned in his office in the Breviary: . . . *frequenti quoque extasi, cum mira interdum elevatione frui*; and it is added that his face would become effulgent during his raptures: *vultuque superna luce radiante conspiciebatur*.[5]

---

[1] *Ibid.*, p. 235.   [2] *Ibid.*, pp. 235-236.
[3] *Vie du bienheureux Paul de la Croix*, vol. i, bk. ii, ch. iii, p. 301 (quoted by Ribet, vol. ii, ch. xxxii, p. 640).
[4] Daras, *ibid.*, p. 235.
[5] *Breviary*, die xxviii aprilis, lectio vi.

Of Benedict Joseph Labre, the mendicant pilgrim, no levitation proper is recorded. Still, the persons who beheld his raptures say that his body, without being raised off the ground, assumed such positions as are hardly compatible with the law of gravitation.[1]

St Alphonsus Liguori, who died in 1787, should be normally inserted here. Owing to the abundant matter, the whole of the next chapter will be reserved to him.

St Maria Francesca delle Cinque Piaghe, a Franciscan tertiary of the Alcantarine Order, died on October 6, 1791. She was born on March 25, 1715, and enjoyed mystic favours from her early years. She was five or six years old when, according to her biographer, Father D. Bernardo Laviosa, she experienced her first ecstatic rapture. Her sister observed her, one Christmas night, rapt near the Crib erected in their house, her body suspended about two feet above the floor.[2] It is also recorded, in the same connection, that on an occasion in later years she was seen to run through the country with such nimbleness that she rather seemed to fly over the ground. Now, the fact was the more striking as before this fit of ecstatic jubilation she had been walking at a very slow pace, being then weakened by sickness.[3]

In her office in the Breviary her risings from the ground are mentioned as pretty usual occurrences: *Coelestibus rebus intenta, frequenter in extasim est rapta et quandoque a terra sublata.*[4]

Mary Frances of the Five Wounds was canonised in 1867 by Pius IX.

[1] Desnoyers, *Le vénérable Benoît-Joseph Labre*, vol. ii, pp. 169-176.
[2] Daras, *ibid.*, p. 125.   [3] *Ibid.*, p. 137.   [4] Oct. 6.

CHAPTER VIII

ST ALPHONSUS LIGUORI (EIGHTEENTH CENTURY— Continued)

ALPHONSUS MARIA LIGUORI, the founder of the Congregation of the Redemptorists, experienced raptures with levitation. Some occurred in public; some were witnessed by one or a few persons. I will describe the circumstances of them as found in the principal biographies of the saint.

The most famous of these phenomena took place in December, 1745, at Foggia, during a sermon delivered by Alphonsus at the cathedral of this town, some time before Christmas. At a certain moment an image of the Virgin called the Madonna with the Seven Veils or the Old Image, venerated at Foggia from the eleventh century, seemed to become luminous and throw a beam on the preacher's face. " Quite out of himself, Alphonsus stammered out the words, ' Good Mother . . . I am yours . . . quite yours.' " But presently he fell into ecstasy, and everybody could see him, with his eyes fixed on Mary, his arms stretched out towards her, lifted in the air several palms above the platform, as if he was about to fly away.[1] The two thousand persons who were listening to the sermon, at first dumbfounded, then uttered cries of admiration which sounded far beyond the walls of the church. " ' A miracle ! a miracle !' was shouted on all sides, and such a crowd of lookers-on rushed to the doors of the church that the Annunciade nuns, whose convent was near the church, thought there was a popular rising in the town."[2]

The remembrance of this scene was still alive fifty years later. " In 1794, as an application was being made to the Roman Court for the introduction of the cause of beatification, the three chief magistrates of Foggia expressed themselves as follows in their petition to Pius VI : ' Everybody in this town knows that, during

[1] Three palms, according to Villecourt's statement, in *Vie et Institut de S. Alphonse*, vol. i, p. 254.
[2] A. Berthe, *Saint Alphonse de Liguori*, vol. i, p. 301. *Cf.* A. M. Tannoja, *Mémoires*, vol. i, p. 291.

the mission preached in 1745 in our cathedral by Alphonsus and his companions, when the Servant of God was preaching on the glories of Mary, a beam of light, sprung from the visage of the Madonna, our glorious protectress, lighted up the preacher's face. Thrown at once into ecstasy, the latter was seen to be lifted three palms above the platform; a prodigy which made everybody in the congregation utter cries of joy and admiration. There are still some old persons in the town who remember the great miracle of 1745 very well.' "[1]

Father Tannoja, who testified to this event in the process, had not been an eye-witness. He spoke after the testimony of Father Garzilli, then Canon at Foggia, and of Dominic Corsano, a secular priest, who were both present at Alphonsus' sermon.[2]

A similar fact—so similar that it might pass for a second version of the same event, were it not for positive evidence to the contrary—took place in October, 1756, at Amalfi. St Alphonsus experienced a levitation again as he was preaching. " In his sermon on the Blessed Virgin, Alphonsus was exhorting the congregation to commend themselves to her for their spiritual and temporal needs; then, all at once, as if by divine inspiration, he exclaimed: ' You do not trust in your Mother firmly enough. You do not know how to invoke her with all your heart. I will pray for you.' And he began uttering the most ardent and touching supplications, when suddenly from the image of Mary placed to the right side of the pulpit streamed a ray of light that shone on the preacher's face. Then we saw him rapt in ecstasy, with brightened face and fixed eyes, and rising two palms above the pulpit, like a seraph about to fly up to heaven. This rapture lasted more than five minutes, during which could be heard, amidst an undescribable emotion, the sobs of the congregation mixed with shouts of ' A miracle ! a miracle !' "[3]

Four eye-witnesses deposed as to this fact in the process: Canons Casanova, di Luca, di Stefano, and Father Criscuoli.[4] The latter ascribed to the miracle the unusual effect of the mission on the conduct of the inhabitants of Amalfi.[5]

The deposition of Dom Francisco di Stefano has been quoted by Cardinal de Villecourt:

" As the Servant of God was preaching a mission in the cathedral, all the exercises of which I followed, trying to stir the piety of the congregation to Mary, who was the subject of his preaching, he said

[1] *Ibid.*, p. 302.   [2] *Ibid.*, n. 1.   [3] *Ibid.*, p. 551.
[4] *Ibid.*, n. 1.   [5] *Ibid.*

113

LEVITATION

once, towards the end of the mission: 'You are too cold in your prayers to this good Mother. Well, I will pray for you.' Presently he knelt down in prayer. Then everybody noticed, as I did myself, that he experienced a kind of ecstasy. His eyes were raised to heaven, and his body rose more than two palms above the place upon which he was standing. His eyes were fixed on the statue of the Blessed Virgin on the right of the pulpit, and his face seemed glowing with fire. It was noticed, and I myself noticed, that Mary's face brightened, and that the beams issuing from it were reflected on the face of the Servant of God. He remained five or six minutes in this situation, without speaking."[1]

Other levitations are reported which are of a more private character. " In the beginning of 1762," says Brother Verdesca, " I was going one morning to our Father's, in order to recite the office with him as usual. On entering his cell, I saw him lifted two or three palms from his chair, in the position of a person half kneeling and half sitting. His arms were outstretched, his eyes open and lifted to heaven, his face was glowing and as it were transfigured. I went gently in and knelt down between the arm-chair and the bed, so as to be able to behold his face by looking round. His ecstasy lasted nearly a quarter of an hour, which to me did not seem to be long. While I was gazing at this heavenly sight, with tears in my eyes, the Servant of God uttered a deep sigh and exclaimed, ' My God! My God!' At this moment he came to himself and sank down to his seat in his natural position. I burst into sobbing, which attracted his notice to my presence and put him to confusion. Turning towards me, he said reproachfully, ' Dear me! so you were here! Mind you do not speak to anybody of what you have seen !' And we began to recite the office, but he seemed rather giddy as a result of his long rapture."[2]

Father A. M. Tannoja also had an opportunity of observing a levitation of Alphonsus, and has given a detailed account of it:
" As I was at Pagani in October, 1784, I went to say Mass, when Alphonsus was at the foot of the altar of the most Blessed Sacrament. I heard him shuffle his feet as if he had been gliding on the floor. Then I heard the same sound some moments after. Suspecting something supernatural was going on about him, I cast a glance sideways, and I saw him rising into the air from his seat several

---

[1] Villecourt, *ibid.*, vol. i, p. 425. [2] Berthe, *ibid.*, vol. i, p. 690.

times; though at the time he could hardly move with the help of his servant and the lay-brother who assisted him, either to go to church or to rise when he was sitting. After Mass I took a place below the choir to make my thanksgiving. I noticed the same motions several times. To ascertain the reality of these more surely, I took the same place several days running, in order to examine him carefully, and I saw the same upliftings of his body, which was repeatedly raised as swiftly and easily as a light feather."[1]

On other occasions, the witnesses reported a lifting on the tips of the toes only, without getting loose from the ground, such as Padre Michella, whose deposition is as follows:

" On a Friday of March, 1770, I was attending his Mass. In the morning I had noticed he seemed more nervous than usual, and as it were under an impression of fright. He said the prayers of Mass to the Canon with ineffable devotion. I knelt down to prepare to celebrate the Holy Sacrifice myself, and left off observing him for a moment. But soon I realised that he could not go as far as the consecration; I looked up and saw him leaning his elbows on the altar, holding the Host in his hand without uttering the sacramental words. By lifting my head a little, I could behold his face. His eyes, wide open, were fixed on the cross. He seemed to be excited to a degree that caused me to tremble. Presently I saw that he touched the ground with the tips of his feet only, as if he were about to fly up. Quite beside myself with emotion, I went out to call Brother Romito or the servant Alexis; but I could not find them, and came back near the altar. The Servant of God was still in the same posture. I then made up my mind to do what I had already done in such circumstances—that is, to shake him by the end of his alb and cassock. This made him come to himself; on recovering from ecstasy he gave out a deep, loving sigh, and pronounced the words of the consecration. He finished his Mass with the fervour of a seraph, then locked himself up in his room, where he remained two hours more than usual in complete silence."[2]

Alphonsus experienced levitations to the last days of his life; in the chair where he was wheeled about when he had become a cripple, and even on his deathbed. Cardinal de Villecourt gives the following account of these facts:

" One day as he was being wheeled through the passage in his wheel-chair, he was noticed talking to himself with great animation

---

[1] Villecourt, *ibid.*, vol. iii, p. 239.　　　[2] Berthe, vol. ii, p. 317.

about the religious duties he was unable to do. Father Volpicelli, wanting to draw his mind off this sad train of thoughts, told him that at his age he was no longer bound to anything, and could with one act of love fulfil all his obligations. ' Indeed !' said Alphonsus, as if coming out of slumber, ' with an act of love.' Father Volpicelli added, ' An act of love is all-sufficient.' As Alphonsus was hard of hearing, Father Volpicelli drew nearer to him and said aloud, ' My God, I love you !' and Alphonsus was at once thrown into ecstasy, lifted more than a palm into the air, and knocked with his head against the chin of Father Volpicelli, who was stooping down to be heard more distinctly."

On another occasion, Alphonsus required Father Volpicelli again to help him to make an act of divine love, but the latter " was careful not to put himself forward as much as before, to avoid another shock, and it was well he did so, for the holy old man was raised off his seat in like manner."[1]

Father Berthe gives an account of the same episode that does not suggest so precisely a levitation proper:

" One day, as he was wheeled along the passage in his chair, Father Volpicelli observed that he was under an impression of fear. ' Make an act of love,' he said to him, ' and Jesus will be satisfied.' Alphonsus asked him what he should say to Jesus. Volpicelli, drawing close to his ear, uttered these words: ' My Jesus, I love you with all my heart !' He had hardly finished the sentence when the saint, in an ecstatic transport, sprang up a palm above his chair and knocked his companion's chin violently with his head. Some days after, coming across Volpicelli in the passage, he asked him again how to make an act of love. Volpicelli was careful to stand away far enough when repeating the formula, and he was right, for hardly had he uttered the name of Jesus, when Alphonsus was again rapt in ecstasy, and sprang up more than a palm above his chair."[2]

When the saint was nearly dying, Joseph of Mauro, the architect of the King, came to Naples to examine the works that were being done on the church of the Redemptorists, and availed himself of it to pay a visit to Alphonsus. " The holy Bishop asked him if the theatres were frequented, and if his nephew Joseph went to the play. ' Monsignore,' said the architect, ' it is now quite a common custom.' Alphonsus did not say a word for a moment; then he added,

'And are the chapels frequented?' 'They are indeed,' answered Joseph, 'and you cannot imagine the great deal of good that is done there, and how eagerly people from the lower classes are crowding in them; you can see there cab-drivers who are regular saints!' His Grace was then on his bed, very much like a dying man, but on hearing of cab-drivers being compared to saints, he exclaimed, 'Cab-drivers who are saints, at Naples! *Gloria Patri!*' And as he said these words, he rose up more than a palm from his bed and repeated three times, 'Cab-drivers in Naples who are saints! *Gloria Patri!*' He was so deeply moved that he did not sleep for the whole night, calling now his servant, now the Brother, and kept telling them, 'Cab-drivers in Naples who are saints!' "[1]

Father Berthe, who quotes the same anecdote, does not refer to any levitation. He simply says that Alphonsus " was in such elation that he did not sleep the following night."[2]

In the office which has been inserted into the Roman Breviary on his feast, levitations are not mentioned. The events of Foggia and Amalfi are only referred to in these terms: . . . *a Virginis imagine in eum immisso miro splendore totus facie coruscare, et in ecstasim rapi coram universo populo non semel visus est.*[3]

---

[1] Villecourt, *ibid.*   [2] Berthe, vol. ii, p. 581.
[3] Die 2 Aug., S. Alph. de Ligorio, lectio v. Still, the curious flitting movements recorded by Father Tannoja are perhaps referred to in the following lines: *Dum vero ad ejus (Virginis) aram oraret, vel sacrum faceret, quod nunquam omisit, prae amoris vehementia, vel seraphicis liquescebat ardoribus, vel insolitis quatiebatur motibus.*

CHAPTER IX

RECENT TRADITIONS (NINETEENTH AND TWENTIETH CENTURIES)

Claude Dhière (1757-†1820).—Anne Catherine Emmerich (1774-†1824).—Mary Crucified of the Wounds of Jesus (1782-†1826).—Blessed Andrew Hubert Fournet (1752-†1834).—Blessed Joseph Benedict Cottolengo (1786-†1842).—St Mary Magdalen Postel (1756-†1846).—Mary Dominic Barbagli (1812-†1859).—St John Mary Baptist Vianney (1786-†1859).—Mary of Jesus (Mother du Bourg) (1787-†1862).—Blessed Michael Garicoïts (1797-†1863).—Mary of Moerl (1812-†1863).—Mary of Jesus Crucified (1846-†1878).—Victoria Claire of Coux (†1883).—Mary Louise Lateau (1850-†1883).—Joseph Baumann (†1898).—Gemma Galgani (1878-†1903).—Mary of the Passion (1866-†1912).—Mary Julia Jahenny (born about 1853, still alive).

THE traditions about ecstatic levitation neither stop nor even grow scarcer as we are drawing nearer to the present time. Here are a few data I have been able to collect concerning the levitation of Catholic mystics in the nineteenth and twentieth centuries.

Abbé Claude Dhière, Director of the *Grand Séminaire* of Grenoble, is said to have experienced levitation during his ecstatic raptures. " M. Dhière," says his biographer, Mlle. de Franclieu—who has written his Life after contemporary testimonies—" very often passed from simple meditation to ecstasy by reason of the divine love that consumed him. His students could then see him lose the use of his senses, stretch out his arms in the form of a cross, and rise from the floor.

" If he uttered some words in these moments of ecstatic fervour they were, as a rule, passages of Holy Scripture or cries of divine love.

" When he recovered from these raptures, he humiliated himself and wanted to be excused by those present for what he called an act of forgetfulness.

" When he experienced ecstasies during his Mass, it was usually at the Memento of the living and the dead, and the students who used to serve his Mass declare that, when enraptured, his feet did not touch the floor any more.

118

" M. Mège, who served his Mass for a time, says that for his own part he never saw him raised off the ground, but that many students in the seminary said they had seen him in that position."[1]

Anne Catherine Emmerich, a stigmatisée, whose visions were made famous by the romantic versions of her secretary, C. Brentano, experienced, according to her own statements, something very closely allied to levitation:

" When I was doing my work as vestry-nun, I was often lifted up suddenly into the air, and I climbed up and stood on the higher parts of the church, such as windows, sculptured ornaments, jutting stones; I would clean and arrange everything in places where it was humanly impossible. I felt myself lifted and supported in the air, and I was not afraid in the least, for I had been accustomed from a child to being assisted by my guardian angel."[2]

Anne Catherine was then in the convent of the Augustinian nuns of Dulmen (Westphalia), where she had made her profession in 1803. When the convent was suppressed by a decree of Jerome in 1811, she went to live at a poor widow's house in the country, where she died in 1824, aged fifty.

Mary Crucified of the Wounds of Jesus (Maria Crocifissa delle Piaghe di N.S. Jesu Cristo), a Franciscan tertiary of the Alcantarine branch of this Order, was also a stigmatisée. She spent her life in her father's house in Naples. She experienced frequent ecstasies, says Dr. Imbert-Gourbeyre, who adds that she was sometimes seen suspended several palms from the ground.[3]

Andrew Hubert Fournet, a priest of Poitou, the founder of the *Institut des Filles de la Croix* (Sisters of St Andrew), was beatified in 1926. Everything that follows about him has been borrowed from the substantial biography published by the Rev. Father Jules Saubat.[4] The latter has himself drawn it from the documents of the process begun after the preliminary inquiry conducted by the authority of the Bishop of Poitiers in 1854.

A. H. Fournet experienced ecstasies with levitation for the first time in presence of witnesses in 1820, while staying at Issy

[1] A. M. de Franclieu, *Vie de M. Claude Dhière*, pp. 283-284.
[2] K. A. Schmöger, *Anne-Catherine Emmerich*, vol. i, p. 243.
[3] Imbert-Gourbeyre, *La stigmatisation*, vol. i, p. 459 (after R. Frungillo).
[4] *André-Hubert Fournet, Fondateur de l'Institut des Filles de la Croix, dites Sœurs de Saint-André*.

(near Paris) in the house of the Filles de la Croix that he had just founded. He was then sixty-eight.

" When the Servant of God was saying Mass, Sister Marie-Alexandrine saw him eight days lifted up from the floor, remaining motionless in this position at the time of the elevation. Quite startled and fearing to be mistaken, she warned the other Sisters, who watched the Father in their turn. They, too, were fortunate enough to behold the same marvel, which took place during a week at each Mass the Father said."[1]

Some Sisters at the convent of La Puye (Vienne) saw him in meditation in the church; he was kneeling and his body was off the floor. The Sister who deposed the fact in the informative inquiry, had it from Sister Monique. This is the text of her testimony:

" The Servant of God was more than once lifted above the earth. Our dear Sister Monique has declared to me that she saw him in the church of La Puye, kneeling with outstretched arms under the bells;[2] Sister Monique was with five or six other Sisters. Some of them who were near Sister Monique were whispering, ' Just look at the Father !' But Sister Monique did not mind their words and continued to pray. When she was out of the church, the other Sisters told her they had seen the Servant of God raised from the floor without touching it at all."[3]

One Lafleur-Peignon, of Paizay, who when a boy used to serve Mass for Blessed Fournet, said that sometimes the latter, when at the altar, " looked like a bird which is going to fly up," and that " his feet were off the floor."[4]

On one occasion Father Fournet was seen levitated while preaching, at the Way of the Cross, in the same church of La Puye. One of the Sisters, Ludvine, gave the following account of the event:

" I will relate a fact that I witnessed in the church of La Puye. The Servant of God was conducting the Way of the Cross in presence of our community, and he preached at each station. I was following him with a candle with another Sister appointed to that office. At the tenth station, as the Father began to preach, I saw him raised above the floor. As I was close to him, I could see easily the light streaming between his feet and the pavement of the church. He was not lifted a foot, but more than half a foot, above the floor. When

---

[1] *Ibid.*, vol. ii, p. 134 (Deposition of Sister Saint-Roger, inform. proc., sess. 64-41).
[2] That is, in the choir, where the bells were.
[3] *Ibid.*, p. 384 (inform. proc., sess. 12-56).
[4] *Ibid.*, p. 296, after apost. proc., sess. 176-34.

I saw the Servant of God so rise off the floor, I was quite bewildered, and I could not help saying to the Sisters near me, ' Oh ! Oh ! Look at the Father in the air !' The Sisters beckoned to me to keep silent and not disturb the ceremony. I do not remember the names of the Sisters who witnessed with me this uplifting of the Father. As for me, I could observe the prodigy quite at my ease, for it lasted all the time the Father preached the tenth station.''[1]

On another levitation experienced by the Father while preaching there are more numerous and detailed testimonies. I will give them in the same order as Père Saubat. These are the depositions of the Sisters of La Puye:

" The Servant of God, on the feast of St John the Baptist, which was also the day of the first communion at La Puye, was preaching in front of a cross standing on the former road to Paisay, near which the parishioners and children of the first communion had been led in procession. Suddenly the children cried out and said to Sister Saint-Vincent de Paul, who led them, ' Sister, look at the Father; he is in the air !' The Sister ordered them to keep quiet, saying, ' I can see it all right, but do not say anything !' And she came gently to tell me what happened, for I was listening with downcast eyes to the Father, who was preaching with extreme animation and fervour. I then saw him lifted a foot and a half over the ground, and presently he sank gradually down. In the evening several Sisters who had noticed the fact talked about it together.''[2]

Another Sister gave the following version of the same event:

" As usual we had a procession to the cross that was at the end of the Sisters' enclosure, on the road to Paisay. We gathered round the cross; the children of the first communion and the men of the parish formed the first row; then came the Sisters, and next the women; as for us schoolgirls, we were behind the Sisters. Father André preached from the foot of the cross. The cross was set in a stone standing on a very low mound. The Father spoke of the bliss of Paradise; we could hear him very clearly. I do not remember if I could see him in the beginning of his sermon; I did not pay attention to it. But owing to my small size and the people that stood before me, it was natural not to see him. I was then about twelve. While he was speaking, I heard a woman near me exclaiming that the good Father was ascending to heaven; she looked quite moved and was weeping. Her exclamation made me more attentive to what was going on. Then I saw very distinctly the Father standing

---

[1] *Ibid.*, pp. 387-388, after inform. proc., sess. 103-56.
[2] *Ibid.*, p. 384, after inform. proc., sess. 12-56.

above the persons in front of me; I could see him down to his knees; next I perceived the edge of his surplice. I could not have seen him thus, if he had not been lifted from the ground. In my simplicity I began looking up to heaven as if somebody had come down from there to fetch the Father. One of my little companions, now Sister Basilie, who had heard my neighbour's exclamation, nudged me with her elbow and asked me what she said; I answered, ' She says that the Father is ascending to heaven; but it is not true, as he is still preaching.' The same woman cried a second time, ' He is flying up ! He is flying up !' and she was shedding more tears than ever; moved by the sight, I began to weep myself. But I did not notice any stir in the congregation. The procession came back to the church. We talked for some days about the event, but the Sisters ordered us not to say any more about it because, they said, the good Father would not be pleased. Later on, Sister Saint-Vincent de Paul related it to us as a fact she had actually seen and accurately observed. She spoke of it as of a most sure thing."[1]

The said Sister Saint-Vincent de Paul's deposition is as follows:
" About six or seven years before the death of the Servant of God, if my memory serves me, I witnessed the fact I am going to relate. It was on the feast of St John the Baptist, which was at the same time the day of the first communion of the children of La Puye. After Vespers, the parishioners and the children of the first communion went in procession to the wooden cross set on a block of stone not far from the village, on the side of the road to Paisay, in the place where the road begins to climb the hill that overlooks La Puye. I should add that the said cross is no longer there, as it was removed when the new road to Paisay was opened. When the Servant of God arrived with the procession at the foot of the cross, he knelt down at once as he used to do, singing *O Crux Ave*; and next the canticle *Vive Jésus, vive sa croix !* Then he rose to his feet, and ascending a little platform of stone round the pedestal of the cross, he began preaching with great zeal and fervour. I was standing at the head of the children of the first communion, whom I led and marshalled. I was listening to the sermon of the Servant of God without looking up at him, when one of the children of the first communion near me cried out, ' Sister, the Father is rising from the ground.' I looked up and saw indeed the Servant of God raised from the earth and suspended about a foot over the step of stone on which he stood before. I saw him in this position and could observe him very plainly. I was about four or five paces from the

[1] *Ibid.*, pp. 385-386, after apost. proc., sess. 38-38.

Father, and there was nobody between us to keep me from examining him quite at my ease. I drew near a Sister who stood some paces from me, and I said to her, ' Look at the Father, who is rising into the air !' This Sister is Sister Saint-Martin, who began to observe him with me. But at this moment the Servant of God had begun to sink and was nearer to the ground. From the time when, on the child's warnings, I saw the Servant of God above the ground, to the moment when I saw him coming gradually down to it again and recovering his foothold, about ten or twelve minutes had elapsed, during which I observed attentively this uplifting into the air. The little girl who had seen the Servant of God lifted in the air and had warned me, was from Cenan, a parish of La Puye; she was then fourteen years old. I do not remember her name, but I know she is dead. The parishioners of La Puye could not see this raising as I did, because they stood behind the cross, which was thus between the Father and themselves. The Servant of God was facing the children of the first communion, who were before him, and I was with them."[1]

Blessed Joseph Benedict Cottolengo of Bra (diocese of Asti) lived in Turin as a secular priest, and devoted himself to many charities, founding different congregations to create them or keep them up. He died at Chieri in 1842. He was beatified by Benedict XV in 1917.

The documents of the process contain many reports about his levitations. I shall quote some of them that come from an eye-witness:

One evening in the year 1836, at nightfall, as Joseph returned to *Piccola Casa*, where he lived, two robbers assaulted him. He escaped, thanks to two policemen who came up in time. The Sister portress of *Piccola Casa* noticed, when he entered her lodge, how pale and agitated he looked, and she was confirmed in her suspicion of his having undergone some serious trouble when she heard him ask for a cup of coffee. After drinking this, Joseph went upstairs to his room that stood above the portress's lodge. The latter noticed after some moments that no noise came from the room, and she judged that Joseph must be unwell. She went upstairs and knocked several times at the door without getting any answer. More and more anxious, she made up her mind to open the door. Then she saw the Blessed Joseph praying before an image of the Virgin, rapt in ecstasy. He was standing, with his arms outspread; his face was bright, and his feet did not touch the floor.

[1] *Ibid.*, pp. 385-387, after apost. proc., sess. 87-56.

LEVITATION

The same Sister beheld a similar spectacle several times. One day as she had called on Joseph to fetch him on behalf of some visitors, she found him rapt and levitated, with his eyes fixed on an image of the Virgin that was hanging on the door. This circumstance enabled the Sister to take a full view of the ecstatic, who was just in front of her. Another time she saw him rapt in front of a crucifix. He was kneeling, but above the ground, and the witness noticed that his cassock had no contact with the floor. These raptures, according to the Sister's observations, used to occur on certain liturgical feasts or when he had undergone some humiliation.[1]

[1] *Positio super virtutibus*, pp. 790-793: *Testis II ex officio juxta* 16 *interrog. Proc. Fo.* 3690 *terg.* 3691, 3692 *respondit: Nello stesso anno* (1836) *una sera verso l' imbrunire, il Servo di Dio ritornava dal Santuario della consolata per restituirsi alla Piccola Casa. A qualche distanza dal Santuario incontrò due guardie municipali, le quali conoscendo che quei luoghi erano pericolosi di notte tempo, si offersero di accompagnarlo: il Servo di Dio accetto l' offerta. Giunti a pochi passi della Piccola Casa ringraziò e licenziò le guardie. Non appena le aveva licenziate, uscirono dai fossi profondi scavati per le fondamenta di un fabbricato della Piccola Casa in costruzione, due sconosciuti, che si erano colà appositamente nascosti, ed assalirono il Servo di Dio. Le guardie essendo ancora a poca distanza . . . arrestarono gli assalitori: il Servo di Dio entrò solo nella Piccola Casa, ed io lo vidi contrafatto e pallido, e quantunque io ignorassi affatto l' avvenuto, mi venne peraltro subito il pensiero che avesse ricevuto qualche affronto. Egli nulla disse, solo chiese una bona tazza di caffè cosa affatto insolita, locchè mi confermò nel pensiero che egli avesse veramente avuto qualche affronto grave, e che ne sentisse tuttavia gli effetti. Il Servo di Dio dopo aver preso il caffè nella farmacia, que era attigua alla porteria, si portò nella propria camera che stava superiormente alla porteria, dalla qualla facilmente si sentiva il Servo di Dio e camminare a muoversi nella sua camera. Trascorso qualche tempo non sentendo alcun movimento nella camera del Serva di Dio ed avendolo per altra parte veduto colla fisonomia alterata, dubitai che gli fosse preso male, onde mi portai a bussare l'uscio della sua camera, picchiai, ripetotamente, senza averne riposta, e questo accrebbe in me l'affanno; allora mi feci lecito di aprire l'uscio, e vidi che il Servo di Dio stava pregando colle braccia aperte davanti ad una immagine della Madonna, accesso in volto, che osservai ch' era ritto e che i piedi suoi non toccavano il pavimento, io così vedendolo, lo credetti in ecstasi, mi fermai per alcuini minuti a contemplarlo, vidi che stava immobile e sempre colla stessa posizione degli occhi fissi all' immagine di Maria, alzato da terra. Io non osai parlare e me ne tornai in Portieria. Non feci parola col Servo di Dio di ciò che io aveva veduto, perchè essendomi già occorso altra volta il vederlo estatico, ed avendone fatto cenno al medesimo, vidi ch' egli se n' era mostrato dispiacente, onde nè con lui nè con altri pendente la sua vita, io non feci parola di questo fatto. Et juxta interro. Proc. Fo.* 3751, 3752 *et terg. respondit: Io vidi il Servo di Dio più volte, mentre stava in orazione nella propria camera, o davanti il Crocifisso, o davanti una immagine della Beata Vergine, rapito in estasi, fuori dei sensi, sollevato da terra, colla faccia accesa, aria ridente, occhi scintillanti e rivolti al cielo. La prima volta che io il vidi fu nel primo anno che io fui*

124

St Mary Magdalen Postel, the foundress of the *Sœurs de la Miséricorde*, was canonised in 1925. Mgr. A. M. Legoux has written a copious biography of her, based on the documents of the several canonical processes, the sittings of which the author has attended in the capacity of a judge. It is from this work that I shall borrow the following facts, resorting, as I did before, to the text itself:

" Her pupils observed her once rapt before the tabernacle of her oratory. She was kneeling with her arms outspread, and did not touch the floor. Her face was radiating a heavenly light, and her eyes seemed to contemplate the infinite beauty. . . . More than once, induced by a curiosity easy to understand and excuse, they wanted to enjoy this beautiful sight again. One of them, among others Adelaïde Lamare, her niece, who was a boarder, would get up during the night, come down on tiptoe, and drawing near the oratory, look through the chinks of the door or the keyhole. ' Indeed,' she would say afterwards, ' my aunt is a saint; last night she was again lifted up from the floor and suspended with bent knees in the air, her eyes lifted to heaven and her face quite transfigured."[1]

---

destinata all' uffizio di Portinaia locchè fu nell' anno Mille ottocento trentasei in prossimità della Festa dell' Ascensione.

Portatami alla camera del Servo di Dio per avvertirlo che in Porteria v' erano persone forestiere che non desideravano parlargli, picchiai per ben tre volte, non rispondendo egli, e sapendo io per altra parte, che il medesimo si trovava in camera, apersi aliquanto, e con riguardo l' uscio, e vidi il Servo di Dio nello stato da me sovradescritto, e potei ben rimirarlo, perchè l' Immagine della Madonna era appesa a lato della porta, ed avendo egli la faccia rivolta verso l' Immagine, io gli era quasi dirimpetto. Mi fermai cinque minuti a rimirarlo, e vedendo che continuava in quello stato, e che non s' era punto accorto che io avessi aperto l' uscio della camera, me ne ritornai in Porteria. Debbo notare, che io entrando nell' uffizio di Portinaia, la Suora Pasquale, ora defunta, che mi precedette nell' uffizio, dandomi le norme che io dovevo tenere alla Portieria (sic), tra le altre cose mi disse, che dovendo chiamare il Servo di Dio quando stava nella sua camera, picchiassi per tre volte l' uscio, e se non rispondeva aprissi pian piano alquanto la porta, e se lo vedeva scrivere, gli parlasse e se stava in orazione non lo disturbassi ed andassi a dire alle persone che il Servo di Dio non c' era. Del fatto da me sopra deposto non ne feci parola con alcuno, nemmeno col Servo di Dio. Poco tempo dopo in un giorno d' una Novena d' una Festa del Signore, che ora non saprei dire quale, mi accadde la stessa cosa, e lo vidi posto come in ginocchio davanti al Crocifisso, fuori dei sensi, sollevato da terra, ed osservai che la veste talare non toccava terra, non potei però vederlo in volto perchè mi trovavo dietro di lui. . . .

Osservo che queste estassi avvenivano al Servo di Dio ordinariamente nelle Novene delle Feste principali del Signore e della Beata Vergine, o quando riceveva qualche affronto.

[1] Legoux, *La vénérable Marie-Madeleine Postel*, vol. i, p. 109.

She was also seen in the same situation by two Sisters, Sister Xavier and Sister Aimable.

" Sister Xavier had once a message to deliver to her. On coming to the passage leading to her room, she heard somebody speak. Believing she was having a conversation with a visitor, she waited about a quarter of an hour. At last she drew near the door. ' How I suffer, my God !' said the Venerable Mother; ' but all for you, my God ! Still more !' Sister Xavier looked at once through the keyhole to see what was taking place inside the room. The Venerable Mother was completely lifted from the floor, without touching it."[1]

Sister Aimable had witnessed a similar scene:

" The good Mother was kneeling with joined hands, lifted off the floor, and she said, ' O my God, have mercy on poor sinners, do forgive them !' and other such burning words."[2]

After Mass, Mary Postel would stay in the chapel to make a longer thanksgiving. The Sister who assisted her in keeping the vestry in order often found her, when she came back from breakfast, " suspended kneeling in the air, her face beaming with celestial light."[3]

A fact of sudden long-distance transport is also reported of the same saint, and should be quoted here in connection with levitation:

" She had gone one afternoon to a neighbouring parish called Gatteville and situated, like Barfleur, on the seaside. She wanted to see her confessor, who remained hidden there in those days.[4] On her way there, as the tide was out, she had taken a short cut by the beach. When she was to come back, the night was closing in and the tide was up. So she must follow a long, unsafe, lonely road, when she heard a voice say distinctly, ' Do not fear.' . . . In the twinkling of an eye she found herself transported a distance of several miles over the bay. She was at Barfleur."[5]

Mary Postel herself gave her opinion on the prodigy in the following circumstances:

" About forty-five years later, . . . her ecclesiastical Superior, M. Delamare, who had heard of the miracle, wanted to have it confirmed by the Venerable one herself, who could not now live very long. The matter was difficult; how was it possible to prevail over a humility which hid the favours she enjoyed more carefully than a miser his treasure ?

" It was agreed upon that Sister Mary, the matron, would recall

[1] *Ibid.*, vol. ii, pp. 295-296.   [2] *Ibid.*, p. 296.   [3] *Ibid.*
[4] It was during the Revolution.   [5] *Ibid.*, vol. i, p. 113.

126

the fact in the presence of M. Delamare and the chaplain M. Lerenard; and so she did, putting the question to the Mother Superior
directly. ' Blessed be God ! He knows everything,' was the only
answer. It was not enough.
" To bring the Mother to confess the thing more plainly, M.
Lerenard added, ' Did not Providence send a man who transferred
you in a boat or on a horse ?' ' There was neither man, nor boat, nor
horse,' said the Mother, with some vivacity; ' when God wills a thing,
it is soon done. After hearing the voice I was carried away in no
time.' "[1]

The Italian ecstatic, Maria Domenica Barbagli of Monte San
Savino, experienced very frequent raptures. Dr. Imbert-Gourbeyre
heard a lady whom he looked after at Royat give the following account
of one of her ecstasies she had witnessed:
" I saw, in 1855, the ecstatic of San Savino, in Tuscany, near
Siena Longa; she was called Miniquina, a corruption of Domenica.
She lived in her own house and had a great renown of sanctity. I
saw her on a Friday. She was in a kneeling position, with her arms
outstretched, and lifted in the air two feet over her bed. Her trance
lasted one hour. I placed my hand under her knees and was able
to lift her further up; she did not weigh more than a feather. I
blew on her, and her body slowly swung about in the air like a leaf
waving in the breeze. I had heard before of these phenomena;
now I could experience them. The following day, during Mass,
she was three times rapt in ecstasy and once lifted into the air.
Thousands of persons have witnessed facts of the kind. Miniquina
died in 1858."[2]
One of the biographers of Maria Domenica, Father G. E. Bini,
confirms in his *Vita* the preternatural lightness of the ecstatic's
body already mentioned by Dr. Imbert's patient, and he says that
it was as light and movable as a small feather: . . . *cosi agile e
leggero che anche per lievissimo soffio ondeggiava quasi sottilissima
piuma.*[3]
Domenica was levitated while lying on her bed. The coverlet
was borne away in the uplifting of the body.[4]

[1] *Ibid.*, pp. 113-114.
[2] Imbert-Gourbeyre, *Les stigmatisées*, vol. ii, p. 244. The date is not
correct. Domenica died on April 6, 1859.
[3] *Vita*, p. 141.
[4] *Ibid.*: *Piu volte però si è veduta sollevata in aria, supina come giaceva ın
letto, transportando seco le coperte a somiglianza di S. Filippo Neri.*

LEVITATION

A. de Rochas, in his essay on levitation, mentions the Curé d'Ars among levitated saints, and refers for fuller statement of the facts to the abridged biography of the Abbé Monnin. Now, the passage referred to (p. 159) is as follows: " One night, the Curé d'Ars was startled out of his sleep and felt himself lifted up into the air. ' My bed was gradually giving way under me,' he said."[1] The author of the biography does not seem to set any objective value on this fact.

In a later Life of J. B. Vianney, by the Abbé Trochu, it is said that M. Jean Gardette, the chaplain of the Carmelite convent at Châlon-sur-Saône, made the following deposition at the apostolic process: " My brother, Curé of Saint-Vincent at Châlon-sur-Saône, was once with me at Ars. In the evening, when the Servant of God was saying the prayers, we seated ourselves in front of the pulpit. About the middle of this exercise, while the Abbé Vianney was reciting the Act of Charity, my brother, who has very sharp sight, saw him gradually lifted up till his feet were raised over the upper edge of the pulpit. His face was transfigured and surrounded with a halo. My brother looked about and perceived no sign of emotion among the congregation. He remained silent, but as soon as he was out he could not help telling everybody with enthusiasm of the prodigy he had beheld."[2]

Mary of Jesus, better known by the name of Mother du Bourg, the foundress of the Sisters of the Saviour and the Blessed Virgin, was the aunt of Mgr. d'Hulst. The latter told Father Bulliot that his aunt had several times been raised off the earth in the eyes of all the community. Father Bulliot made a report about it to the *Société des Sciences psychiques* (sitting of Feb. 3, 1897).[3]

The two biographers of Mother du Bourg, the Abbé Bersange and G. du Bourg, give us more details about the facts. According to G. du Bourg, " it was nearly always at the end of her raptures that Mother du Bourg was suddenly raised from the ground. She would endeavour to withstand the impulse, but a supernatural force carried her away. Then she would abandon herself to this attraction."[4]

Dr. Imbert-Gourbeyre was personally acquainted with Mother du Bourg and her relatives. Some of these had seen her lifted in the air while praying.[5] This is how he describes one of those raptures:

---

[1] A. Monnin, p. 159. *Cf.* ed. in 2 vols., vol. i, p. 336; also Trochu, p. 290.
[2] Trochu, p. 635. [3] Rochas, *Recueil*, p. 92.
[4] Du Bourg, *Une Fondatrice au XIXe siècle*, p. 254.
[5] *Les stigmatisées*, vol. ii, p. 234, n. 1.

128

"Nearly always the ecstasy ended in a sudden uplifting of Mother du Bourg, who exclaimed, 'O charity! O divine love!' Then she tried to resist the divine attraction. She would grab her seat or prie-dieu in vain, then cross her arms on her breast or stretch them out to heaven, and abandon herself to the force that raised her swiftly up. She would always keep the posture in which she had been rapt, and remained suspended in a kneeling or sitting posture."[1]

According to the same author, these aerial raptures occurred with some regularity: "Every night at evening prayer, Mother Mary of Jesus could not hear the Act of Divine Love recited without being rapt at once in ecstasy. She would then be raised into the air to the height of her chair; then she suddenly sank down on her prie-dieu. One day the fall was so heavy that the board was broken. I have it from an eye-witness."[2]

The latter fact has been recorded by Mother Mary of the Cross, an eye-witness:

"On April 7, 1856, when I was saying the Act of Divine Love, at evening prayer, the Reverend Mother was lifted up with overwhelming force, and, as she clutched her prie-dieu to resist the divine attraction, the seat was also raised and dropped down again with a crash. The step was broken. The next morning I came to see her. 'They ask me if there is anything the matter with my knees,' she said, with some confusion, 'but they are quite all right.' 'It is not so with the prie-dieu,' I observed. 'My heart was cleft and rapt; it was a purifying love that gave me exquisite pains,' answered the good Mother. And some moments after she came softly down to the chapel to see the condition of her prie-dieu; and stooping to examine the split, she murmured, 'O feeble and wretched creature! See what you have done.'"[3]

The Mother's prie-dieu has been kept, and may be seen in the

---

[1] *La stigmatisation*, vol. i, pp. 505-506.
[2] *Ibid.*, p. 506.
[3] Bersange, p. 312. I found it difficult to render into English the allusion of the Venerable Mother to her mystical state. The original is: *Mon cœur se partageait et partait.* I suppose the ecstatic refers to the feeling described by St Francis of Sales, who says of the soul wounded with the "wound of divine love": *A mesme temps qu'elle est attirée puissamment à voler vers son Bien-Aimé, elle est aussi retenue puissamment et ne peut voler, comme attachée aux basses misères de cette vie mortelle et de sa propre impuissance; elle désire des aisles de colombe pour voler en son repos et elle n'en trouve point. La voilà donc rudement tourmentée entre la violence de ses eslans et celle de son impuissance (Traité de l'Amour de Dieu, bk. vi, ch. xiii).*

chapel of the house of her congregation at La Souterraine (Creuse). It is a bulky prayer-desk set on a base. It has not been repaired. A photograph of it is given at the end of G. du Bourg's biography of the Venerable one.

On October 24, 1854, at the close of a retreat, Mother du Bourg was two hours rapt, and rose twice up into the air.[1]

The ecstatic herself alluded to levitation in a letter to the Baronne de Barante. The latter questioned her about her mother's salvation. This was Mary's answer:

" Ah ! How good God is ! How powerful our prayers are through this ineffable bounty that we shall never have been able to love, value, and acknowledge as it should be ! Not long ago—it was last night—a person to whom God sometimes deigns to reveal his secrets was kneeling in her cell; suddenly she was lifted off the floor, and she knew your mother was in heaven."[2]

It is said that when she heard of Pope Gregory's death (1846), Mother du Bourg knelt down and experienced an aerial rapture.[3]

Blessed Michael Garicoïts, the founder of the Congregation of the *Prêtres du Sacré-Cœur de Jésus* of Bétharram, was born in the diocese of Bayonne in 1797, and died in 1863. He was beatified in 1923. When saying Mass he would often be lifted to the tips of his toes. Sometimes he was actually raised two or three spans (nearly a foot) above the floor. Several *Filles de la Croix*, nuns of Bétharram, seminarists, and other people, according to his biographer, were witnesses of these facts.[4]

Mary Moerl, a famous stigmatisée of Tyrol, was almost con-tinually rapt, but none of her numerous visitors ever saw her levi-tated; though it is reported by some of them that at times she would be raised on her bed so as to touch it only by the extreme tips of her toes.[5] M. E. de Moy, Professor of Law in Munich University, has given the following description of an ecstasy of Mary's:

" With her hands joined, her head and eyes lifted to heaven, on her knees, her body leaning forward, she seemed carried by angels invisibly supporting her, for according to the slope of her body she ought to have lost her balance, and her knees were hardly pressed on the bed-cover."[6]

---

[1] *Ibid.*, p. 296.   [2] *Ibid.*, p. 361   [3] *Ibid.*, p. 362.
[4] R. P. Bourdenne, *La vie et l'œuvre du Vénérable Michel Garicoïts*, pp. 347-348.
[5] L. Boré, *Les stigmatisées du Tyrol*, pp. 16, 26, 175-176.
[6] *Ibid.*, p. 185.

RECENT TRADITIONS

Lord Shrewsbury, who had visited the ecstatic in 1841, gave a similar description to a correspondent, A. L. Philipps.[1]

Sister Mary of Jesus Crucified, a lay Carmelite nun, was born in 1846 at Abellin, a little village of Galilee. She died in 1878 in the Carmel of Bethlehem in the odour of sanctity. Her cause was recently introduced into the Roman Court. This ecstatic was sometimes lifted up into the air, but never without some purchase to start with or some support to poise herself on. When she flew to the top of the lime-trees in the garden of the convent at Pau, she would first clutch at some twig and haul herself up to the top of a high tree, where she would perch on a small branch. This kind of ecstatic ascent took place for the first time on June 22, 1873, and was renewed on July 9, 19, 25, 27, 31, August 3, of the same year, and on July 5, 1874. But it is believed that Mary was lifted to tree-tops many other times. She would sometimes remain perched several hours.[2] Her later biographer, Father D. Buzy, S.C.J., was kind enough to send me different details on Mary Baouardy which are not in his book. I will transcribe them literally:

" Sister Mary lifted herself up to the top of a tree by the end of the branches. She would take her scapulary in one hand; with the other she seized the extremity of a twig, and, in the twinkling of an eye, she glided along the outer surface of the tree up to the top. The witnesses emphasise the fact that she climbed up instantaneously. She even passed directly from one tree-top to another.

" When she was up, she stood on branches too small normally to support a person of her weight (the more so as she was rather stout). These are the depositions of some witnesses in the process:

" The late Sister E. told me that one day, as she was with the Servant of God in the garden, the latter said to her, ' Turn round.' She had hardly turned round when, looking again, she saw her already sitting on the top of the lime, on a small branch, swinging like a bird and singing the song of divine love."

" ' I saw her once rapt in ecstasy on the top of a lime-tree,' says another person. 'She was sitting on the very end of the uppermost branch, which in usual circumstances could never have supported her. Her face was beaming with light. I saw her climb down the tree like a bird, passing from the end of a branch to another, very lightly and modestly. I noticed that these lime boughs, which

[1] *Ibid.*, p. 108. *Cf.* pp. 199, 229.
[2] D. Buzy, *Vie de Sr. Marie de Jésus Crucifié*, pp. 213-217.
131

LEVITATION

were very slender, should have broken under the weight of the Sister,
who was pretty heavy. She was still rapt when she climbed down.'
" ' When she climbed down the tree,' states another witness,
' she passed from one branch to another like a bird, and her dress
followed her as if she came down a stair.'
" On one occasion she came down with difficulty; the Prioress
had ordered her to come down, as she often did. Sister Mary
hesitated for a moment. Then she began climbing down, but very
clumsily. She ascribed this breakdown to her not having complied
at once with her Superior's command. ' If me obey quick,' she said
in her broken language, ' the trees grow as small as that,' and she put
her hand close to the ground."[1]

A stigmatisée from Ardèche, Victoria Claire of Coux, who
died in 1883, experienced levitations which were sometimes of a
still more incomplete character. De Rochas publishes the following
evidence about her that he had from an eye-witness, Madame D.:
" I saw her with great amazement remain with her eyes fixed
but lively, and gradually raised above the chair whereon she was
sitting. She stretched forth her arms, leaned her body forward, and
remained thus suspended, her right leg bent up, the other touching
the earth but by a toe. I saw Victoire in this position, impossible
for anyone to keep up normally, every time she was in an ecstatic
trance, when I was fortunate enough to pay her a visit twice a week.
During my visits, she would experience two or three raptures that
lasted from ten to twenty-five minutes. I saw her in this state
more than a thousand times, chiefly during the first years of our
friendship."[2]
Dr. Imbert-Gourbeyre received a similar testimony about this
person.[3]
No printed literature on Victoria is available. A Jesuit, Father
Rousset, wrote a work about her which was not published. The
Abbé Combes, who was the parish priest of Coux in Victoria's lifetime, kept a diary of the notable facts in the life of his ecstatic
parishioner. In this document, made accessible to me through the
kindness of a friend, I could pick out some facts which are of some
interest in respect of the present essay. For instance, Victoire
experienced many transports and aerial suspensions which are to be
classed, by their form and circumstances, among so-called demoniac

[1] Extract from a letter of Feb. 14, 1927.
[2] Rochas, *Recueil*, p. 27.
[3] *La stigmatisation*, vol. i, p. 562.

molestations. But no other witness of these is recorded than Victoria Claire herself. I also find in this document the testimony of one Mlle. Régnier, whose evidence, I am told, is of considerable value, regarding a levitation proper, the circumstances of which are as follows:
" We were in the chapel of the Sacred Heart. Victoire Claire was behind us, kneeling, close to the confessional. Looking round, I saw her lifted in the air more than three feet over the floor. The Sister, seeing my bewilderment, ordered us out at once."
The witness was only six years of age when this took place. The Abbé Combes never witnessed any scene of levitation or even of pseudo-levitation, but he had noticed that a halo of light sometimes surrounded the head of the ecstatic, especially after Communion.

Positions contrary to the law of equilibrium were observed, according to Dr. Imbert-Gourbeyre, with Mary Louise Lateau, a famous stigmatisée of Bois d'Haine (Belgium), whom this author examined carefully.[1]

In July, 1898, the liner La Bourgogne sank off Newfoundland. To this catastrophe is connected a scene the account of which fits into the present recital. The hero of it is a Dominican friar, the brother of the well-known French novelist E. Baumann, who has written what follows:
" Of my brother's last moments here is an unexpected testimony, which reached me not long ago, like a message from heaven. I will not indeed warrant the supernatural truth of this strange and miraculous fact. But it shows in what state of rapture my brother passed from the gloom of the sea to the everlasting sun. When La Bourgogne was about to sink, a Protestant lady, who was in a boat rowing away from the ship—one of the few women who escaped—turned round towards the wreck, the sloping deck of which was now close to the waves. Then she saw the three Dominicans in the midst of ship-wrecked people on their knees: the eldest, the Father Prior, held out to them his rosary and a crucifix; the youngest—my brother—lifted his eyes to heaven, as if rapt in ecstasy; he seemed to be raised off the deck, and round his head was a circlet of light."[2]
" I have the episode," says M. Baumann, " from the Rev. Father Hugon, Professor in the Angelic College in Rome, a self-restrained theologian, adverse to illuminism. The Protestant lady had reported it, in a New York hospital, to a Sister of the Bon Secours

[1] Les stigmatisées, vol. i, pp. 106, 111.
[2] E. Baumann, Mon frère le Dominicain, pp. 391-392.

of Troyes, Mother Henry Joseph, a person of sound judgement, incapable of inventing a miracle. She wrote about it to Father Hugon. The latter told her to keep the story secret, and he did not himself speak of it to anybody. He avoided investing with an untimely aureole a young monk prematurely gone. Lately, when somebody spoke to him about Father Joseph, he thought it advisable to impart the fact to me, and to mention its precise origin. The wrecked lady did *see* something; but as she was the only person who did so among the other survivors, we cannot decide whether her excitement wrought the phenomenon or if God, to enlighten her, disclosed to her the anticipated glory of one of the elect."[1]

Gemma Galgani of Lucca died in the odour of sanctity in 1903. She is said to have experienced ecstasies with levitation; but her biographer refers but very vaguely to the fact. He is content with saying that occasionally she would be lifted up in her raptures high enough to embrace a crucifix that she could not have reached otherwise.[2] Gemma Galgani was a stigmatisée; she belonged to the Passionists.

Mary of the Passion, of the *Crocifisse Adoratrici di Gesù Sacramentato*, is not reported to have experienced levitations proper, but only ecstatic agility. Sister Mary Prassede, of the same congregation, says in a letter dated June 3, 1913, that one day, still being a novice, she was bidden by the Mother Superior to take back to her cell Mary of the Passion, because the latter was so ill that she had to return to bed immediately after Communion. "We had hardly left the choir, when I noticed that the Servant of God, though she was very weak, ascended the stairs in no time, as if she was flying, while I was unable to follow her, though I was in good health. She seemed not to tread the floor but actually fly up the stairs that led to her cell."[3]

---

[1] *Ibid.*
[2] Félix de Jésus Crucifié, *Gemma Galgani*, p. 181. P. Germano di S. Stanislao, *Life of Gemma Galgani*, Engl. trans., pp. 270-271 (quoted by H. Thurston, p. 334).
[3] L. M. Fontana, *Vita della vittima riparatrice*, etc., p. 297: . . . *Io era ancora Novizia e la Madre Superiora, negli ultimi giorni che Suor Maria della Passione scese nel Coro per fare la S. Comunione doveva immediatamente ritornare in letto. Ebbene, appena uscite insieme dal Coro, osservavo che la Serva di Dio, quantunque sofferentissima, saliva le scale in un istante, come se volasse, ed io in buona salute non potevo seguirla, sicchè a me sembrava che non toccasse terra, ma che realmente volava per le scale che conducono alla cella.* . . .

An ecstatic from Brittany, who is still alive, Mary Julia Jahenny of La Fraudais (near Nantes), is said by Dr. Imbert-Gourbeyre to have experienced for two years repeated raptures with levitation. He adds that at his request competent persons ascertained her loss of weight when in a state of rapture.[1]

I endeavoured myself to verify the accuracy of this statement, but I was unable to obtain any confirmation of it by the parish priest of Blain—who serves the parish of La Fraudais—who wrote to me that he had never seen anything of the kind.

[1] *La stigmatisation*, vol. ii, p. 268.

BOOK II
THE FACTS

PRELIMINARY NOTE

I SHALL examine in this book the amount of reliance that may be placed on the traditions reported above. It is plain that, in consenting to inquire into the historic value of beliefs contradictory to the data of daily experience, I oppose the view of those historians who, by criteria foreign to their science, exclude from it any uncanny event they happen to come across. It is my hope to be able hereafter in the present book to throw discredit on this dogmatic process.[1]

CHAPTER I

DIVERS TRADITIONS OUTSIDE CHRISTIAN HAGIOGRAPHY

§ 1. ANTIQUITY AND THE ORIENT

UNDER these heads, in Chapter I of Book I, we have met with theoretical beliefs rather than with records of facts of pseudo-historic character. Leaving temporarily aside our experimental repugnance to admit that the human body might be suspended in or fly through the air without the action of some detectable physical force, to consider merely the historic value of the traditions referring to the prodigy, we easily find that the anecdotes collected in the course of our inquiry are surrounded with a fabulous atmosphere which is very apt to discourage any critical research into the origin of the said documents, had that ever been possible.

Some modern accounts of the yogis might, in theory, deserve better credit, as they come from authors who do not attempt the vindication of some religion or philosophy; but to the natural motives

---

[1] To speak with more modesty and accuracy, I had better say " to contribute to throw discredit . . .," for this urgent work has been performed with all necessary talent and knowledge by Father H. Pinard de la Boullaye (*L'étude comparée des religions*, vol. ii, par. 322 *ff.*) and J. de Tonquédec, whose *Introduction à l'étude du merveilleux et du miracle*, so wise and penetrating, seems to me to settle the speculative bearings of the problem.

LEVITATION

for being incredulous in such matters should be added others derived from the character of the so-called witnesses. I for my part have transcribed the accounts of Jacolliot in the same way as many records of dubious hagiographic facts, because no elimination seemed to me justified in a *statement* of beliefs. But now, on critical grounds, I will say that the author of the *Voyage au pays des faquirs charmeurs* does not inspire me with the least degree of confidence.

This severe judgement should be extended to most of the writers who have written of the pseudo-marvels of Indian ascetics. Among others, the American journalist who explained the illusion of the rope-trick by a collective hypnotisation,[1] confessed later on that he had simply tried to enliven a somewhat worn-out anecdote with a scientific flourish to the taste of the day.

Indeed, the lives of genuine mystics escape superficial observation in India as elsewhere, and the travellers who used to recount the prodigies of so-called mystics have merely met with conjurers. The orthodox Buddhist mystic should not display his magic powers before the profane, according to the rule of Buddha himself, as the following story testifies. One day a Bhikkhu rose into the air to fetch a plate of santal-wood placed high above the floor, and, holding it, flew three times over the head of Rajagriha. Buddha rebuked him with these words: " How can you, Baravâja, for the sake of a paltry platter, reveal to laymen the superhuman character of your power ?"[2]

Besides, the term *ascetic* implies in India ways of living, outwardly and inwardly, which are most diverse and even opposed in nature. If, in a study of levitation, the psychological circumstances of the phenomenon should not be left aside—as I expect to prove— it is necessary, when we speak of the prodigies worked by Indian mystics, to state the kind of ascetic we refer to. From a spiritual and simply moral point of view we should be careful to discriminate between a sincere contemplative like Râmakrishna and some devotee of Çakti, a regular wizard, or a nâga, whose poverty is robbery in disguise.

Practically, a scientist who has been studying comparative mysticism for a number of years told me he had tried in vain to

[1] *Cf.* R. Schmidt's *Fakire und Fakirtum*, p. 168.
[2] *Vinaya Texts*, 3, 1 (quoted by C. Godard, *Le Fakirisme*, p. 34). Future Buddhas are cautioned against using their clairvoyance for profane ends, and generally, observes M. de la Vallée-Poussin, " A supernatural power should never be prostituted to worldly purposes " (*Bouddhisme*, p. 354 and n. 1).

140

obtain from missionaries whom he knew to be well aware of native ways any definite information as to the abnormal facts commonly ascribed to yogis or other Indian ascetics.[1]

These remarks hold true of Chinese and Japanese sects. In India or in the Far East, the tradition we have to deal with is of a purely speculative nature: none of the facts it produces stands on a ground that may be critically explored.

It is much the same with Islam, with maybe the exception of the deposition of Al-Sâmarri, declaring to the Vizier he had seen Al-Hallaj lifted in the air. This testimony, given by a witness for the prosecution, who had only to lose by lending the culprit mysterious power, is the first document on which we may set the slightest amount of historical value. Such is the opinion of the biographer of Al-Hallaj himself, M. L. Massignon, the well-known Islamic scholar, Professor at the Collège de France.[2]

§ 2. WIZARDS

(a) Among Savage Tribes

We have seen that the Australians, Amerindians, and Negroes regard their sorcerers as capable of rising into the air and flying through it. The credulity of these tribes, the cunning of those who are concerned in keeping it up, forbid us to look upon these beliefs as based on experimental ground. At best these superstitions might induce inquiries to ascertain in each particular case the substratum of truth upon which they are possibly founded. Indeed, Father Papetard affirmed to Dr. Imbert-Gourbeyre that he had seen sorcerers of Oregon actually skimming in their flight the tips of the

[1] I was pleased to find a confirmation of my assertions regarding the difficulty of ascertaining the reality of the preternatural phenomena of Oriental mysticism in the following statement of Mme. Alexandra David-Neel, who has lived fourteen years in Tibet: " The anchorets and their disciples are quite unlike our Occidental mediums who hold séances for money and accept to have their manifestations critically examined.

" The humblest disciple of a Tibetan *Gomtchen* would be very much surprised if such a proposal were made to him. I think I can hear his answer: ' I do not care whether you believe or not in these phenomena. I do not want to convince you. It is fit for jugglers to expose themselves to public view. There is no public performance with us.' "

And the author adds that the investigators would not even have to listen to such a declaration, " for they are not at all likely ever to reach the mystic masters or their disciples " (*Le Thibet Mystique*, p. 891).

[2] *Al-Hallaj*, vol. i, p. 136.

grass blades. This evidence is not altogether negligible. The missionary is likely to have witnessed some out-of-the-way thing. But was the thing levitation ? To assert it would be most daring. Sorcerers in every country know very well how to throw themselves into somnambulistic fits, or they have often become sorcerers because of some morbid condition of theirs. Possibly Father Papetard had seen a wizard seized with corybantism, and the latter so lightly ran and sprang over the grass that he thought he glided in the air over it. . . .

As to the evidence of Father Trilles about the ceremony of the pole on the end of which the initiates of the Ngil society are said to be lifted into the air by the attraction of the hands of the chief sorcerer, it is hard to ignore it, but it should be observed, (1) that even if the fact be true, there is no levitation proper in this case, as the bodies of the initiates are raised off the earth on a support and by the seeming attraction of a visible agent; (2) that the circumstances of the fact suggest the possibility of some subtle piece of jugglery bringing the phenomenon about.

(b) Among Civilised Peoples

A great number of sorcerers and witches have been imprisoned, judged, and sentenced to death in European countries. Big treatises have been written on their ways and marvels by those who interrogated and judged them. But none of them was ever capable of producing serious evidence of wizards having been actually carried through the air. Among others, Del Rio, who has compiled a number of facts in connection with the aerial transports of magicians, is far from being convincing.[1] The weakness of their reasons is amply proved by the fact that theologians who had no theoretical objections to raise against demoniac powers in man preferred to resort to more rational explanations, and thought that the witches' journey to their Sabbat was only the subjective result of their demoniac raptures. Such was the opinion expounded by Benedict XIV in his famous treatise.[2] Again, it is remarkable that Abbé Ribet, so ready to welcome in his work any kind of the marvellous, divine or diabolical, could find no better example of Sabbat transport than an anecdote drawn from Görres, who himself has quoted it from

---

[1] M. Del Rio, *Disquisitionum magicarum libri sex*, l. ii, quaestio xvi. *De nocturnis sagarum conventibus et an vera sit illarum de loco ad locum translatio.*

[2] *De Serv. Dei beat.*, l. 4, p. 1, c. 3, n. 3, t. 4, p. 14.

another author, with his too frequent disregard of accurate references.[1]

The upliftings of Magdalen of Cordova are recorded in more reliable documents, but in too vague and episodical a way—neither dates nor names of places and witnesses are mentioned—to deserve much attention.

As a rule, the prodigies of black magic are considered with much scepticism by modern theologians. As Father Gardette sensibly observes in his article on the matter in the *Dictionnaire de théologie catholique*, one would prefer half a dozen facts carefully ascertained to " a multitude of doubtful ones the sources of which are almost impossible to criticise."

§ 3. DEMONIACS

(a) Among Savage Tribes

Some missionaries have said they had come across strange cases of aerial transport of the human body, which the natives regarded as caused by the action of malignant spirits. Here again we should admit a positive origin for these rumours; but there is no evidence that the carrying away of the so-called possessed victims is due to a supernatural cause. A far less onerous hypothesis may be resorted to to explain away the carrying of them up to the top of a baobab than the action of a spirit, since we know that a somnambulistic fit is more likely to be responsible for it. Indeed, it is most remarkable that there is nothing more in this than hearsay evidence; no missionary has himself ever seen the transport of the molested person upwards or downwards. They have been called up by the natives; they have seen somebody tied up with lianas to the top of the tree; sometimes they have seen him climbing down the tree with unusual nimbleness, as the apparent result of some ceremony. But their experience, as far as I know, never goes further.[2]

(b) Among Civilised Peoples

On the other hand, some writers are quite positive about the uplifting of the possessed that they have—or have seen—exorcised. Sulpitius Severus, among others, in this respect, makes use of expressions of unmistakable clearness.[3]

[1] Ribet, vol. iii, ch. xvii, par. xix, p. 397. *Cf.* Görres, vol. v, ch. xvii, p. 165.
[2] *Cf.* Mgr. A. Le Roy, *La religion des primitifs*, p. 348.
[3] *Cf. supra*, Bk. I, pt. 1, ch. ii, par. 2, b, p. 13.

LEVITATION

Nearer to our time, Dom La Taste has described with minute accuracy the convulsions and raisings of Mlle. Thevenet. But it is to be noticed that, if he speaks of her having been lifted up to the ceiling, he does not refer to any duration of the suspension; which he would have certainly done if he had ground to, as his aim in this description was to prove the demoniacal possession of the Jansenist convulsionaries. Therefore, there is no exaggeration in supposing that his expression "s'élever" does not mean more than to spring up with bounds of unusual height and force, such as may be witnessed in the course of an hysterical fit.[1]

This rational explanation is more difficult to resort to in the case of Françoise Fontaine, the possessed woman of Louviers, if the terms of the official report are to be accepted literally.

Anyhow, in the cases of so-called possession observed lately, levitation is never referred to, but simply feats of abnormal agility akin to somnambulism. Dr. Ch. Hélot, who has investigated a series of such cases without rationalistic prejudices, never came across anything like a suspension in the air.[2]

In one of the last books written on possession many a case is to be found, indeed, when the "possessed" person is carried away or lifted up into the air, but, remarkably enough, none of these occurrences was ever witnessed by anyone else than the would-be victim of the devil, and never were they observed during the exorcisms.[3]

On the other hand, it seems exaggerated to deny a priori the possibility of levitation as one of the symptoms of possession—whatever may be the meaning given to the word—and it is strange that a scientist like Dr. Österreich, in his work on possession, has not alluded to the phenomenon in his description of the outward signs of this state. If he himself refuses to admit the reality of this

[1] The same holds true of Nicole of Vervins, another possessed woman sometimes mentioned as having been levitated during her exorcisms. *Cf.* in *Histoire de Nicole de Vervins*, by J. Roger, the reproduction of an old print. The comparison of the picture with the explanatory text shows very clearly that the writer never meant that the demoniac was actually suspended in the air.

[2] Ch. Hélot, *Névroses et possessions diaboliques*, Observations i-xvii, pp. 9-88.

[3] L. Champault, *Une possédée contemporaine* (1834-1914), pp. 140 ff., 188, 204, 210, 225, 237, 262. *Cf.* still a reference to something like levitation in C. M. de Heredia's *Spiritism and Common Sense* (N.Y., 1922), where the author speaks of two young girls of Natal who, in their fits, "sometimes are lifted off the ground in spite of the Sisters holding them" (p. 116). The said girls have been exorcised by Mgr. Delalle, Apostolic Vicar of Natal, but it does not seem that the latter has ever witnessed the phenomena. This took place in 1907.

particular symptom, it should be well to account for his position, and, at any rate, the mentioning of the *belief* in its existence was, from an historical point of view, quite indispensable.[1]

§ 4. MEDIUMS

Dr. Richet, so little averse to believing in so-called metapsychic phenomena, still evinces some scepticism regarding mediumistic levitation. What is reported in this respect of Eglington, Ruggieri, Cecchini, seems to him " frightfully doubtful."[2] As to the phenomena obtained with Eusapia Palladino, Zuccarini, W. S. Moses, if they appear more worthy of belief, the former ones (Eusapia's) are acknowledged to lack completeness.[3] This severity is extended even to the feats of D. D. Home by Professor Richet, whose conclusion on the matter is as follows: " These strange facts of levitation, either with St Joseph of Copertino, Stainton Moses, or D. D. Home, deserve our attention. However, despite the authority and number of the witnesses, I think that inexorable science is not yet entitled to regard levitation as a proved phenomenon."[4]

Indeed, it is to be wondered whether in some of the above quoted instances actual negation ought not to be substituted for Dr. Richet's suspicion. For example, regarding Zuccarini, whose levitation does not seem to him improbable, the experiments organised by Professors Vicentini and Lori by means of special controlling apparatus, have shown that the said phenomenon was of a quite natural character, as the medium was not suspended—if we may put it so—more than half a second, whereas another time when he was thought to be raised above the floor, an unexpected flash of light disclosed him to be standing on the table.[5]

Nevertheless, it should be acknowledged that outside doubtful cases and obvious pieces of trickery, some instances of mediumistic levitation present themselves with an impressive aspect of veracity. For instance, it is difficult to reject the whole evidence establishing the reality of this phenomenon with D. D. Home. Indeed, Frank Podmore thought himself entitled, after a searching scrutiny into the circumstances of the case and of some others, to conclude that every supernatural manifestation of the kind had infallibly its origin in the fraud of the medium or the hallucination of those present.

[1] T. K. Oesterreich, *Les possédés*, ch. ii *passim*.
[2] *Traité*, p. 696.   [3] *Ibid.*, p. 697.
[4] *Ibid.*, p. 699.   *Cf.* p. 692: " . . . the facts, *as yet so uncertain*, concerning levitation." (The italics are mine.)
[5] Dr Grasset, *L'occultisme*, pp. 408-411.

But the subtleties he is compelled to resort to to carry his point disclose at every line the weaknesses of his criticism, the actual basis of which appears to be more metaphysical than historical. Practically, I even think that no reading is more fitted to suggest to the unbiassed inquirer the reality of Home's preternatural faculties than that of Podmore's criticism.[1] If so resolute a sceptic, so patient, well-informed and carping a critic was incapable of drawing up a more convincing array of arguments against the genuineness of the medium's power, is it not the best proof of the sturdy resistance he must have found in the facts ?

Still, this does not mean that Podmore's criticism of the prodigies of spiritualism, and particularly of mediumistic levitation, is altogether devoid of value. Far from it. Its conclusions should, on the contrary, be retained from a general and theoretical point of view. They may be summed up under this threefold head:

1. The facts are nearly always observed in the dark or in a very subdued light, which leaves ample room for cheating or illusion;

2. They take place in the presence of carefully picked witnesses, who expect to behold abnormal manifestations, consequently whose imagination is open to suggestion;

3. So many pieces of trickery—conscious or not—were detected in the past that the candid observer must be excused if better conditions of experimentation in the present are unable to dispel at once his now instinctive feeling of suspicion.

§ 5. MAGNETISED PERSONS

Cases of levitation as a result of magnetic practices have been—so far as I know—but very scarcely reported, and they were of quite a private character. Ch. Lafontaine says in his *Mémoires* that he had been able to draw up hypnotised persons placed on one of the scales of a balance, and this in the presence of scientists of different countries, but he has omitted to give any particulars of his remarkable experiments.[2] At any rate, it is strange that none of the most famous magnetists have ever mentioned levitation among the phenomena obtained by their passes, and that it is not recorded in the very complete Report on magnetism presented in 1831 to the *Académie de médecine* of Paris by Dr. Husson. The seemingly genuine facts recorded later on in this connection amount to trifling phenomena

---

[1] *Cf. Modern Spiritualism*, vol. ii, bk. iv, particularly ch. iii and iv.
[2] *Mémoires d'un magnétiseur*, vol. ii, pp. 94-95.

that cannot be compared with levitation.[1]   As to the more characteristic manifestations described by Lafontaine, their relationship with
magnetism is far from being established.   Lastly, were the attraction
of a magnetised person by the hands of the hypnotiser proved, it
need not follow that the phenomenon has anything to do with levitation proper.[2]

In these circumstances, magnetic levitation cannot be safely
acknowledged as a proved category of this phenomenon.   Indeed,
not only is its very existence doubtful, but if it were demonstrated,
its specificity might still be questioned, until the causal relationship
between the magnetising process and the uplifting of the body were
experimentally established.[3]   And even then, the observed phenomenon might be denied to be levitation proper if it is admitted—
as it seems it should be—that the term implies the spontaneous
rising of a human body in conditions excluding the agency of any
contrivance or apparatus—even a live one—on the levitated body.

§ 6. Conclusion

On the whole, the traditions concerning levitation—outside Christian hagiography, which is still to be examined—appear to be of a
rather elusive character.   The magico-religious facts of the Oriental
sects, far-distant and fabulous, baffle all criticism.   The feats of
savage or civilised wizards belong also to an uncontrollable folk-lore.
As to the somersaults of demoniacs, their gradual subsidence as they
draw nearer to our time may well suggest some exuberance in the
accounts of old.

Only mediumistic levitation has been the subject of reports circumstantial enough to solicit our attention.   The sincerity of a
number of investigators, their desire for serious experimentation,
however, are not enough to make us forget the unfavourable material
conditions under which they are bound to work; the darkness where
they are confined must always affect positive minds with insuperable
repugnance.

[1] Boirac says that by extending his hand over his subject sleeping a
natural sleep, he caused his feet to rise.   He observed his right hand only
possessed this power (Sudre, par. 143).   Similar facts were observed by
Drs. Bourru and Burot, by Baragnon, and by Moutin, a disciple of du Potet
(Bourru et Burot, *La suggestion mentale*, pp. 206 *ff.*).

[2] *Cf. infra*, Bk. III, ch. iii, par. 2, *b*.

[3] There would be no theoretical difficulty in ranging such instances as
those of Lafontaine under the heads of witchcraft or possession.

CHAPTER II

THE DOCUMENTS OF CATHOLIC HAGIOGRAPHY :
SEARCH FOR SOME CRITICAL TESTS TO BE
APPLIED TO THEM

WITHOUT anticipating the issue of this inquiry, we may mark, in the first place, that Catholic hagiography provides exceptionally rich matter for it; by the abundance, antiquity, continuity, and often by the accuracy of its traditions. Nothing here is to be compared with the tales of Buddhism; the levitations of the saints fit into the daily train of history; they occur on definite spots of the globe, at precise dates, before identified witnesses. All this does not preclude, of course, every chance of deception, exaggeration, or error —and in particular it would be very naïve to regard topographical information as a standard of veracity—but it puts at least a check on their occurrence, and, for that matter, provides a firm basis for argument.

§ 1. Is the Critical Examination of the Documents Permissible ?

Some will object that it is vain to try the value of testimonies concerning facts manifestly false. History, they say, has not to ascertain if those who tell tales are deceiving or deceived. The tale shows that there is a liar or a fool, and that is enough. The manner in which the deception has been contrived or the error committed may be a matter of study for the psychologist; the historian is not concerned in it.

It may be at times useful and even indispensable in history to ignore certain facts; but such *a priori* elimination should always be carried out with caution. When we have to deal with traditions, the facts of which are not only out-of-the-way but fantastic, when we are confronted with a kind of marvellous where gratuitous prodigies form a sort of concatenation of nonsense, then it is plain that an inquiry into the real value of the evidence would be a needless and somewhat unreasonable performance. But we should not confuse nonsense and the marvellous, by which we only mean here: *any*

148

phenomenon that seems to escape the action of usual natural forces and suggests the interference of an occult and intelligent cause.
One day an enemy of Buddha's set loose a herd of mad elephants against him and his five hundred *arhats* in order to crush them. When they saw the charge, the Buddhist monks rose prudently into the air. As to Buddha, he was content to hold out his hand; his five fingers became five lions whose roars shook heaven and earth. Struck with awe and remorse, the elephants fell prostrate on the ground and started crying. . . .

This tale of Chinese Buddhism, which I have picked out almost at random from Father Wieger's valuable book,[1] belongs to what I call the fantastic. The historian is not required to tax his erudition to find out reasons for doubting it. The normal use of common-sense is quite enough here.

Now, when I read that Venerable Mother Agnes of Langeac, when rapt in ecstasy, appeared one day to the Abbé Olier, who was then two hundred leagues from her; that the fact is known by the holy man's report; that eighty depositions were made about it in the process of the beatification of Mother Agnes;[2] contrary as the event may be to my daily experience, is not the impulse of incredulity it rouses in my mind less spontaneous and insuperable than in Buddha's adventure?

Levitation, in Catholic hagiography, belongs to a marvellous but not to a fantastic order of things. It presents itself as a queer, baffling fact, contradictory to everything we know of natural forces; and this entitles us to assume a prudent defensive attitude against it; but reason does not require any more from us.

Neither does it regularly assume the form of these hagiographic themes whose fictitious character is obvious, such as the miraculous arrival of relics in a derelict ship, or something thrown into the sea which is found again in the stomach of a fish. . . .[3] The accounts of levitation have mostly a sober, accurate historical form, which may conceal illusion or fraud, but does not suggest popular legend or poetic fiction.

To flinch from the historical test of abnormal facts, lest we should light on miracle, would perhaps indicate an exaggerated prudence.

[1] Léon Wieger, *Histoire des croyances religieuses et des opinions philosophiques en Chine*, p. 477.
[2] De Lantages, *Vie de la vénérable Mère Agnès*, p. 251.
[3] *Cf.* other instances in H. Delehaye's *Légendes hagiographiques*, pp. 32 *ff.*

LEVITATION

For, after all, who knows if we are going to be confronted by
it ? Will not this or that fact, regarded today as miraculous, be
explained tomorrow in a way consonant with unsuspected natural
laws ?
To make history subservient to the dicta of experimental science,
though it may be commended by some masters, is a very perilous
process. Indeed, if facts are to be historically recorded but with the
imprimatur of the physicist, chemist or biologist, we simply run the
risk of finding science ready to sanction five hundred years too late
the fact that had just been passed over by the historian and has
remained unrecorded. . . .
It was because Joan of Arc revealed the secret of the King that
people believed in her mission. Whether science accounts for the
fact or not is quite immaterial on historical grounds, for, as Quicherat
has it, " it is founded on such a firm basis that it cannot be got rid
of without shaking down the foundation of history itself."[1]
Now, it is for the theologian or philosopher to decide on clairvoyance being a supernatural or simply uncommon power. As an
historian, all I should do, if I am to play my part fairly, is not to
juggle it away. An honest and exact informer, I will never do away
with any of the unwonted facts that may account for, or even simply
accompany, the events I relate, whatever their metaphysical connotations may be. As L. Massignon wisely observes, " The duty
of the historian is to criticise the personal authority of the witness
before the contents of his testimony; and if he accepts the witness,
not to curtail his testimony according to *a priori* theories."[2]
Moreover, experimental science has no other function than to
observe the customs of nature, and to hand over to us, for our con-
venience, in schematic form, the uniformities it has been able to
collect. Therefore, it is none of its business to declare for or against

[1] *Aperçus nouveaux* (quoted by A. Lang in *La Pucelle de France*, p. 102
and Appendix D).
[2] *Al-Hallaj*, vol. i, p. 136. A remarkable instance of this scientific
fairness may be drawn from the attitude of the German exegetist Adolf
Harnack, who, though he did not personally admit the possibility of miracles
or prophecies, did not let his *philosophical* bias interfere with his *historical*
conviction that many marvels recorded in the New Testament were genuine,
and particularly that the prediction of the ruin of Jerusalem was actually
previous to the event. All that sort of thing, he said, remains *undurch-
dringlich* (unaccountable), but the historian has to be reconciled to it. *Cf.*
Das Wesen des Christentums, Leipzig, 1906, pp. 16, 17, 19, and *Neue Unter-
suchungen zur Apostelgeschichte und zur Abfassungszeit der Synoptischen
Evangelien*, Leipzig, 1911 (quoted by de Tonquédec, *Introduction à l'étude
du merveilleux*, p. 291, n. 1).

singular facts, even if of exceptional rarity. To deny these in the name of daily experience would be grossly tautological.

So we are entitled to try the worth of the documents where it is recorded that saints were lifted up over the earth and remained floating in mid-air. If the statement originates from a cheat or mistake—as sensory experience suggests—let us hope that a minute investigation may succeed in proving it at last.

§ 2. HAGIOGRAPHIC AMPLIFICATIONS

Mere fraud is not to be ignored on principle. Leaving aside the innocent cases where old hagiographers made no scruple to embellish the lives of their heroes for the edification of the reader, authors better informed of the requisites of history have been known, in their eagerness to convince, to alter documents in a way that was cognate to forgery.

When, for instance, the works of Mary Lataste were published, some theologians noticed that different passages in her revelations that had been much admired were translated verbatim from St Thomas Aquinas. There were exactly thirty-two such passages. " The objection," observes Father Poulain, " was imparted to the writer who was regarded as having collected the revelations. He did not deny the fact, but he answered with an air of dignity that since our Lord had inspired these pages to St Thomas, he might have recited them to Mary Lataste." Father Poulain, from whom I am borrowing these details, adds that " A more simple explanation was preferred which proved later on to be correct."[1]

The well-known instance of Catherine Emmerich, whose visions were revised and augmented by her over-imaginative poet-secretary C. Brentano, reminds us again that excessive apologetic zeal is a tendency to be forestalled in a hagiographic inquiry.

But how are amplifications to be detected ? To surmise generally the interpolation of any marvellous fact is a radical means, but, as we have seen above, rather crude and fraught with danger. We want nothing but truth, but we want the whole truth. We will try to lay hold of it with a more gentle procedure.

Experience has proved that fictitious additions come oftener from late compilers than direct and contemporary biographers. For, in the interval, the popular imagination has had the time to contrive its legends, from which later biographers will be tempted

[1] A. Poulain, *Des grâces d'oraison*, ch. xxi, 33, n. 1, p. 355.

to draw such features or events as are likely to give more body and beauty to their work.

The temptation of such legendary matter is not even always needed. Some hagiographers are quite able to devise the legend by themselves, not perhaps by inventing wholly spurious facts, but at least by misrepresenting those they meet with.

When St Bernard came to preach the Crusade in the diocese of Constance, an incredulous archer laughed at the preacher and his miracles. " He does not work more miracles than I do !" the man is reported to have exclaimed. Now, at this very moment, as the saint was drawing near to impose his hands upon the sick, the archer fell inanimate on the ground, and remained for some time out of his senses. " I was close by him," says Alexander of Cologne, " when the thing took place. . . . We called the Abbot, and the poor fellow could not rise before Bernard came down to him, made a prayer, and raised him to his feet again."[1]

Now, observes Father Delehaye, " none of the eye-witnesses has ever said a word suggesting the resurrection of a dead man. Still, one century after, Herbert, who compiled a collection of miracles of St Bernard, Conrad, author of the *Exordium*, and Caesarius of Heister-bach, affirm that the archer was dead, and that the saint restored him to life."[2]

On other occasions it may happen that the text itself suggests to the imagination some prodigy that was not meant in it.

In the Life of St Elisabeth of Hungary, Thierry of Apolda says that the Duke, angry with his wife because she allowed a poor leprous boy to lie in their bed, snatched the coverlet off it. And at this moment, he adds, God opened his spiritual eyes (*tunc aperuit Deus interiores principis oculos*), and the prince, instead of the leper, saw on the bed the image of Jesus on the cross.

The symbolic story has been materially interpreted by subsequent biographers, and the Duke's vision has become a physical miracle: " in the place of the poor boy, a great bleeding Christ was lying, with outspread arms."[3]

It will therefore be our duty to suspect feats of levitation with the saints to be the offspring of dramatic imagination, and even to surmise such an origin whenever they are not recorded in primitive documents.

[1] H. Delehaye, *Les légendes hagiographiques*, pp. 101-102.
[2] *Ibid.*
[3] *Ibid.*, p. 102.

§ 3. EYE-WITNESSES

Eye-witness evidence should not be regarded as a proof. First of all, some will declare themselves eye-witnesses without being so. The formula " I saw," observes Father Delehaye, has been used by authors who drew the facts from their imagination or from written documents.[1] Besides, genuine eye-witnesses may deceive or be deceived. The more honourable and numerous the witnesses, the fewer the risks of fraud; and these may be regarded as non-existing in the case of persons whose life was but a patient effort towards the realisation of a moral ideal excluding the most innocent lie. In default of such heroic virtue, the social situation of the witness, his culture, his independence, will be elements to be taken into account in the appreciation of the testimonies.

Regarding the number of the witnesses, should the legal rule *testis unus testis nullus* be enforced here ? On the one hand, levitation is too abnormal a phenomenon for us not to be very strict about the dispensation of evidence; and we cannot consider this or that levitation as genuine on the statement of one witness. On the other hand, it would be greatly abusive not to take any account—at least temporarily—of what is brought by a single deposition of a reliable witness. It does not prove, by itself, that *this* levitation is true; but confronted with another *independent* deposition, also single in its case, it may suggest the reality of the phenomenon itself, irrespective of any particular case; in other words, several testimonies whose intrinsic value is lessened only because each of them is based on a solitary experience, are not enough to establish the individual veracity of the facts they record, but taken as a whole and applied to proving the fact in general, they should, by their convergence, forcibly incline our minds to admit the truth of it.[2]

The cases, apparently more certain, where the facts are reported by several witnesses who have simultaneously observed them offer more security, but not every chance of error is done away with; for instance, if the witnesses have experienced a so-called collective hallucination. The example of the physicists of Nancy who declared

---

[1] Delehaye, *ibid.*, p. 80.

[2] " Probable proofs," observes J. Butler, " by being added not only increase the evidence but multiply it " (quoted by Newman, *Grammar of Assent*, pt. ii, ch. viii, par. 2). On demonstration by converging signs, called by some authors " cumulative proof," see the keen and substantial note I in vol. ii of *L'étude comparée des religions*, pp. 380 ff., by H. Pinard de la Boullaye.

they had perceived the N rays[1] is a proof that the culture of the individuals making up a group is not enough to remove all possibility of illusion; and hence some will be tempted to think that the congregation who cried out, "A miracle !" when they saw St Alphonsus Liguori rise above the pulpit in the cathedral of Foggia, were also a prey to mental contagion. . . .

Practically, it should be observed that, according to those who have studied what is called crowd psychology, collective hallucinations are usually the result of expectant attention, and are only experienced by minds intent on something that *must* happen. Such was the case—often quoted in textbooks of psychology—of the crew of the French frigate *La Belle Poule* when they mistook some floating bushes for the wrecked people they were looking for.

Moreover, even in the case of expectant attention, neither every crowd nor everyone in a crowd is a prey to hallucination. " L'attente," says Renan, " crée *d'ordinaire* son objet."[2]   No sensible reader will object to substituting here *sometimes* for *usually*.

So let us admit that, occasionally, persons gathered with a view to examining a definite phenomenon will imagine they have really seen something non-existing, through the agency of some mistaken sign.   And applying this to the present subject-matter, if we hear of a levitation observed by people specially meeting for the purpose of ascertaining the phenomenon, we shall stand within the bounds of reasonable scepticism by surmising their illusion.   But these conditions are never realised in hagiography, whereas expectant attention naturally arises in spiritualistic or even metapsychic meetings, where the observers, whatever their private critical sense may be, are exposed in a group, to yield to the glamour of the marvellous.

To the problem of the suggestibility of witnesses is connected the following question: Should the witnesses be scientists to deserve to be believed ?

We have just found that scientific competence may be at times an insufficient security; scientists not only are not proof against suggestion, but as scientists—that is, through their own scientific prejudices—they may be particularly subject to it.

However, scientific culture is apt in most cases to bring a fair amount of safety into the observation and ascertaining of apparently marvellous facts: the scientist who knows the symptoms of some strange neurotic affections will not be inclined to construe them into

[1] *Revue scientifique*, Oct., Nov., Dec., 1904.
[2] *Les Apôtres*, ch. i, p. 16.

154

prodigies as the layman might do; or the knowledge of the resources of subconsciousness will, for instance, reduce many a case of so-called premonition to a vulgar phenomenon of reminiscence. . . .

Now, let us observe that, in the case of levitation, the nature of the fact is not so subtle that a special scientific training or a particular self-control should be required to ascertain its existence. To *know* if the recoveries from some diseases are contradictory to natural laws a minimum of ætiological information is necessary; to *report* faithfully a series of intricate facts requires a development of visual memory, a spirit of method, a sense of discrimination, that are not commonly to be found.[1] But to *see* that a human body is lifted above the ground and is floating in mid-air, it is enough for the witness to enjoy common-sense and not be short-sighted.

Here the disciple of Hume or Renan will object that I presume in believers a faculty which they are altogether lacking, any religious assembly being, according to these authors, infected with the crassest credulity. So I have to indulge in a short digression to warn the reader against the gullibility too liberally bestowed on religious folks in the *Essay on Miracles* and *La vie de Jésus*.

A fair inquiry into historical facts shows, indeed, that the credulity of the witnesses in hagiography should not be overrated. And it is remarkable that those who impute it to them usually confine themselves to general considerations without attacking the problem on its experimental—historical—ground. Let us take another course and see whether, in fact, the extraordinary phenomena of the mystical life have not raised, in all times and countries, among believers as among others, natural reactions of mistrust and a critical examination of the facts. Some instances will suffice.

Ecstatics have been in most cases put to severe tests; watched, burnt, pricked about by people who thought them simulators; stigmatisées have been carefully watched and medically attended. When Lucy of Narni was known to have developed stigmata, the clergy did not act otherwise than any sceptic such as Hume or Renan themselves might have done in the same case. The Bishop of Viterbo went to the convent, visited the stigmatisée, had her wounds washed with hot wine, and treated her as a cheat. One year later,

---

[1] Witness the experiment tried some years ago in a congress of psychology held, I think, in Göttingen. At a certain moment, a man rushed into the room where the congressists were gathered and performed all kinds of most unexpected feats. The reports that the flabbergasted psychologists were afterwards requested to draw up on their experience are said to have been of distressing unlikeness.

as the marks had not healed, the Inquisitor Dominic of Gargagno went in his turn to the convent with the Bishop of Castro, several magistrates of Viterbo, and Dr. Alexander Gentiali. After an examination they deemed that the origin of these unfestering wounds was preternatural. But many persons remained incredulous. To settle the matter, Pope Alexander VI sent to Narni his physician, Bernard of Recanati, a Franciscan Bishop, and the Master of the Sacred Palace. The stigmata were examined and dressed again, and the hands were put into sealed gloves. After a week the inquirers found there was no alteration in the wounds, and drew up a report about it (1497). This document did not satisfy the Pope, who ordered the magistrates of Viterbo, on January 18, 1498, to send Lucy to Rome to examine her himself, and it is only when he had ascertained the holiness of her life that he was willing to treat her with reverence.[1]

This example is not exceptional. Similar ones might be drawn from the lives of Ursula Benincasa,[2] Joan of Jesus-Mary,[3] Veronica Giuliani,[4] etc.

Cases of abnormal abstinence were not received with less caution, and this in times when simple-minded or prejudiced people believe that common-sense had still to be born.

When Hugh, the Bishop of Lincoln, learnt in the year 1225 that there lived at Leicester a nun who fed only on the Eucharist, he instantly despatched fifteen clerks, charged to watch her carefully for a fortnight.[5] And when the parishioners of Saxlen knew that Nicholas of Flühli could do without any food, they went and kept sentry night and day over his hermitage to see if they were not deceived. This occurred in 1487.[6]

Why should we suppose that doubt and caution were less easily aroused in those who witnessed feats of levitation, a phenomenon far more startling than ecstasy, stigmatisation, or abstinence ? And does not history itself show that, in many instances, those present at levitations were instinctively urged to check the evidence of their eyes by additional sensory data ?[7]

[1] Imbert-Gourbeyre, *La stigmatisation*, vol. i, pp. 142 *ff.*
[2] *Ibid.*, p. 214. *Cf. St Philip Neri*, by Louis Ponnelle and Louis Bordet, p. 86.
[3] *Ibid.*, p. 280. [4] *Ibid.*, p. 390.
[5] *Ibid.*, vol. ii, p. 197. [6] *Ibid.*, p. 197.
[7] In the Lives of Douceline, Teresa, Joseph of Copertino, Alphonsus Liguori, Domenica Barbagli, etc., we find the witnesses ascertaining whether the levitated person is actually lifted off the ground, doubting at first the testimony of their sight.

Lastly, even if the witnesses were too credulous, we must take into account the critical sense and prudence of those who took their testimonies in the canonical processes. We should not lose sight of the fact that the *Promotor Fidei*, or Devil's Advocate, has the special duty of impugning the assertions of too credulous witnesses, and that his *animadversiones* are often of a most carping character. As an example of this kind of criticism I will mention the remarks made by the *Promotor Fidei* in the process of beatification of Alphonsus Liguori in answer to those who declared that the saint had attended Clement XIV at his deathbed by bilocation, while he was rapt in ecstasy at Arienzo:

" This long absence of motion does not prove an ecstasy but only a state of great weakness. Such accidents must have taken place often enough, for the people around him were not surprised at it. . . . This sleep came from a morbid condition which people in the Bishop's palace were well aware of. . . . As to the words uttered when he woke up, they express the dream of a sick person.[1] The Servant of God knew that the Pope was very ill. He was greatly affected by it. He often spoke of it. He prayed to God to help him. . . . Therefore, it is quite natural that Alphonsus dreamt during his two days' lethargy that he had attended Clement XIV at his death, and that when he woke up he mistook his dream for reality. His waking and announcing the Pope's death at the very time when Clement was breathing his last is but a coincidence, which is the less surprising as he expected to get the fatal news any moment."[2]

It might be added that the servants of the Bishop's palace themselves had not received their master's assertion with less scepticism, for when he had told them, on awaking, that he had just been attending the dying Pope, " we were all tempted to burst out laughing," confessed Sister Agatha Viscardi to Father Tannoja.[3] They only changed their minds when they knew of the strange coincidence that went to confirm the words of Alphonsus.

Not only the character of the facts is seriously discussed, but all care is taken lest the witnesses overstep the limits of sober truth. Among others, the report on the deposition of Tobias da Ponte, in the process of Bernardino Realino (Bk. I, pt. ii, sect. ii, ch. 4, p. 77), shows that at least in some instances the interrogatory is conducted

[1] These words were: " You thought I was asleep, but I was attending the Pope who has just died."
[2] A. Berthe, *St Alphonse de Liguori*, vol. ii, pp. 360-361.
[3] *Ibid.*, p. 360.

with much caution, the witnesses being duly warned against any fanciful adornment of their narrative.

Indeed, every process of beatification[1] does not offer the same degree of security,[2] but the fact that levitation has been found an objective phenomenon in modern processes is not to be slighted.

In some cases—pretty rare indeed—the only witness of the alleged uplifting is the person held to have experienced it. Are we, then, to consider this subjective impression as an additional security? Some authors have thought so,[3] but they are obviously wrong.

Have we not all of us experienced in our dreams the strange feeling of floating in mid-air, of flying through free space with an intoxicating sensation of supernal lightness?

" All kinds of hallucinations," observes A. Maury, " complete the ecstatics' bewilderment. They believe themselves suspended in the air, like St Joseph of Copertino, St Thomas of Villanova, St Teresa. The same illusion is to be found again among Buddhist religious, and may be accounted for by the power of some hysterical persons to stand firmly on the tips of their toes or to keep up the most tiring positions. Demoniacs, for the same reason, have been held to enjoy this marvellous faculty."[4]

The American psychologist J. H. Leuba has also recalled, after many others (Baillarger, Cabanis, etc.), the feeling of aerial buoyancy experienced by some ecstatics, and mentions that Blessed Henry Suso has referred to it. This feeling may be artificially brought about, and Leuba says that he could make two persons experience it by giving them ether or nitrous oxide, and adds St Teresa's upliftings amount to nothing else.[5]

These remarks are not without significance. We should profit by them. Let them serve as a warning in our search for the objective phenomenon, if any such exist, and let us lay this rule down:
" On no occasion is a levitation to be considered authentic when

---

[1] Canonisation has no important bearing upon our subject-matter, as it is only concerned with miracles wrought by the saint after his death.

[2] Before Urban VIII's decrees (1625 and 1634), for instance, when beatification was not necessarily decreed by the Holy See.

[3] J. de Maistre, speaking of St Teresa's statement on her levitations, says, " Are we going to question the facts reported by the saint herself, in whom genius and candour rival with holiness?" (*Soirées de Saint-Pétersbourg*, 10ᵉ entretien.)

[4] *Magie et astrologie*, pp. 416-417.

[5] *Extase mystique, Mercure de France*, Feb., 1911, p. 673.

the only report about it comes from the person who is supposed to have experienced the phenomenon. In every such case let self-deception be taken for granted." But, of course, we will add this qualification: " The said presumption of error will not remain unshaken, if reliable eye-witnesses confirm by their testimonies the statement of the alleged levitated person."

§ 4. PATHOLOGICAL PHENOMENA THAT MIGHT BE MISTAKEN FOR LEVITATION

Now, if *bona fide* eye-witnesses of so-called instances of levitation had been mistaken through natural facts of a delusive character, this would satisfy the requirements both of physics and of historical criticism. For instance, there might be cases where the human body by its paradoxical attitudes or unusual agility might suggest its temporary freedom from the force of gravity. Then we should have at last a clue to this enduring tradition that cannot be regularly accounted for by fraud or groundless delusions.

Indeed, some neuropaths are endowed in their fits with extraordinary acrobatic abilities. The wonderful feats of strength and nimbleness they are then able to perform have caused a certain phase of their fits to be named " clownish " by French psychiatrists.

" The tetanic period," says Charcot, " with its two phases of tonic and clonic spasms does not last long. . . . After some minutes' rest the neurotic begins to shriek, and enters upon the second act or period of extensive motions. The hysterical person is suddenly lifted as if by a spring, her whole body is raised from the ground; she is thrust into the air, springs back over and over again, more than twenty times without a stop."[1]

Some somnambulists also have fits during which, according to Dr. Jousset, " the diseased persons are not affected with convulsions but perform perfectly coherent—though quite violent and swift —motions; dancing, tumbling feats, and somersaults such as are executed by acrobats."[2]

This form of somnambulism is not especially to be observed in the night; the fit will occur unexpectedly in the day, in the midst of the usual occupations of the neuropath.

" The fit begins with a pain in the head and some difficulty in making answers; the eyes are wandering, and then close; the face colours slightly, the head droops on to one of the shoulders or the

[1] Quoted by C. Hélot, *Névroses et possessions diaboliques*, pp. 175-176.
[2] Quoted by C. Hélot, *ibid.*, p. 218.

159

breast; the body collapses, the breath grows quicker, the patient is now fast asleep; then, after some minutes, he suddenly rises, and with wonderful agility leaps to the top of some piece of furniture. He performs the most prodigious feats, then throws himself down on the ground, and swiftly rolls over the floor up and down the room; after some minutes of this performance, his body is stiffly raised as if by a spring; then he flings himself backward, touching the floor only by his feet and the top of his head, or assumes the reverse position; sometimes, in this position, he stands on one foot and revolves with amazing swiftness; at last the body collapses again, and the fit is over. The patient does not remember anything, but feels tired and stiff. But for this sense of fatigue, appetite and general health seem to be preserved."[1]

To this description should be added several varieties of acrobatic impulses; among others, climbing up tree-tops and walls, and rhythmic dancing.[2]

We will not examine now whether the feats ascribed to the saints may be reduced in some instances to such effects of acrobatic somnambulism; but we will observe that, for safety's sake, any phenomenon more or less cognate to this pathologic tumbling must be systematically ignored in reports of levitation. Feats of agility or lightness where the body has been off the ground or any other support for but a few seconds should be carefully discriminated from lasting aerial suspension.

§ 5. Five Test Formulas

The preceding remarks may be summed up in five critical rules whose application is likely to afford some degree of security in an inquiry into genuine cases of levitation—if there are any. They may be put under this form:

Rule I.—Every account of levitation without necessary topographical and chronological details, mention of witnesses, and graphic original details as to the circumstances and characteristics of the phenomena, should be regarded as an edifying embellishment of no historical purport.

Rule II.—Any account—even if it be circumstantial enough—whose details convey a general impression of triteness should be held a commonplace hagiographic topic.

Rule III.—The only available testimonies should come from genuine eye-witnesses, whereas the statements of the levitated

[1] *Ibid.*   [2] *Ibid.*

persons are always assumed to be of a purely subjective character.

Rule IV.—Any additions to primitive biographies should be looked upon as suspicious.

Rule V.—We should never admit the likening to levitation proper of any apparently cognate phenomena (such as standing on tiptoe, assuming abnormal positions, performing capering feats); and we must, in every instance, examine whether the mentioned facts are not reducible to the said natural exercises.

CHAPTER III

APPLYING THE TESTS TO SOME HAGIOGRAPHIC CASES : NEGATIVE INSTANCES

§ 1. ELIMINATION OF INSUFFICIENTLY CIRCUMSTANTIAL ACCOUNTS

MANY cases—chiefly among the older ones—will be eliminated by applying to them what may be called the *test of accuracy*. Such are those of St Luke the Younger, St Joannicus, St Andrew Salus, St Ladislaus, St Elisabeth of Hungary, Blessed Philippinus, Peter of Monticello, St Jutta, St Hedwig, Blessed Margaret of Hungary, St Albert, Blessed Bartholus (Bk. I, pt. ii, sect. ii, ch. i); of Peter Armengol, Blessed Margaret, St Agnes of Monte-Pulciano, Blessed Robert of Salentum, Blessed Venturino of Bergamo, Nicholas of Ravenna, St Colette of Corbie, St Peter Regalati (*ibid.*, ch. ii); of Blessed Giovanni Angelo Porro, Blessed Bartholomew of Anglario, Blessed Colomba of Rieti, Blessed John Marinoni, Luke of Medina del Campo (*ibid.*, ch. iii); of Mary Raggi, Alphonsus Rubius (*ibid.*, ch. v); of Claude Dhière (*ibid.*, ch. vii). This list is by no means exhaustive.

§ 2. TYPES OF ACCOUNTS SUGGESTIVE OF THE WORKING OF A HAGIOGRAPHIC THEME

Some narratives are not wanting in details, but the details in them are of such a nature, both so accurate and commonplace, so often met with before, that they do not make us more confident than the vague above-mentioned reports. I am tempted to class in this category those nocturnal feats of levitation descried by an inquisitive witness peering through the convenient chinks in a cell door, who, at this very moment, sees the saint rapt in ecstasy, " the body lifted about two palms above the floor, surrounded with a blazing light."

This episode which Eunapius told of Iamblichus, who is said to have been thus surprised in levitation by his servants, has been often repeated since by hagiographers. And the similar scenes in the lives of St Luke the Younger, St Dominic, St Vincent Ferrer, St

Francis of Paula, St Ignatius of Loyola, may be *temporarily* regarded as simple variants of it.

By grouping under this head the levitations or some levitations of these saints, I do not assume that *practically* every fact is counterfeit, but I want to mark that they are open to *theoretical* suspicion, and therefore should be left aside in an inquiry aiming at making good unquestionable facts.

§ 3. HEARSAY EVIDENCE

In some stories, the biographer says that the levitation was witnessed by this or that person whom he names. It is plain that such statement is not equivalent to the deposition of an eye-witness. Such testimony is only available when the eye-witness has made an official statement of what he has seen and his declaration has been duly recorded. Therefore, it is hardly possible to set much value on facts which have not been regularly set down in a sworn deposition.

Consequently every levitation mentioned in lives of saints whose cult has simply been approved by the ecclesiastical authority without any regular procedure of beatification, should be thus eliminated; and even in the case of canonical beatification, the principle of systematic elimination should also be applied to the lives of the saints for whom the informative inquiries were begun too late, and where the testimonies may be supposed to express but a legendary tradition more or less alien to reality.

Neither the levitations of Agnes of Assisi († 1253, cult authorised in 1777), nor those of Gaspar de Bono († 1604, beatified in 1786), of Giles of Santarem († 1267, cult approved in 1748), of Giovanni Angelo Porro († 1506, cult authorised in 1737), etc., will therefore be likely to inspire us with sufficient confidence.

Now, as we have seen, in some rare instances, the descriptions of the aerial raptures come from the ecstatics themselves. It has been justly observed that such reports could hardly be regarded as objective. *A priori*, there is no reason why we should not suppose that the saints who have believed they were levitated have not laboured under self-delusion as we do ourselves in our dreams or after taking various drugs. So, for safety's sake, we will hold the impressions of levitation described by St Teresa, St Catherine of Siena, or St Philip Neri, as pure imaginations.

We are the better entitled to distrust them as it is proved that some saints, when rapt in ecstasy, would feel as if they were lifted up very high into the air. St Mary Magdalen of Pazzi, according to

Cepari, when she was rapt, would answer very loudly to those who talked to her, because she thought she was far up in the air. And she was heard to whisper to herself: " They cannot hear me down there, they are too far off."[1] Silvano Razzi, the biographer of Blessed Oringa, says also that she felt as light as if she had no body.[2]

Therefore, when Teresa writes that during her ecstasies her body became so light that it had no more weight, and that she did not feel the earth under her feet, we have good reason to think that she experienced a feeling of uplifting, without any actual raising of her body from the earth, and Leuba is justified in saying that the saint's account does not prove her levitation but only her illusion as to levitation.[3]

§ 4. REJECTION OF LATE ADDITIONS

By application of the fourth rule, an account of levitation cropping up in a late biography, when contemporary or former documents do not mention any facts of the kind, should be considered interpolated.

Several instances will prove that this danger of late amplifications is not imaginary in the domain we are now exploring.

St Dunstan, according to one of his biographers, was lifted up to the vault of the cathedral of Canterbury, on Ascension Day, May 17, 988. The accuracy of some particulars, in default of other documents, would suggest the honesty of this account. But there is just *another* document; along with the biography of St Dunstan where the marvel is reported, there is a Life written by an anonymous author who claims to be a contemporary and eye-witness. Now, the said author does say, like the other, that Dunstan, on the same date, delivered a homily in his cathedral, but he omits to point out that the preacher flew up from the pulpit.

A no less notable discrepancy is to be found between two biographies of St Dominic. While the depositions made twelve years after the death of the saint (1233) do not mention any levitation, the phenomenon is reported, fifty years later, by Thierry of Apolda. So the tradition is very likely to be legendary, and in particular we have ground to believe that the uplifting of St Dominic, on the day

[1] Cepari, *Vita di S. Maddalena di Pazzi*, pp. 82-83 (quoted by H. Thurston, p. 312).
[2] *A.S.*, Jan. 10, p. 652, par. 15: . . . *corporis agilitatem, quae, aliquanto tempore tanta fuit, ut saepius sese palpando corpore sibi carere videretur.*
[3] See *supra*, p. 158.

when he miraculously brought to life again the nephew of Cardinal
Orsini, was interpolated to improve the event, in spite of its being
reported by Sister Cecilia, who is said to have been an eye-witness
of the scene.[1]

As Father H. Thurston prudently observes, we are the better
justified in doubting St Dominic's levitations as the depositions made
in 1233 by his familiars, if they do not mention this fact, contain
very accurate details about his devotion in prayer. The witnesses
" tell us about his groans and sighs, his intense fervour and his
penitential exercises, but there is no word which suggests that he was
ever seen by any of them raised from the ground, or that there was
any tradition among his first companions that this was known to have
happened."[2]

The same criticisms hold good in the case of Francis of Assisi.
Neither the first nor the second Life by Thomas of Celano mentions
that Francis was ever lifted from the ground. Now, Thomas has
certainly questioned the witnesses of the saint's life, and particularly
Brother Leo, who is believed to report in the *Actus* the levitations
he had seen on Mount La Verna. St Bonaventure, it is true, in a work
chronologically intermediate, says that Francis was seen in the night
with his radiant body lifted from the earth, but nobody knows where
he took that from, and, anyhow, he was not a witness of it.

The silence of Thomas of Celano in his *Vita Secunda* is the more
striking as, when he composed it, about 1247, he intended to complete his former Life of the saint, and treated with peculiar care the
subject of his contemplation, to which he gave a long chapter,
De studio orationis S. Francisci.[3] Ignorance being excluded as a cause
of this omission, some underhand hostility might be suspected in this
biographer. In fact, some authors—among whom M. P. Sabatier—
have regarded Thomas of Celano as a secret opponent of the Franciscan ideal, and his *Vita Prima* as a disguised libel. Indeed, the
supposition would help much in throwing light on the discrepancy
between the *Actus* and Celano's writings regarding Francis's levita-

---

[1] Sister Cecilia's narrative is taken into account by Father Lacordaire
in his *Vie de Saint-Dominique* (pp. 188-189), and by Mother Francis Raphael
(quoted by H. Thurston, p. 272), but M. J. Guiraud does not refer to it in
his *Saint-Dominique*. He gives the reason for this omission in his biblio-
graphy, where he points out that Sister Cecilia's account was dictated about
1280—that is, sixty years after the events—to Sister Angelica; that the document, though it comes from an eye-witness, has a tendency towards exaggeration and the marvellous, and consequently requires careful criticism (p. 208).
[2] H. Thurston, p. 273.   [3] *Ibid.*, p. 274.

LEVITATION

tions, but it is now rather obsolete, and an author so versed in Franciscan questions as J. Jörgensen not only does not share in this suspicion of Thomas's honesty but has no hesitation in showing him as a most candid and ingenuous soul utterly incapable of such wickedness.[1] Therefore, we have reason for thinking that, if Thomas had collected any evidence on Francis's rising into the air, we should find some vestiges of it in his Lives of the saint.[2]

St Francis Xavier's upliftings rouse similar distrust. It is noteworthy, observes Father Thurston, that we find nothing about his levitations in the affidavits of the sixty witnesses or so who gave evidence at Goa, Cochin, Baçaim, and Malacca in 1556, *four years after his death*. Now, all these witnesses had known the saint personally, and had repeatedly assisted at his Mass, where he is said to have especially experienced his aerial raptures. However, in the later inquiries which were held in 1616—that is, sixty years after—levitation was referred to in the depositions. Though it might be argued that the said depositions concerned other places than the first, it is impossible to find that the evidence for levitation in this instance is satisfactory.[3]

How did simple reality come to be tampered with in these different cases? It would be interesting to trace back the adulteration to its starting-point. Very likely no actual lie was told, at any particular moment, but a series of minor warpings of the original facts issued at last into a regular sophistication. Or, maybe, the error originated from misconstruing a text. For instance, speaking of St Francis of Assisi, Thomas of Celano had said: *Suspendebatur multoties tanta contemplationis dulcedine, ut supra semetipsum raptus, quod ultra humanum sensum experiebatur nemini revelaret.*[4] And the

---

[1] *Bien loin d'avoir été un imposteur plein de malice, Thomas se révèle toujours à nous comme une âme simple et presque ingénue et son unique défaut en tant que biographe est sa préoccupation excessive de l'élégance du style.* (*Saint François d'Assise*, Introduction, p. xxxiv, n. 1.)
[2] I was not aware, when I wrote these lines, of Father F. M. Delorme's discovery at Perosa of the important text (*Legenda Antiqua S. Francisci*) attributed to Brother Leo, which is regarded by the erudite Franciscan as the chief source of Celano's *Vita Secunda*. Now, it is remarkable that the said *Legenda Antiqua* does not record any levitation of St Francis. The text of the *Legenda Antiqua* has been published by *La France Franciscaine*, Paris; it has been translated into French by Abbé F. Fagot under the title *Saint François d'Assise raconté par ses premiers compagnons*, Paris, 1927
[3] H. Thurston, p. 274.
[4] II Celano, 64 (quoted by Thurston, p. 272).

166

expression *suspendebatur ad coelum* is also to be found in the *Speculum Perfectionis*.[1] This spiritual figurative suspension may have been made out later on to be a material one. The supposition is the more probable as we have already met with an instance where a positive miracle had been inferred from a simple metaphor,[2] and that in St Francis of Assisi's life another case of levitation very often mentioned has no other origin than a lax interpretation of an ambiguous text. Indeed, it is said in the *Actus* that Francis lifted Brother Masseo into the air and thrust him forward the length of a spear. Whereupon Görres—perhaps not the first—improves upon it, and writes that the saint " carried away in his flight Brother Maffei." Then Dr. Imbert-Gourbeyre borrows the formula from him, and seems to have been again the source of Mgr. Farges.[3] Thanks to the disfigurement of Brother Masseo's name, the successive borrowings are traceable, and we can realise how perilous is in this domain the disregard of original sources. Another instance of misinterpretation, or of over-generous interpretation, of a text may be drawn from St Zita's Life. The *Acta* say about her *suspendebatur frequenter in ecstasi*, without any suggestion of a concrete acceptance of the expression in the context. Still, the saint is mentioned among those who have experienced levitation.[4]

§ 5. APPROXIMATE PHENOMENA

We have seen that some neuropaths in their fits can perform strange acrobatic tricks, either assuming paradoxical attitudes by muscular contraction or tumbling about in a most uncanny fashion.

The agility of a Christina the Admirable or of a Catherine Emmerich, it should be acknowledged, is not without reminding us of somnambulistic feats. And when Joseph of Copertino springs upon the table in the room of a sick person, and alights among the bottles and cups without breaking anything, the comparison with the fits described by Dr. Jousset recurs naturally to our mind.[5] Again, we have observed that the same saint was not always lifted off the ground. He sometimes simply stood on the extreme tips of his toes like Douceline, in an attitude rather suggestive of a pathologic state than of a divine rapture. The same thing happened to St Alphonsus Liguori and to some others.

[1] vii, 93 (*ibid.*).   [2] *Supra*, Bk. II, ch. ii, par. 2, p. 152.
[3] *Cf. supra*, Bk. I, pt ii, ch. xi, p. 42, n. 6.
[4] *Dictionnaire pratique des connaissances religieuses*, fasc. xvii, *s.v.* Levitation, by Father Roure.
[5] *Supra*, Bk. II, ch. ii, par. 4.

Without caring, for the present, if these facts have a relation of causality with levitation proper or not, we will judge that the one safe policy is to regard them *a priori* as having a natural origin, and to ignore any assimilation to levitation of such feats of agility or deftness as keeping one's balance on tiptoe or climbing up trees and standing on their tops—however slender the boughs may be on which the ecstatic was poised. For here, indeed, gliding from the extraordinary into the extranatural is too tempting and easy.[1]

On the same principle, we will not class with levitation the walking on the water which is sometimes met with in the Lives of the Saints.[2] The phenomenon, indeed, is rather unimportant; if it were proved that the human body is able to rise and float in mid-air, it would become easily credible that it can be buoyed up on a fluid a thousand times as dense as air. The evangelic story makes a rather modest figure compared with the aerial exploits of Joseph of Copertino. . . .

*   *   *   *   *

The strict application of the five critical rules laid down in the preceding chapter to every case of levitation mentioned in the present work would issue, it is plain, in doing away with *many* of them. Would it mean suppressing *most* of them ? It may be. *All* of them ? I do not think so.

I shall try in the next chapter to show that at least some privileged cases can undergo unharmed the trial of the most ruthless criticism.

[1] It may be seriously questioned whether the levitation of some saints did not simply amount to this tiptoe rising. Possibly it is the case with Philip Neri, for whose levitation proper there is no first-hand evidence. Still, Gallonio, an eye-witness, says he saw Philip actually lifted from his bed (*Vita*, p. 227. *Cf. St Philippe Néri*, by Louis Ponnelle and Louis Bordet, p. 68, n. 2).

[2] This phenomenon is mentioned, among others, in the Lives of the following saints: Bernardino of Siena, Francis of Paula, John Capistran, Peter of Alcantara, Raymund of Pennafort, etc.

CHAPTER IV

APPLYING THE TESTS (*Continued*): *SOME POSITIVE CASES*

§ 1. St Joseph of Copertino

IF there is a collection of testimonies regarding levitation that, on the face of it, is likely—being so plentiful and varied—to stand successfully the trial of the above-mentioned tests, we shall certainly find it in St Joseph of Copertino's life.

The purpose of the first paragraph in the present chapter is to check the value of this impression.

Previously I want to warn the reader that he is invited to share in a fair experiment, and not to attend a got-up affair the events and outcome of which are known to me beforehand. My own impression is, I confess, that the case of Joseph is a very strong one, but so far my conviction is rather of an intuitive character; and practically, when I am writing these lines for the first time, I am not satisfied that the fivefold test will leave it undamaged. . . .

First and Second Tests

Every levitation mentioned in Joseph's life is locally determined. Not only do they occur in Italy, at Nardo, Assisi, Osimo, Fossombrone, Naples, or Rome, but in such and such a monastery: the Grotella, the Sacro Convento; and even in a particular chapel of the monastery, in front of this or that statue.

Most of the facts are duly dated, and sometimes the exact time of the day is mentioned.

Witnesses are mentioned by name.

As to details, they are abundant and so vivid that nobody would take them for hagiographic commonplaces.

Third Test

Joseph's levitations are not known to us by his own descriptions. We do not know what his impressions were, nor even whether he was aware at all of his being lifted up into the air.[1] The facts have been set down in depositions by eye-witnesses, and their evidence has been officially recorded, for the informative inquiries were started hardly two years after the saint's death, in the different places where he had lived (preliminary inquiries at Nardo, Assisi, Osimo). In the year of his death, the General of the Conventuals, James of Ravenna, had bidden Robert Nuti of Assisi to write a Life of Joseph,[2] and the biographer, who had known the saint personally, had collected testimonies from persons who also had been on friendly terms with him: Martelli of Spoleto, Bernardino Benaducci, Archangelo Rosimi. The second biography, that of Domenico Bernino, published in 1722, was based upon the results of the inquiries. Lastly, the third biography, by Angelo Pastrovicchi, though it was published ninety years after the saint's death, cannot be regarded as a late document, for it is only a compendium of the facts recorded in the official documents. It was composed by order of Benedict XIV, *Promotor Fidei* in the process, a renowned authority in canonical matters, who wished that for each fact related the episcopal and apostolic processes should be cited.

Fourth Test

Under these circumstances the chances for legendary amplifications seem very much reduced; but it would not be safe to regard any exaggeration as impossible. On the contrary, it is highly probable that among the hundred and more levitations recorded in the process, several have been somewhat embellished. It is even doubtful whether such impressive facts may in every case have left to the witnesses the self-control indispensable for a perfectly objective narrative.

Nevertheless, even if a large allowance is made for possible exaggeration, the reality of the facts stands unimpaired.

The exaggerations are likely to have concerned the computation of the heights or distances flown by the ecstatic. The comparison of the account given by Pastrovicchi of the flight of Joseph towards the calvary[3] with Bernino's statement is an example of such possible alteration. We read there that Joseph flew a distance of eighty paces, whereas Bernino mentions only fifteen paces. This difference does not necessarily suggest an exaggeration—for, after all, the wrong

[1] At least generally, When he warns Balthazar Rossi not to be afraid before lifting him up into the air, he seems to know what is going to happen. As to his other references to his ecstasies, they do not show that he was aware of his being levitated.

[2] It was published only fifteen years later (Palermo, 1678).

[3] *Supra*, p. 92.

estimate may be the smaller one—but it reminds us that in such instances the calculated figures should be regarded as approximate.

Besides, it is not certain that in this particular case the fact was reported by eye-witnesses. Joseph had left Grotella in 1632, and the scene of the calvary took place more than thirty years before it was set on record in the inquiry at Nardo. . . .

Consequently we will conclude that everything is not of equal value in the accounts of levitation which are now being examined. In events so apt to stir the imagination, the least we can do is to get reconciled to *minor inaccuracies* in the records of some—and perhaps of all—of them.

If the levitations mentioned in Joseph's life had all taken place at Copertino, their authenticity would be open to discussion, for the saint left the town in 1638, and the first depositions in the inquiry prescribed by the Bishop of Nardo were collected only in 1665; that is, thirty years elapsed between the events themselves and their official recording. Such an interval is quite enough for most of the eye-witnesses to have died, for the memories of the survivors to have grown dim, for the legend to have gradually but deeply performed its work.

But the case is different with the facts of Assisi that occurred during the sojourn of the saint in the Sacro Convento (1639-1653), and with those of Osimo (1657-1663). All these were deposed by eye-witnesses and deserve to be carefully considered.

Among the facts of Assisi, one of the last and most notable is the ecstatic flight that took place in the presence of the Duke of Brunswick.[1] This event was related by Pastrovicchi and Bernino according to the official documents. Among witnesses, two, the Duke and one of his chamberlains, gave a token of their conviction more striking than a deposition: they passed from Lutheranism to Catholicism. He who would reject these testimonies must believe in the most elaborate mystification or in a strangely powerful collective hallucination. But—leaving aside other special reasons against it—how could we allow ourselves to be misled by such suppositions, when so many similar facts, that cannot be ignored in mass, had occurred before this historical scene, followed itself by so many other facts no less strongly asserted ?

Of course, as was pointed out above, allowance should be made for a possible or even probable exaggeration as to this or that detail; but even if we lessen the height and duration of the risings and the distance of the flights as much as we like, it is hard to believe that

[1] *Supra*, p. 99.

every witness of these scenes was simple or shifty enough to turn mere high or long jumps into prodigies.

Besides, if soberness is required, it is easy to select the very plainly honest, sedate, and matter-of-fact account of the surgeon Francesco Pierpaoli, who could closely observe the levitation of his patient.[1] Here, nothing in the matter itself or in its expression is suggestive of the least vehemence of imagination. No desire, no idea of edification, appears in his dry, meticulous report. No surprise, no emotion. Nothing, it seems, but the desire not to be misled by one's senses. Francesco kneels down to see whether the ecstatic is actually off his chair.

No experiment carried out with more calm and caution, set down in more accurate terms, could ever be dreamt of.

By a curious coincidence, the life of St Joseph of Copertino seems to have been especially contrived to demonstrate levitation, for to the number and varied circumstances of his aerial risings is to be added the intellectual, social, or moral value of the persons who witnessed them: Pope Urban VIII, John Frederick of Brunswick, the Great Admiral of Castile, Princess Mary of Savoy, the surgeon Francesco Pierpaoli, the physician Giacinto Carosi, Cardinal Facchinetti, Bishop of Spoleto. Some days after Joseph's death, the Cardinal wrote to the person who had announced it to him: "The raptures that he experienced are known to everybody. I saw him, as several persons in my palace did, lifted off the floor the breadth of four fingers."[2]

To make the case still safer, it happened that the documents of the process were examined by Prosper Lambertini, the future Benedict XIV, who was *Promotor Fidei* (Devil's Advocate), and were most searchingly criticised by this renowned authority in canonical matters. Now it appears that his *animadversiones* were victoriously answered in the discussion before the Congregation of Rites, for not only did he publish himself as a Pope, in 1753, the decree of beatification of Joseph, but he pointed out in his classical treatise on canonisation the particular reliability of the testimonies concerning the saint's levitations:

"Whilst I discharged the office of Promotor of the Faith, the cause of the Venerable Servant of God, Joseph of Copertino, came up for discussion in the Congregation of Sacred Rites, which after my retirement was brought to a favourable conclusion, and in this *eye-witnesses of unchallengeable integrity* gave evidence of the famous

[1] *Supra*, p. 101.
[2] Letter of Oct. 2, 1663, quoted by Bernino, ch. xvii, p. 249.

upliftings from the ground and prolonged flights of the aforesaid Servant of God."[1]

Lastly, we must not lose sight of the fact that during his own lifetime the prodigies of Joseph were submitted to critical observation, and even to hostile suspicion. If he roused popular enthusiasm, this popularity itself brought on him the mistrust of the Inquisition that summoned him before its tribunal at Naples. If he was juridically discharged, his case continued to inspire a great deal of suspicion, for when he came to Rome from Naples to hand over to the Father-General of his Order, John Baptist Berardicelli, the message of the Holy Office directing him to be sent to some solitary monastery, the latter received him with a rather forbidding mien; and later on, in the Sacro Convento of Assisi, where he had been sent by order of Pope Urban VIII, he was treated with contempt and severity by Father Antony of St Maure, who took him for a hypocrite and publicly reproved him as such.[2]

Fifth Test

A fifth objection should be examined. Are there not in Joseph's life such facts as we named *approximate*, raisings from—but not off— the ground, that recall the muscular contractions of hysterical people; dizzy spinning suggestive of the whirling dance of some neurotics? There is no doubt about it. Sometimes, when saying Mass, Joseph would be lifted on the tips of his toes and stand thus for a long time. Or he would spring to the top of a tree and remain poised on a twig. It would be easy to show that even in these instances his physical abilities outdid the possibilities of nature; but we need not resort to any argument of that kind. For simplicity's sake, we will admit the natural character of every " approximate " fact, and we shall say: " These feats may be pathological or not; certain it is they do not lessen the worth of preternatural facts, but rather increase it by showing that the witnesses were quite able to discriminate the raptures where the saint was lifted off the earth from those where, being lifted from it, he nevertheless kept contact with the ground or some other support.

To admit that every levitation in Joseph's life originates from a

[1] *Dum autem munere fungebar Fidei Promotoris, in Sacrorum Rituum Congregatione, discussa fuit causa venerabilis servi Joseph a Cupertino, super dubio virtutum; quod post dimissum a me Promotoratus Officium, feliciter fuit resolutum, in qua testes omni exceptione majores et oculati celeberrimas a terra* elevationes et ingentes volatus retulerunt de eo Servo Dei extatico. *(De Servo* Dei, etc., III, xlix, 9.) (Not underlined in the text.)
[2] Laing, pp. 19 *ff.*

natural fact magnified by the imagination or deliberately strained is a view incompatible with a respect for history.

So let us not be surprised if a mind as penetrating, free, and well-informed as that of Andrew Lang did not hesitate in giving credence to these prodigies.[1] Many will deem with him that taking part against history cannot be done here without an act of intellectual violence that jeopardises the very reason we wanted to preserve.

§ 2. Some More Cases: St Teresa, St Alphonsus Liguori, Blessed Andrew Hubert Fournet, Blessed Bernardino Realino, F. Suarez, Blessed Joseph Benedict Cottolengo

The depositions on St Teresa's levitations are chronologically favourable; the informative inquiries were started in 1595—that is, thirteen years after the saint's death. Eye-witnesses were still alive, and ten of them are mentioned in the *Acta*. One of the testimonies, that of Sister Anne of the Incarnation, the Prioress of the convent founded by Teresa in Salamanca, is really striking in its sober accuracy. Illusion seems by no means probable: it was broad day-light (between 1 and 2 p.m.); the phenomenon lasts half an hour; and the feeling of awe experienced by Sister Anne does not keep her from looking for an experimental confirmation of what she sees: *she puts her hands under the feet of the ecstatic.*[2]

Shall we surmise fraud—even pious fraud ? But how could we, when we know that the witness passed for a paragon of Christian virtues, and that Teresa herself thought very highly of her intellectual and moral qualities ?[3]

After reading this deposition, the import of the saint's declarations is completely changed. *A priori*, her impressions might be considered as purely subjective; it was historically a duty to suspect their objectivity. But now the coincident accounts of Yepes, Maria

[1] I do not refer here to the rather non-committal remarks of *Cock Lane and Common Sense* (p. 101), but to private confidences to a friend. Another non-Catholic writer, Norman Douglas, has acknowledged the historical value of the evidence for Joseph's upliftings: " . . . it may be urged that a kind of enthusiasm for their distinguished brother monk may have tempted the inmates of his convent to exaggerate his rare gifts. Nothing of the kind. He performed flights not only in Cupertino, but in various large towns of Italy, such as Naples, Rome, and Assisi. And the spectators were by no means an assemblage of ignorant personages, but men whose rank and credibility would have weight in any section of society " (*North American Review*, vol. cxcviii, July, 1913, p. 103). (Quoted by Laing, p. iv, n. 3.)

[2] *Supra*, p. 72.

[3] " No Prioress," she said, " was so helpful to me as Mother Anne of the Incarnation " (*The Book of the Foundations*, ch. i, Medina del Campo).

Baptista, and Sister Anne invite us to give up our prejudice and to a plain admission of the facts.

With St Alphonsus Liguori the facts are varied: we have public levitations (Foggia, Amalfi)[1] and private evidence. On one occasion we have seen the witness, Father Tannoja, take particular precautions not to be deceived by his senses: he posts himself several days in the same place to observe the phenomenon, and, every time, he sees the saint—then an invalid—lifted off his wheel-chair.[2] In this case, as in Joseph of Copertino's, the canonical procedure was started early enough to allow many eye-witnesses to be heard. St Alphonsus died on August 1, 1787. Eight months later (April 5, 1788) the informative process of Nocera was begun. Thirty-six witnesses made depositions in it, among whom were Fathers Villani, Mazzini, Corsano, Criscuoli, etc., who had long lived near the saint; his servants, his secretary Felix Vezella; priests and laymen of Nocera. At Santa Agata the process began in September, 1788, and lasted one year. Fifty-six witnesses were heard, among whom were Fathers Tannoja, Costanzo, Cajone, the Archbishop of Amalfi, Mgr. Puoti. The legal delays were exceptionally shortened, and the cause was officially introduced on May 4, 1796.[3]

The levitations of Blessed Andrew Hubert Fournet deserve also to be carefully examined, for part of them have been sworn to by eye-witnesses, and some depositions have quite a vivid accent of veracity. Indeed, the witnesses report very old impressions, but the character of what they report is so simple, they have been so forcibly struck by what they have seen, the style of their account is so convincing, that the whole evidence is far from suggesting a legendary tradition. The state of mind of the witnesses—at least of the Sisters —is also quite remarkable; they evince no exaltation, but prove quietly observant of details, and we should not be sure to find the same composure in bystanders of higher culture. The story of the curé of Châlons, who said he had seen the Curé d'Ars lifted over his pulpit, and who, as soon as he is out of the church, begins expatiating on the " miracle," contrasts pleasantly enough with the good Sisters of La Puye, chiefly anxious to follow the sermon or the ceremony, and not

[1] *Supra*, p. 112 ff.
[2] *Supra*, p. 114. To the objection that the upliftings were nothing but natural movements, it must be answered: (1) that Alphonsus was at the time completely crippled with age; (2) that the very fact of Father Tannoja's watching the saint several days running shows he had observed something quite unusual.
[3] Berthe, vol. ii, pp. 620 ff.

175

to be distracted from it even by a levitation of their venerated founder.[1]

On the other hand, in one particular case the fact that the parishioners of La Puye are said not to have seen the Father levitated near the calvary prevents us from setting on the Sister's deposition all the value it seems otherwise to be worth. Her statement that the said parishioners were kept from seeing the phenomenon by their being placed behind the cross is not satisfactory, even if we make allowance for the Father's having been unusually thin.

Some levitations have been formally recorded by single witnesses. Consequently, the application of the legal maxim *testis unus . . .* might, from a theoretical point of view, be sufficient to ruin their respective evidence. But practically the whole of these depositions, considered in connection with the reality of the phenomenon, generally speaking, and not of each particular case where it was manifested, forms a demonstration by convergence that may be regarded as final. In order to show *in concreto* the *general certitude* created here by the convergence of signs *severally probable*, I shall sum up, in synoptic form, the chief points of five depositions from single witnesses regarding levitations mentioned before:

TERESA OF AVILA.	BERNARDINO REALINO.	F. SUAREZ.	JOSEPH OF CO-PERTINO.	J. B. COTTO-LENGO.
Deposition by Sister Anne of the Incarnation.	*Deposition by Tobias da Ponte.*	*Deposition by Jerome da Silva.*	*Deposition by Francesco Pierpaoli.*	*Deposition by the Sister-portress of Piccola Casa.*
" As I looked at her, she was lifted about 12 inches from the ground, which her feet did not touch. She was shaking all over her body. I drew near and placed my hands under her feet." Duration: half an hour.	" I saw the Father in kneeling posture, his face lifted to heaven, the eyes closed, the body raised more than four palms above the ground." Duration: some moments.	" I saw him in kneeling posture, before a crucifix, bareheaded, with joined hands and his body lifted five palms from the floor, level with the crucifix where the crucifix stood." Duration: three minutes.	" I found that the Father was rapt in ecstasy. His arms were spread out, his eyes open and lifted to heaven. I noticed that he was lifted about a palm above his chair. In order to observe the phenomenon better, I knelt down. . . . He was actually suspended in mid-air." Duration: a quarter of an hour.	" I saw him in ecstasy in front of a crucifix. He was in kneeling position, lifted from the ground; his frock did not touch the floor." Duration: not stated.

[1] Cf. *supra*, p. 121.

The exceptional morality of these witnesses should be emphasised, for it precludes any likening of their depositions to the average type assumed by law, against the lies or blunders of which it has wisely protected the accused. Sister Anne and Jerome are not simply virtuous people; their lives were bordering on sanctity. Tobias da Ponte was a gentleman of rank and of high character. Francesco, the surgeon, by his experimental training, affords peculiar security. As to the Sister-portress of Turin, it will suffice to suggest how sedate and self-controlled she was, to recall that never before her official deposition did she tell anybody of what she had seen at Piccola Casa.

Lastly, we should pay particular attention to the character of some realistic details of the testimonies which prove that the witnesses have not imagined the scene under the influence of religious zeal and with a purpose of edification; for instance, Teresa is said to have been shivering all over while she was lifted over the ground, and the posture of Joseph, raised above his chair, with his extended leg, is rather ridiculous than suggestive of divine rapture. . . . If such details have been reported, it is, undoubtedly, because they have been seen.

On the other hand, nobody can admit that Sister Anne of the Incarnation, Tobias da Ponte, Jerome da Silva, Francesco Pierpaoli, and the Sister-portress of Piccola Casa, who never knew each other any more than they heard of their respective experiences, were all deceived by hallucinations so similar as regards the matter itself, though rather different as regards the details.

Indeed, to every unprejudiced mind the fivefold coincidence of these independent testimonies creates a strong conviction that nothing but metaphysical obstinacy can resist.

These are a few cases where the reality of levitation seems to me well-established, or at least based on sufficient evidence to deserve the attention of any serious mind. I think it would be easy to pick out of the long recital in the first book of the present work quite a number of instances no less reliable. I leave it to the reader to do the sifting for himself. I am content with pointing out as particularly reliable the upliftings of St Catherine of Siena, Mary of Agreda, Mother du Bourg, Domenica Barbagli. My impression is that a careful investigation would only strengthen each of these cases.

LEVITATION

§ 3. General Purport of the Foregoing Remarks

If, indeed, the common standards of historical criticism warrant us that it was neither *always* a mistake nor a deception to assert that human bodies have been lifted from the ground without any apparent physical cause, and have remained floating in mid-air without any visible support, it follows that the material possibility of the phenomenon is established. Hence the critical tests that were like insuperable obstacles set against every doubtful case may be now slightly tempered, not, indeed, to let them through and receive them on an equal footing with the proved ones, but to grant them the benefit of friendly doubt. In other words, if the levitations of a Joseph of Copertino are historically founded, other facts of the kind cannot be systematically excluded from the saints' lives any longer, even when their claims to our acceptance are of a more humble character.

We should, of course, keep still a sharp lookout; we should require the safest proofs of authenticity, but our mistrust has to grow less suspicious, our demands less captious. Besides, this attitude has now become easy, nearly spontaneous, for it is the natural result of the kind of indifference we feel regarding the problem, the general solution of which is now found. Particular cases with difficulties of their own remain to be resolved, but we do not feel so keen an interest in them. We are not sure that in this or that life of a saint the levitations are genuine, because the evidence is slender or the tradition too late; and even sometimes, as in St Francis of Assisi's case, or St Dominic's or St Dunstan's, history invites us to surmise an interpolation, but these flaws in the block of tradition are now incapable of seriously impairing its steadiness, for we know we have found a solid foundation for it.

On the other hand, if levitation is a real fact, historically proved, it rouses a fresh interest in us, a more direct, more concrete interest. As long as we were entitled to believe that it could be reduced to a subjective impression or some pious symbol, the circumstances of the phenomenon were rather immaterial. Now that we know we have to cope with an objective physical manifestation of the mystical life, we feel inclined to examine it more closely, to mark more curiously its external conditions or details, to explore more searchingly its moral and physical surroundings. Such methodical analysis will disclose to us what may be permanent and uniform in the phenomenon; and it will enable us later on to take a more synthetic, systematic, and clear view of it.

Lastly, if any light may be thrown upon the causes of the prodigy, is this not the only means to get a gleam of it ?

178

CHAPTER V

ANALYSIS OF THE PHYSICAL AND PSYCHOLOGI-
CAL CHARACTERISTICS OF LEVITATION AMONG
CATHOLIC MYSTICS

I INTEND, in the present chapter, to examine levitation;
first, from a physical point of view—that is, to mark its visible
peculiarities; then I shall try to trace out its psychology—that is,
to investigate the psychic conditions which seem to be connected
with the phenomenon.

I will continue here to examine only hagiographic data. More
abundant, better described, more certain than the others, they are
specially suitable to serve as terms of comparison.

Having thus determined by this analysis the more general characters of levitation among the saints, we shall return to non-hagio-
graphic data, to see whether we should practically discriminate
between the two or, on the contrary, identify both categories.

§ 1. PHYSICAL CHARACTERISTICS

(a) Peculiarities of the Movement of the Body

1. *Direction.*—Levitation consists nearly always in a vertical
uplifting of the body, followed with a state of equilibrium in mid-
air. Horizontal translation is more scarcely met with. This type
of levitation is commonly found only in Joseph of Copertino's Life.
It is also observed in Peter of Alcantara's, and two curious instances
of it—for which one would like better evidence—are to be found in
St Gerard Majella's.[1]

2. *Height.*—Usually the body does not rise at all high. The
instances where the levitated person is said to have been raised very
high into the air (Dunstan, Colette of Corbie, Francis of Assisi,

---

[1] To avoid too great a number of references, I refer, once for all, to the
alphabetic list at the end of the present book, which will enable the reader
to consult at once the useful passages.

LEVITATION

Philippinus) happen to be rather uncertain.[1] In most cases the figures
mentioned in the accounts are very moderate. I noticed the following estimates concerning levitations founded on serious evidence:

St Teresa	25 cm.
Blessed Bernardino Realino	100 „
Francis Suarez	100 „
St Alphonsus Liguori	50 „
Blessed Andrew Hubert Fournet	25 „
Mother du Bourg	50 „
Domenica Barbagli	60 „

This gives an average of 50 cm. (2½ cm.=about an inch).
Even with Joseph of Copertino levitation was usually very close
to the ground. When he was lifted up at the altar, saying Mass,
it was not more than a few centimetres high. " I saw him," wrote
Cardinal Facchinetti, " lifted from earth four fingers' breadth."
We remember that the same saint was not always actually raised
off the ground. He would sometimes keep connected with the floor
by the tips of his toes. St Douceline remained poised for hours
together on one toe. And so did Victoria Claire of Coux. I have
said that we should not regard these phenomena as levitation,
deliberately ignoring the relation that may exist between the two.
Some will ask, perhaps, why in such instances the ecstatics have
not gone beyond this seemingly embryonic levitation. Though I
am unable to answer in a satisfactory manner, I want to point out:
(1) that these facts cannot be the origin of the belief in levitation
proper, as the mere lifting with contact with the ground has been
distinguished by the witnesses from true levitation, with saints like
Joseph of Copertino and Douceline, who are said to have experienced
both kinds of raisings; (2) that it is not extraordinary that the causes
of levitation—whatever their spiritual or supernatural nature may be
—find a check on their working in certain physical or psychical
conditions undiscernible to us. Theologians admit that simple
movements of the body are enough to dispel certain states of lower
contemplation. Why should it not be so with some physical phenomena ? The notion that a mystic phenomenon must be or not be,
that it should always have a perfectly clear-cut form, is pretty natural

[1] It is possible to account for the vanishing of the levitated person that is
referred to in certain Lives (Colette of Corbie), not by the incredible height
reached by the ecstatic in his ascent, but by a phenomenon of invisibility,
some instances of which are to be found in the Lives of several saints (Vincent
Ferrer, Gerard Majella, Hermann Joseph of Steinfeld, Mary Raggi).

with us, but it proceeds from a purely speculative and rather crude view of the facts. If a mystic favour be a gratuitous gift, that does not imply that it should break in upon every reality. Human freedom assigns to its working definite conditions that vary in each individual case. This is a reason why the search for a law, in the physical acceptation of the word, seems to be here quite needless.

3. *Distance.*—The longest distance reached in a case of ecstatic flight seems to have been about thirty yards (Joseph of Copertino). The very far-distant aerial transports recorded in some other saints' Lives (Gerard Majella, Mary Magdalen Postel) cannot be taken into account here, because they are not unquestionable.

4. *Swiftness.*—It does not seem possible to give any standard as regards the speed of the uplifting. Usually the ascent is gradual and very slow; but swift risings are also mentioned, as in Thomas of Cori's Life. In horizontal transports the movement is, on the contrary, impetuous.

(b) Position of the Body

The body always keeps the position it had when the levitation began; it remains in kneeling, standing, lying, or sitting posture. When the levitated person was abed, as was the case of Alphonsus Liguori, the phenomenon does not seem always to be capable of being seriously ascertained, as it is impossible to make sure that the whole body is really off the couch—I mean, of course, if the body is but slightly raised. In the case of Domenica Barbagli, on the contrary, it is pointed out that the bed-cover was carried off.

(c) Sphere of Influence of Levitation

Levitation does not affect only the body of the ecstatic. The objects in contact with the said body are equally freed—at least in certain cases—from the power of attraction. So it has been noticed that in the flights or upliftings of Joseph of Copertino his clothes remained in good order in spite of his swift and sometimes capricious evolutions.[1] The same thing has been observed with possessed people and mediums. Some ecstatics, such as John of the Cross and Mother du Bourg, have been seen to lift their chair or prie-dieu along

---

[1] *A.S.*, vol. v of Sept., p. 1041 A.: . . . *id admirabile accidebat quod . . . vestes quoque congruo modo compositae permanerent inter tot tamque varios corporis raptus, quibus prorsum, rursum, sursum ac deorsum et in omnem partem ferebatur. Cf.* Bernino, p. 297.

LEVITATION

with them into the air. But it is not certain that they did not draw them up by clutching at them. If that is so, facts of the kind had better be mentioned in the following paragraph.

(d) Ascensional Power

Not only the levitated person finds in the air a position of equilibrium, but he sometimes proves capable of developing considerable ascensional power. So we have seen Joseph of Copertino carrying up with himself into the air Balthazar Rossi the lunatic. And he is said to have done the same thing with two fellow-religious. The same feat is also reported of Dominic of Jesus-Mary. As to Francis of Assisi, we have found that the often-mentioned lifting of Brother Masseo had no historical foundation. Regarding the raising up of lesser burdens than a human body, we may recall the very certain feat of Mother du Bourg, who carried up into the air her heavy praying-desk, but fell back with it almost instantly.

(e) Lightness

Is the lightness of the body during levitation real, or is levitation to be explained as if the body, keeping its natural weight, was pushed from beneath or drawn upwards ? It seems impossible to answer the question, because the experiments have been too few to throw any light on this physical aspect of the phenomenon. Let us, however, recall the following fact: the lady who lifted up Domenica Barbagli some inches above her former level, when she saw her floating in mid-air above her bed, did not experience the least resistance, and the body of the ecstatic remained suspended in the place where it was pushed. Such would not be the case if the body, with its normal weight, was supported invisibly, unless we suppose such support extensible at will. Besides, a light breathing was sufficient to make it wave about, as had already happened in the cases of Mary of Agreda or Dominic of Jesus-Mary, or Mary of Jesus Crucified, the Syrian Carmelite, when she was swinging like a bird on the top of a twig of a lime-tree.

Examples are mentioned when ecstatics have given to those who carried them in their arms an impression of unusual lightness, even without any levitation. Dr. Imbert-Gourbeyre says that Isabella Sanchez, a Franciscan tertiary, when rapt in ecstasy—which generally happened to her at Mass—lost much of her natural weight and could be carried about without the least effort.[1] The same thing is re-

[1] *La stigmatisation*, vol. ii, p. 262.
182

ported by this author of Francis of Cocogliedo,[1] who, being rapt into ecstasy while serving Mass, had to be carried away to the sacristy by the Father Prior, which the latter could do as easily as if he had borne a feather.[2] De Rochas mentions another case of ecstatic lightness which seems genuine. It is that of an ecstatic who lived in a convent near Grenoble. " This person," he says, " remained laid up at the time of her trances;[3] then her body would sometimes become stiff and so light that it was possible to lift her up like a feather by holding her by the elbow."[4] The fact had been affirmed to de Rochas by three eye-witnesses: the parish priest of a village near Grenoble, a professor of the University of the said town, and an engineer, formerly a student of the *Ecole polytechnique*.

On the other hand, the case of Blessed Giles of Santarem, who could not be moved about when he was floating in mid-air, would prove that an extreme mobility of the ecstatic body is far from being the rule; but the case seems to be unique and is too uncertain to be taken into account.[5]

(f) Luminosity

In a great number of cases the bodies of the levitated ecstatics are said to have been radiant with light. This light in certain instances was actually dazzling, as in the case of Blessed Bernardino Realino, whose body, according to Tobias da Ponte, emitted such bright rays that the room was lighted up like a smithy.

(g) Sinking and Alighting of the Body

The body comes gradually down and alights gently. At least, such is the general rule. But there are exceptions. Upon one occasion, Joseph of Copertino, having recovered his senses on the top of a tree, could not come down again—a ladder had to be brought; Mother du Bourg sank abruptly on her praying-desk; Mary of Jesus Crucified, awakened from ecstasy, could hardly climb down the lime-tree on the top of which she was standing. Thus the often-quoted expression *suaviter demittebatur* which has been applied to St Albert, is far from being a reliable formula.[6]

[1] I think the author means Cogolludo ?   [2] *Ibid.*, p. 263.
[3] " Elle restait couchée au moment de ses *crises*," writes the author, using a rather ambiguous word.
[4] Rochas, *Recueil*, p. 91.
[5] I refer, of course, to the fact of heaviness *connected with levitation*. Heaviness coupled with simple ecstasy has been reported in several instances. *Cf.* Ribet, vol. ii, p. 602; Görres, vol. ii, p. 288.
[6] Farges, vol. ii, p. 273. *Cf. La stigmatisation*, vol. ii, p. 272.

(h) Duration of the Phenomenon

Some very long levitations have been mentioned, such as Peter of Alcantara's (three hours), Pacificus of San Severino's (four hours), Louis of Mantua's (three days), Thomas of Villanova's (twelve hours), Christina of Aquila's (twenty-four hours), Mabille of Simiane's (two days). But these extraordinary durations do not belong to verified cases. The best evidenced levitations seem to have been usually pretty short: five minutes (Alphonsus Liguori), ten minutes (Andrew Hubert Fournet), half an hour (Teresa). As to Joseph of Copertino, he is in this respect, as everywhere else, exceptional. He is said to have remained suspended two hours, and if the levitation he experienced in the presence of Francesco Pierpaoli did not last more than a quarter of an hour, it is due to Father Silvestro Evangelista's command to the ecstatic to come back to himself.

(i) Locality and Surroundings

Locality seems to be entirely immaterial. The ecstatic is lifted in his cell, in a church, in a garden, in the open country; alone or in the middle of a crowd.

(j) Light

The same remarks hold true about light. Levitations have taken place in full daylight, in the dark, or by artificial light.

(k) Physiological Aspects

1. *Ecstasy.*—It does not seem that levitation has ever occurred without the accompaniment of ecstasy; hence it is followed with the same physiological symptoms. The ecstasy is sometimes attended with alienation of the senses; but the levitated person also manages to continue the same occupation as before, as was the case with Blessed A. H. Fournet, who kept preaching when levitated near the calvary or during the Way of the Cross. This activity did not mean that ecstasy did not exist, for several mystics have been known to be able to attend to their usual business when rapt in ecstasy (Mary Magdalen of Pazzi, Mother Agnes of Langeac, Catherine of Siena). But this kind of mobile ecstasy is exceptional. This is probably the reason why the authors who have studied the question superficially believe that ecstasy is regularly followed with immobility. " Ecstatics," says Maury, " are thrown at last into a state of immobility and insensibility that nothing can tear them from; their limbs grow stiff,

their muscles lose their flexibility and the power of motion itself."[1] It is rather wonderful that these lines should have been written by an author whose varied information cannot be denied. Indeed, it is still more wonderful that they have enjoyed some credit, when history teaches us that the greatest among ecstatics were so far from having lost " the power of motion " that their ecstasies afforded them the most paradoxical power of aerial motion.

If levitation involves ecstasy—mobile or immobile—the physiological features which seem to characterise it are common to both states, they have nothing specific. So it is reported that Elisabeth of Hungary and Paul of Sogliano were quite exhausted after levitation;[2] that Adelaide of Adelhausen and Dominic of Jesus-Mary vomited blood.[3] These symptoms are not interesting from our point of view because they cannot be ascribed with certainty to levitation itself. The same holds true of the loud cries uttered by Joseph of Copertino,[4] which are also to be met with in the lives of Peter of Alcantara, Francis of St Nicholas, Gerard Majella, etc.[5]

The other symptoms of ecstasies with levitation have been described with accuracy as regards Joseph of Copertino by the surgeon Francesco; they are the usual symptoms of simple ecstasy: alienation of the senses or general anæsthesia, weakening of the breathing, muscular rigidity. St Teresa, during the levitation observed by Sister Anne, " was trembling all over," and Biagio of Caltanisetta also was shivering from head to foot as if a fit of fever had been upon him.

2. *Age.*—As in the case of ecstasy, there is no fixed rule. Alphonsus Liguori experienced levitations when he was ninety-one, Teresa when forty. Several saints are said to have had raisings into the air from a very early period of their life, such as Passitea of Siena, Catherine of Siena, Lucy of Narni; but it must be acknowledged that these instances are not very certain.

3. *Health.*—Sick persons have been known to be levitated (Joseph of Copertino), and even dying persons (Alphonsus Liguori,

[1] *La magie et l'astrologie,* p. 408.
[2] *La stigmatisation,* vol. ii, p. 274.
[3] Görres, vol. ii, pp. 25 and 229.
[4] *A.S.,* vol. v of Sept., p. 1023 A. As Cardinal de Lauria questioned him about these cries, he answered: " The powder ignited in the arquebus explodes with a loud noise; so explodes the heart ignited by divine love " (Bernino, p. 284).
[5] *La stigmatisation,* vol. ii, pp. 246-247.

Peter Claver). The organic condition of the body has apparently no influence on the production of the phenomenon.

4. *Sex.*—The saints, holy personages, or mystics mentioned in the present book include 93 women and 112 men; but as women have at all times been more numerous in religious Orders than men, it may be asserted that levitation—which has been mostly experienced by members of religious Orders—is far more frequent among men. The same proportion has been found for simple ecstasy. Contrary to the common opinion, there are more men than women among ecstatics; according to Dr. Imbert-Gourbeyre, the proportion is fifty men to a woman.[1]

(*l*) Rarity of the Phenomenon

Levitation is of very rare occurrence. The contrary notion is quite common. The anthropologist E. B. Tylor has gone so far as to say that levitation had become " a usual attribute of Christian saints."[2] The same mistake is, curiously enough, to be met with in authors better informed than Tylor of the phenomena of the mystical life: Father Maréchaux,[3] Mgr. Farges,[4] J. Ribet,[5] Dr. Imbert-Gourbeyre.[6] Father H. Thurston himself, so thoroughly conversant with the subject, who has written on it the one substantial and original essay, thought himself entitled to write: " of similar incidents (regarding levitation) there is literally no end."[7] Lastly, I have just read in a recent book that " the whole lives of the saints are full of this frequent miracle."[8]

Now I want to insist that the assertion, in spite of this unanimity, is founded on a pure illusion. By dint of repeating the same names of levitated saints, people have certainly deluded themselves into a

[1] *La stigmatisation*, vol. ii, p. 435. M. de Montmorand arrives at the same conclusion (*Psychologie des mystiques orthodoxes*, p. 423).
[2] *Primitive Culture*, vol. i, p. 151.
[3] *Le merveilleux divin*, p. 226: *Les faits de ce genre sont innombrables dans la vie des saints. Cf.* p. 22: *Le plus souvent le corps de l'extatique est soustrait aux lois de la pesanteur.* . . .
[4] *Les phénomènes mystiques*, vol. ii, p. 271: . . . *ils* [the feats of levitation] *sont* . . . *fréquents dans la vie des saints extatiques.*
[5] *La mystique divine*, vol. ii, ch. xxxii, p. 639: *Il est peu d'extatiques qui n'aient été vus, une fois ou une autre, dans leurs ravissements, élevés au dessus de terre.*
[6] *La stigmatisation*, vol. ii, p. 239: *Rien n'est plus fréquent que de voir les saints s'élever en l'air pendant leurs ravissements.*
[7] *Some Physical Phenomena of Mysticism*, p. 330.
[8] Garçon et Vinchon, *Le diable*, p. 91.

fanciful multiplication of them. Of the fourteen thousand saints or thereabouts contained in the Bollandists,[1] sixty or so are mentioned in the *indices morales* as having experienced levitation, which gives a proportion of 0·4 per cent., or 1 case only in over 230. Supposing that the indices are not absolutely complete—I mean, that they do not include the totality of the cases of levitation—it is still unlikely that the true proportion in this collection is above 1 per cent. The list of levitated saints contained in the present work, which is the completest published to this day, consists of hardly more than two hundred names. Supposing, again, that I have not been able to bring out more than a third of the names of the levitated saints or mystics—which seems a rather liberal allowance for error—and that the total number of the saints is not over fourteen thousand —which it certainly is—we arrive at a proportion of 4 per cent.

Not only the ascertained facts of levitation are very rare, but even the allusions to the phenomenon in the lives of saints are quite exceptional.

Moreover, why should it not be so? Levitation, as we have found, implies ecstasy, and ecstasy itself is far more unusual among mystics than is commonly supposed. According to Dr. Imbert-Gourbeyre's calculation, only 500 members of the Franciscan Order have experienced ecstasy in the course of the last five centuries— that is, about 1 in 6,000.[2]

Rare in the lives of the saints regarded as a whole, levitation is rare, again, in the life of each particular saint; at least, if we go by the number of ascertained cases. The one exception to this rule is Joseph of Copertino, who stands quite apart in nearly every respect, as has already been observed. And even in his case, if we take as a basis the number of upliftings officially recorded (about 100), it appears that for a period of thirty-five years during which the phenomenon took place, its average frequency was not over three times a year! One might object that the small number of *ascertained* facts does not allow us to infer the scarcity of *existing* facts; if Father Suarez was only once seen levitated, it does not follow that he never experienced the same phenomenon at other times. One might even add logically enough that if a casual visitor could witness a levitation, it is most likely that the phenomenon had occurred before, and most unlikely that it never occurred afterwards. Satisfactory as the deduc-

---

[1] This is but an approximation. My estimate is based on the number of pages of the general index (144), at the rate of 100 names a page.
[2] *La Stigmatisation*, vol. ii, p. 437.

tion may sound, it is unable, on practical grounds, to shake this concrete observation: with one exception, the upliftings of the saints who are known to have experienced this phenomenon are mostly to be reckoned on the five fingers.[1]

Now, someone will perhaps ask how it comes that both believers and unbelievers in levitation have so agreed in over-estimating the number of assertions regarding this phenomenon? This is, I think, accounted for in the following way: the two parties have instinctively taken the thing for granted, because they imagined it afforded a more rational foundation for their opinion. The believer's implicit argument is: if levitation is so often mentioned in hagiography, how could people have been so invariably deceived into fancying it to be real? Whereas the unbeliever regards the same assumed frequency of accounts of levitation as an evidence of its falsity. For, he thinks, how could any sensible-minded person admit that such an uncouth phenomenon—supposing it for a second to be true—could have occurred so frequently?

§ 2. Psychological Atmosphere of Levitation

First of all, let us observe the legitimacy of an inquiry into the psychological circumstances of levitation.

Though we have to deal with a material physical phenomenon, we are entitled, we even feel it indispensable, to scrutinise its moral surroundings.

It would never occur to anyone to try to determine the spiritual atmosphere favourable to the dissolution of sulphuric acid in water, because nothing at all suggests that the success of the operation depends on the way of living or the religious opinions of the operator. But here, with us, the matter is somewhat different, for everything suggests that the moral dispositions and the way of living of the levitated persons had something to do with the phenomenon, and even that they might set working the cause or causes of it. Therefore, it is scientific and it may be fruitful—since an unbiassed examination of the facts induces us to do so—to recapture the moral atmosphere which seems instrumental in the production of the said phenomenon.

---

[1] Besides, the above-mentioned inference of possible frequency is of a purely logical order, and there is no reason why the facts now examined should depend on any formal logic of ours. In our deep ignorance hitherto as to the cause of levitation, may we not suppose that the presence of a particular person had possibly something to do with the production of the phenomenon? Cf. infra, Bk. III, ch. iv, par 2.

LEVITATION AMONG CATHOLIC MYSTICS

(a) Spiritual Physiognomy of the Levitated Saints

As we are examining the levitation of the saints, or at least of Catholic mystics, it is plain that we are likely to find among them a primary psychological uniformity: in every instance the levitated person is a being whose whole powers are bent towards the attainment of definite moral and spiritual ends.

But since every saint has not experienced levitation—indeed, since very few have—we may be sure that levitation has not its sufficient reason in the effort towards moral perfection or the longing for divine union which are the characteristics of the interior life of the saint. Are the levitated saints promiscuously mixed with the rest, or, on the contrary, can we, without straining things, find any distinctive marks in them? For instance, is levitation more frequent among active or contemplative mystics? (By these expressions, I mean those upon whom this or that form of life has been imposed by circumstances, for any mystic is by preference a contemplative.) The answer to this question is not easy, because the number of genuine cases of levitation is unknown, and we run the risk of a false generalisation if we take into account imaginary cases.[1] But in any way we can hardly get to any generality: Joseph of Copertino is a pure contemplative, but Alphonsus Liguori is a preacher, a Bishop and founder of an Order; Paschal Baylon, Gerard Majella, Diego, Alphonsus Rodriguez, Andrew Hibernon, Antony of Nardo, James of Illyria, John Baptist of Mastena, John Massias, Onofrio of Fiammenga, Salvator of Orta, are ignorant lay-brothers; Suarez is a celebrated theologian, Alphonsus Liguori a Doctor of the Church. Among women the same contrasts offer themselves.

The one common feature that appears is, perhaps, a more exclusive seeking after ruthless means of corporal penance. And yet, hardly have I ventured the supposition than I am wavering in defending it, when I think of Francis Suarez, the theologian, whose life was all spent in books and speculation, not leaving much room for the practices of a violent ascesis. On the other hand, Joseph of Copertino, the paragon of levitated saints, is distinguished by a rare inaptitude to every kind of physical or intellectual work, by an eager pursuit of the most refined ascetic torture.[2]

As far as the small number of historically proved levitations

---

[1] As is the case, for instance, with Father Poulain when he takes for granted the giddy flights of St Francis at La Verna in his estimate of the possible height reached by levitated saints (ch. xiii, 12).

[2] *A.S.*, vol. v of Sept., pp. 1017 F and 1018 A.

entitles us to any inference, I think the last psychological feature is to be discerned, in some degree, in every mystic who has experienced aerial raisings.[1]

(b) Psychological Occasion of Levitation

It is easy to see that the motion of the soul to which the aerial rapture corresponds in the mystic, is, as in ordinary ecstasy, a vehement transport of fervour. This fervour may be kindled by the most varied causes and, on the face of it, by the most futile: Gerard Majella is thrown into ecstasy because he hears an old blind beggar piping the canticle he loves, Joseph of Copertino because the view of a sea-urchin imparts to his mind an insight of the Almighty's splendour.

Are the impetuosity of the take-off, the height of the rising, the length of the flight, the duration of the suspension, functions of the soul's fervour? It seems impossible to give the question a definite answer. However, certain facts incline us to suppose that such relationship between the exterior and interior phenomena is not imaginary, though the dependence excludes any quantitative expression. For instance, Caesarius of Heisterbach reports that a priest of his diocese who happened to be levitated when he said Mass did not experience the phenomenon unless he officiated with the required slowness and recollection. Any noise around him and the necessity of making haste were enough to put a check on his bodily ascents.[2]

With the latter fact is to be paralleled the bewilderment of Mary of Jesus Crucified, whom hesitancy in obeying robs at once of her buoyancy, and we may wonder if the similar breakdowns of Joseph of Copertino and Mother du Bourg are not also the external effect of some momentary spiritual shortcoming.

It would be indeed a very rash inference to think that levitation manifests in one saint a more intense habitual fervour than in

---

[1] I need not say that I do not ascribe to ascesis any compelling power. It is plain that no abstinence was ever able to produce of itself any preternatural phenomenon. The beggar and the savage are, sometimes, more destitute than the most mortified coenobite, but it does not raise them into the air. There is not even any reason to believe that corporal penance has here any causal value. It is but the sign of an inner state that may be regarded as the occasional cause of levitation. Catholic mysticism, as everybody knows, does not attach any intrinsic value to the material practices of asceticism, and the English mystics among others have laid peculiar stress on the vanity of corporal penance unattended with inner mortification.

[2] *Historiarum memorabilium*, l. ix, c. 30 (quoted by Görres, vol. ii, ch. xxi).

another who lacks this exterior sign. If it were so, at what distance from a Joseph of Copertino a Vincent of Paul, a John Berchmans, a Francis of Sales, would have to stand ! The comparison would be the more delusive as we are now investigating a phenomenon whose efficient cause and mechanism are thoroughly mysterious to us. Saints, indeed, were never seen in levitation, but this is all we know about it. First, they may have experienced it privily, without anyone detecting the secret; secondly, if they have had no actual levitation, who knows if they were not responsible for the apparent deficiency which might then disguise the deepest degree of humility ? Do we not already know of several saints who would struggle fiercely against what they deemed to be too conspicuous tokens of divine favour ? Teresa flung herself down to the ground when she felt she was going to be caught up by her rapture; she prayed to be freed from these singular manifestations of grace. Mary of Agreda did not fight less persistently and vigorously against the same privilege, which she hated to be made public. Philip Neri was so afraid of being levitated before other people that he hardly dared enter a church with some friend.

Who knows if these saints or others, abandoning themselves more freely to their natural impulse, would not have equalled the prodigious Franciscan ?

(c) *Consciousness of the Phenomenon*

Every mystic does not seem to have known this physical aspect of his ecstasies. Mary of Jesus Crucified was not aware of being raised to the tops of the lime-trees in the conventual garden at Pau. Francis of Posadas would say to his confessor that he did not understand what was the matter with himself, that the ground under his feet seemed to give way. Mary of Agreda did not know that she was levitated after Communion, and heard casually of her having been exposed in this state to the view of the public. As to Joseph of Copertino, he certainly knew his raptures, and wanted to be excused for what he regarded as a physical blemish.[1] Referring to the ecstasy he had experienced before the Legate of Spain, he accounted for it by saying that something in the machine had got out of order; but possibly he only spoke of the state of ecstasy itself. On the other hand, it appears that on certain occasions he felt himself capable of bringing the " disorder " about, for his uplifting of Balthasar Rossi along with him into the air is plainly premeditated: " Do

[1] Bernino, pp. 133-134.
191

not fear !" he said, grasping the lunatic by his hair. But the fact is quite exceptional. As to Teresa of Avila, we have seen that she did know she was lifted from the earth, and at first used to be greatly awed by the prodigy.

(d) Awakening by Command

Orthodox mystics are known to come out of ecstasy by the command of a person having spiritual authority over them. The command is said to be always effective if given orally, but only in some cases if it is given mentally.[1] As may be expected, when the rapture is attended with levitation the command of the spiritual Superior puts an end, at the same time, to the suspension itself. The awakening of Joseph of Copertino by the order of Father Evangelista, when he was levitated in presence of Francesco, may be recalled as an instance of the fact. Another Franciscan, Vito de Martina, according to Mazzara, would sometimes fly up in the garden when rapt in ecstasy, and come down to the ground again as soon as his Superior ordered him to do so from his cell.[2]

* * * * *

Having thus described the physical characteristics of levitation, having also—as far as we could—restored the psychological atmosphere, as it develops among orthodox mystics, we may now attempt a comparison with the similar phenomena outside Catholic hagiography.

It would be interesting to include in the comparison cases of levitation from every source (yogis, sorcerers, demoniacs, etc.), but the facts are too uncertain and too vaguely described to admit of such a procedure. The comparison will be effective only as regards mediumistic levitation which has been the object of circumstantial records.

[1] Poulain, ch. xviii, 12-13.
[2] Imbert-Gourbeyre, La stigmatisation, vol. ii, p. 282.

CHAPTER VI

PHYSICAL AND PSYCHOLOGICAL CHARACTERISTICS OF MEDIUMISTIC LEVITATION

THE following analysis is in some degree of a theoretical character, for if the levitation of the saints appears to be of unimpeachable authenticity — at least in several instances — the same phenomenon is surrounded, in the case of mediums, with different circumstances very likely to discourage confidence. Nevertheless, genuine or not, it has seemed interesting to me to compare mediumistic levitation methodically with the manifestations mentioned in hagiography in order to mark their common features and, if need be, their differences.

This comparison requires the same analysis as in the previous chapter. It will be carried out on the same plan.

§ 1. PHYSICAL CHARACTERISTICS.

(a) Circumstances of the Motion of the Body

1. *Direction.*—The mediums are lifted up vertically and sustained in the air or carried away horizontally as it happens in hagiographic records. The motion of translation is reported of Home and Stainton Moses.[1]

2. *Height.*—The following heights have been reached by levitated mediums: Home, from some inches to five feet;[2] Stainton Moses, six feet;[3] Eusapia, from some inches to three feet;[4] Ruggieri, twenty feet;[5] French, two feet;[6] Maria Vollhart, one foot.[7]

3. *Distance.*—The transport of the body, when it occurs, is necessarily limited, as it usually takes place in a room. Home forms

---

[1] About Home, see *supra*, Bk. I, pt. i, ch. iii. About Stainton Moses, F. W. H. Myers, "The Experiences of Stainton Moses," *Proceedings of the S.P.R.*, vol. ix, part 25, and vol. ii, part 27, 1893–1895.
[2] *Report on Spiritualism*, sittings of April 13, July 6, June 22. *D. D. Home*, p. 299.
[3] Rochas, *Recueil*, p. 67.
[4] *Ibid.*, pp. 74, 81, 83.
[5] *Ibid.*, p. 89. [6] *Ibid.*, p. 57. [7] Sudre, p. 248.

an exception to this in his flight at Ashley House, but the distance was no more than the seven feet separating the two windows. Another transport of the same medium is said to have taken place at the Abbey of Adare, when he flew about twelve yards.[1] At Stockton, in a garden, he flew about a hundred feet.[2] The evidence for the last two cases is very slender indeed.

4. *Quickness.*—As a rule the lifting is slow and gradual. At least, such is the case with Stainton Moses,[3] Home,[4] Eusapia;[5] but I find that Willy came to be raised with a jerk.[6]

(b) Position of the Body

The levitated medium is lifted up in any position. Home rose in sitting, kneeling, standing, lying postures.[7] Willy " was raised horizontally, and seemed to rest on an invisible cloud."[8]

(c) Sphere of Influence

The objects in touch with the levitated person are influenced by the phenomenon: Stainton Moses rose with his chair,[9] and so did Maria Vollhart.[10] Eusapia's skirt was once seen " to stick to her legs as if it had been bound or sewed to her," while the medium was horizontally extended, with her head and a portion of her back propped on the table edge.[11]

(d) Ascensional Power

According to Dr. Santangelo, Ruggieri rose about twenty feet above the floor, lifting two persons along with him.[12] Mr. Falcomer said to de Rochas that he had seen a medium at Florence who had lifted up to the ceiling a sceptical person, and had dropped him on the floor so unfortunately that he had had his arm broken.[13]

---

[1] *D. D. Home*, p. 299.
[2] *Report on Spiritualism*, sitting of May 11.
[3] Rochas, *Recueil*, p. 67 (quoting Myers).
[4] Crookes, *Researches* (quoted by Rochas, p. 60).
[5] Rochas, p. 80.   [6] Sudre, p. 248.
[7] Crookes, *D. D. Home*, p. 298.   [8] Sudre, p. 248.
[9] Rochas, p. 67.   [10] Sudre, p. 248.
[11] Rochas, p. 75 (quoting report of Chiaja to the Spiritualist Congress of 1889).
[12] Rochas, p. 89.   [13] *Ibid.*, pp. 90-91.

MEDIUMISTIC LEVITATION

(e) Lightness

During the séances held at Naples in 1889 with Eusapia, Professors Otero Acevedo of Madrid and Tassi of Florence are said by Chiaja to have proved that the medium could be lifted as easily as a feather. But it does not seem that their impression was derived from an actual lightness in Eusapia; the fact that they followed the body with their hands in its slow elevation is quite enough to account for it.[1] Besides, it should be remembered that the phenomenon of lightness could not be ascertained by a series of experiments carried out with the same medium, some of which, indeed, afforded definite negative results.[2]

With the medium Alberto Fontana, the opposite phenomenon of heaviness was observed just after a levitation. The medium remained as if he were "nailed to the floor," and nobody in the company was able to move him about. The phenomenon ceased after an invocation of what the experimenters call the familiar spirit of the medium.[3]

(f) Luminosity

I am aware of but one instance when levitation was accompanied with luminosity,[4] and I know that in some cases an artificial phosphorescence of the medium's body had to be resorted to in order to observe its rising; Willy, the subject of Dr. von Schrenck-Notzing, was dressed in black tights studded with phosphorescent pins.[5] On the other hand, frequent luminous phenomena were observed during mediumistic séances, but they were not an accompaniment of levitation. It should also be observed that this manifestation has often been shammed. Possibly Home did not "rub odic lights with ends of phosphor match," as Browning sarcastically suggested in a well-known satire of the medium, but it is proved that some others did.[6]

[1] Rochas, p. 74.   [2] Ibid., pp. 76 ff.   Cf. Grasset, pp. 408-409.
[3] Ibid., p. 88.
[4] Cf. Incidents in my Life, vol. ii, pp. 120-122: "Just before this took place [a lifting of the medium up to the ceiling], we saw his whole face and chest covered with the same silvery light which we had observed on our host's [Mr. S. C. Hall's] face."
[5] Sudre, p. 248.
[6] Grasset, p. 366. As regards Home, it is only fair to mark that Browning's phrase, "I cheated when I could," in Mr. Sludge, was purely gratuitous, at least as far as the poet's experience was concerned. From F. W. H. Myers' investigation into the matter (Journal S.P.R., July, 1889, quoted by Podmore, vol. ii, p. 230, n. 3), it appears that Browning had never detected Home cheating. His allusion to this medium's using phosphorus to produce luminous manifestations was based on a second-hand rumour. F. Podmore observes also that the alleged exposure of Home at the Tuileries was never supported by any first-hand testimony.

Anyhow, it may be noted here that the luminous phenomena will assume the shape of balls, tongues and jets of flame (Stainton Moses, Home), or of bluish will-o'-the-wisps (Eusapia).[1]

Dr. Féré says that he has observed that the head and hands of two neurotics were radiant with an orange light during their trances. In one case the halo had a radius of about twenty centimetres.[2] The observation is, I think, unique.

(g) Sinking and Alighting of the Body

The levitated medium sinks usually back to the ground in a slow, progressive way (Home, Stainton Moses, Eusapia).[3] But sometimes he comes suddenly down.[4]

(h) Duration of the Phenomenon

It is remarkable that no duration was recorded of the levitations of Home by the witnesses who made depositions about them before the Committee of the Dialectical Society. According to other documents, it appears that in his case this phenomenon would last from a few seconds[5] to about five minutes.[6] As regards Eusapia, the estimates are very modest; they hardly refer to more than a few seconds. Upon one occasion a duration of five minutes is mentioned, but it is about an incomplete levitation.[7] As for Willy and Maria Vollhart, the figures mentioned by M. Sudre are respectively five minutes and one minute.[8]

(i) Locality

The experiments are as a rule carried out within four walls. With the exception of Home's, no levitation is known to have been experienced in the open. But this may be regarded as a natural consequence of the phenomenon taking place in the course of a regular séance, which is scarcely held out of doors. The room where the séance is to be held must not be just any kind of room; the best mediums are said to grow inefficient whenever they are placed in a room too bare of furniture or looking too much like a laboratory. These are, according to M. Sudre, the best conditions of success as far as surroundings are concerned: " . . . Not too large a room should be selected, with rather comfortable and pleasant-looking

[1] Sudre, pp. 250-251, *D. D. Home*, p. 302.
[2] *Revue de médecine*, April 10, 1905.
[3] Rochas, pp. 60, 67, 81.   [4] Sudre, p. 248.
[5] Rochas, p. 60 (quoting Crookes).   [6] Rochas, pp. 62-64.
[7] Rochas, pp. 75, 81.   [8] Sudre, p. 248.

furniture. . . ." The least details are to be carefully attended to; the wall should be hung with a plain, sober paper, the seats should be comfortable enough, and it is advisable to reserve an armchair for the medium. "Some pictures, books and flowers, and if possible a piano," will complete the cheerful look necessary to the production of mediumistic phenomena.[1]

(j) Light

The séances where physical phenomena are to be obtained, observes M. Sudre, are usually to be held in the dark.[2] And the author admits that this necessity makes it hard to ensure a safe control—and even the mere *observation*—of the phenomena.[3] According to him, darkness is necessary, owing to an autosuggestion of the medium which, he hopes, may be done away with some day. As far as the past is concerned, the number of upliftings observed in full light is extremely slender. The only instances that I know of in this regard are those of Home, whom Lord Lindsay,[4] W. Crookes,[5] and Dr. Karpovitch,[6] said they had seen lifted up over the ground in full light. However, it is to be remarked that no detailed record of such full-light séances is available.

According to Lord Lindsay, the famous séance of Ashley Place took place on a moonlight night. "The moon," he said, "was shining full into the room." But Lord Adare in his testimony said, on the contrary, "It was so dark I could not see clearly how he (Home) was supported outside."[7] And besides, it was observed that it was new moon on that day.[8]

Light seems as a rule so contrary to levitation that MacNab having, he says, "awkwardly lit up" while the medium, Mr. F——, a sculptor, was lifted in the air sitting on a piano stool, "the latter sank heavily from a height of 50 to 60 centimetres; so heavily that one leg of the seat was broken."[9]

The medium of Dr. von Schrenck-Notzing, Willy, when he is entranced, says his observer, "is intensely scared by light," and the "spirit" who "controls" the medium, Mina, insists on the light being lowered as soon as the phenomena grow more important.[10]

[1] Sudre, pp. 70-71.
[2] Sudre, p. 65.
[3] Sudre, p. 66.
[4] *D. D. Home*, p. 299.
[5] *Ibid.*, p. 344.
[6] *Ibid.*, pp. 368-370.
[7] *D. D. Home*, p. 301.
[8] Cf. *supra*, p. 23, n. 2. Even if the date of December 16 is correct, the moon was but two days old, and the light must have been very dim.
[9] Rochas, p. 69.
[10] *Les phénomènes physiques*, p. 160.

LEVITATION

To throw a beam of light unexpectedly on the medium when he is entranced, observes M. Sudre, would produce a nervous fit capable of depriving him for a long time of all power.[1]

All this shows that Eusapia's exclamation *Meno luce!* remains the watchword of mediumistic séances.

(k) *Atmospheric Chills*

" Every observer of metapsychic phenomena," says M. Sudre, " has pointed out the draughts of chill air and the fall in temperature that take place in the séances. Mrs. Speer observed that during a séance with Stainton Moses (Feb. 7, 1874) the room seemed to have filled with cold air and the self-registering thermometer had actually fallen by 6° F."[2] This feeling of cold was noticed by many persons attending Home's séances. The phenomenon was alluded to by W. Crookes; he says that this medium's manifestations were " generally preceded by a peculiar cold air, sometimes amounting to a decided wind." And he stated that he had had " sheets of paper blown about " by this wind, " and a thermometer lowered by it." " On some occasions," he adds, " I have not detected any actual movement of the air, but *the cold has been so intense* that I could only compare it to that felt when the hand has been within a few inches of frozen mercury."[3]

The same phenomenon was observed in the cases of Eusapia and Willy, and H. Price experienced it with his medium Stella.[4] The greatest falls of the thermometer are said to correspond to the most strongly marked phenomena.

Though the phenomenon is not particularly concomitant of levitation, it does not seem either that it should be considered unconnected therewith, as it is especially mentioned as accompanying the levitation of objects.[5] I thought it should be mentioned, though in fact I have not come across any reference to it in accounts of human levitation.

(l) *Physiological Aspects of the Phenomenon*

1. *Trance.*—According to M. Sudre, the particular organic condition of the medium, called *trance*, is absolutely necessary to the production of metapsychical phenomena. This state of trance may

[1] P. 67.
[2] P. 249.
[3] *D. D. Home*, p. 341.
[4] " A Record of Thirteen Sittings for Thermopsychics, and other Experiments," *American Journal of the S.P.R.*, No. 5, 1924.
[5] Sudre, p. 250.

have different degrees, from a simple condition of absence of mind to a convulsive fit.[1] Trance, which is comparable to hypnotic sleep, may be produced—and, indeed, has often to be produced—by a magnetist. Some mediums can get into a trance of their own free will. This is how Dr. von Schrenck-Notzing describes the entrancement of his medium Willy, who sometimes experienced levitation:

" As soon as Willy has sat down and held his hands out to the controllers, the red light is substituted for the white one. After about a period of half a minute to two minutes, the subject falls usually into autohypnotic sleep, this change being accompanied with a swift contraction of the body as if the medium was suddenly frightened. . . . The passing into the somnambulistic state is often so rapid that Willy has not the time to finish a started sentence. Sometimes when he awakes (after several hours) he finishes up his sentence and goes on with the conversation begun when he was awake. . . . The physical condition is quite suddenly altered. The muscles . . . become stiff. The body is convulsed with sudden spasms—specially in the arms—the violence of which increases regularly before the manifestations appear. . . . The production of the phenomena is usually announced with exclamations such as ' Form the chain !' ' Do not cut off !' ' Look out !' At the same time the spasms grow more violent; the subject is struggling about with gasps and groans. . . ."

When the phenomenon is taking place (the author refers to a séance of so-called materialisation) the subject is growing more and more excited: " His whole body is agitated, affected with cramps; the medium often rises on his chair, breathes hard, and groans like a person who tries to lift a heavy load. As in bacchic trances, which are known from ancient sculpture, the phenomenon is accompanied by a turgescence which has often been mentioned by doctors who were controlling the medium."[2]

According to the same writer, this sexual concomitant of the mediumistic manifestation, which in his subject issues sometimes in the orgasm, is not absolutely necessary to the production of the phenomena.[3]

As regards levitation, the necessity of trance does not seem as absolute as M. Sudre suggests. Stainton Moses, if his descriptions are to be trusted, experienced levitation in a conscious waking state: " I was quite conscious of what was going on, and could describe the progress of the phenomenon to the persons seated round the table. . . . My mind was quite clear, and I realised very well the strange phenomenon."[1] According to Morselli, Eusapia could also produce manifestations in waking condition and full consciousness.[2] And Home declared before the Committee of the Dialectical Society that he need not be entranced to produce every phenomenon; but he did not point out what manifestations required this particular state.[3]

2. *Age.*—Age is said by M. Sudre not to impair mediumistic power.[4] On the other hand, it has often been stated by those who had experimented with Eusapia that her power had sensibly declined with the years.

3. *Health.*—We should distinguish the general condition of health of the medium and his particular state of weakness or disease at a given moment. Indeed, bad health, generally speaking, is no obstacle to the production of metapsychic phenomena, since mediums like Home were all their life in an extremely poor condition; since Stainton Moses, Eusapia, and many others were regular neurotics;[5] but it should be noticed that this general neuropathic condition must not be made worse by some acute disease, or even, in certain cases, by a trifling ailment. For instance, Stainton Moses said that if he felt at all poorly his manifestations were of the vaguest character.[6] Willy's power may be paralysed by a slight disorder, a fit of ill-humour, and even by uncomfortably thick clothes.[7] On the other hand, Home said that his manifestations were not influenced by illness of any kind.[8]

4. *Sex.*—No influence.

5. *Heredity.*—Mediumistic power is said in certain instances to be transmitted by parents to children, and certain cases are mentioned in support of the assertion.[9] Practically, it is difficult to know if the alleged instances are not sufficiently explained by the moral influence of the surroundings, and even by the regular training of the child.

[1] Rochas, p. 67.
[2] Schrenck-Notzing, p. 111.
[3] Sitting of June 22.
[4] P. 50.
[5] Sudre, par. 29, *Metapsychic and Pathology.*
[6] A. Erny, *Le psychisme expérimental*, p. 61.
[7] Schrenck-Notzing, p. 172.
[8] *Report*, sitting of June 22.
[9] Sudre, pp. 50-51.

MEDIUMISTIC LEVITATION

(m) Rarity

Levitation is quite an exceptional mediumistic phenomenon, not only among mediums in general, but in the case of those who are said to have enjoyed this particular power.[1] D. D. Home, according to W. Crookes, had been raised from the ground at least a hundred times. Now, this assertion was written in 1874; that is, at a time when Home had given séances for about twenty years. If we consider that he managed to give several séances a day, the figure suggested by Crookes, if it is accepted without discussion, shows that levitation, even with Home, who was considered as a prodigious levitator, was of exceptional occurrence.[2]

§ 2. PSYCHOLOGICAL ATMOSPHERE

(a) Moral and Spiritual Character of the Medium

The psychological uniformity that asserted itself among Catholic mystics is not, of course, to be found with mediums. Still, it does not seem impossible to discern common features in them, both moral and spiritual, for, if need be, we may be content with recording negative features; I mean to say, were we unable to state what mediums *are*, we can attempt to clear up the matter by pointing out what *they are not*.

The general morality of the professional medium—in default of specific information—might be inferred from the calling he has chosen, or accepted. The quite natural suspicion he is under, the physical control he is submitted to (meticulous examination of the whole body, chaining up to the controllers, etc.), the surrender of his personality—in the case of hypnotism—into the hands of a magnetist, all these may already help us to form an idea of his moral standard, of his sense of personal dignity.

The consideration of some concrete cases does not destroy this speculative view. D. D. Home's character, though it has been vouched for by respectable people, can hardly be cleared from the conspicuous blemish of his being an adventurer.[3] Eusapia was a poor

---

[1] Richet, *Traité*, p. 692. [2] *D. D. Home*, p. 298.
[3] Some would even say an impostor. *Cf.* Elie de Cyon, *Dieu et science : Essai de psychologie des sciences*, 2nd ed., pp. 265-279. Still, it must be acknowledged (*cf.* p. 195, n. 6) that no definite evidence was ever produced in favour of his having cheated. What I am referring to here by calling him an adventurer is the general fact of his having managed—very cleverly indeed—to make a living, and an opulent one, out of his mediumship; not to mention the most suspicious incident of his adoption by Mrs. Lyon.

stray girl, depraved from early childhood, an hysterical woman with a marked tendency towards erotomania.[1] Stainton Moses, from a social point of view, offers more security. He was for a time a teacher at University College School, and F. W. H. Myers honoured him with his friendship. Still, his psychic condition was not of the best; he was a somnambulist.[2] Of a contemporary medium who happens to experience levitation, Willy Sch., with whom Dr. von Schrenck-Notzing had many experiments, we possess the information imparted by the latter, which I will sum up in a few lines: Willy (he was eighteen when Dr. von Schrenck-Notzing wrote down these particulars) is morbidly sensitive and lacks power of will; his humour is so fickle that he passes suddenly from the brightest state of mind to a state of gloom. On the one hand, he is said to be " mild, kind, docile, modest," and he has " very keen moral and religious feelings "; on the other, he is shown as full of ambition, lacking self-control, stubborn, an inveterate liar. " He will," says the author, " make false statements about trifling matters, with the accent of the deepest conviction, as if he delighted in deceiving others." Then, " when somebody sets the facts right and impresses him with a sense of his error, he bursts into tears of remorse."

After these few touches nobody will be greatly surprised in hearing Dr. von Schrenck-Notzing declare that his subject " has a certain tendency to hysteria."[3]

So not only is mediumship occasionally to be met with in subjects of doubtful morality, but, according to Dr. Paul Gibier, the training for developing mediumistic power results nearly always in moral deterioration.[4]

The crowded chapter of the conscious or unconscious frauds of mediums adds to their character some rather ungraceful features.[5] Even if we accept the supposition that in certain cases fraud is quite unconscious and derived from the eagerness of the entranced medium to produce the desired phenomena,[6] certain it is that the

---

[1] Cf. on her private life, Paola Lombroso's article in Echo du merveilleux, 1907, p. 229; and on her neuropathic taint, C. Lombroso's study in Annales des sciences psychiques, 1908, p. 29.

[2] Sudre, p. 51. [3] Schrenck-Notzing, pp. 156-158.

[4] Analyse des choses, p. 153, . . . l'entraînement destiné à développer les facultés supérieures d'abmatérialisation conduit presque toujours à la démence ou à une péjoration des penchants, et parfois à l'éclosion de nouvelles passions dépendant le plus souvent d'une aberration du sens génésique. Dr. P. Gibier is a spiritualist.

[5] A summary of mediums' deceptions may be found in Grasset, pp. 56 ff., 347 ff. Cf. Lucien Roure's Le merveilleux spirite, passim.

[6] Sudre, p. 68, par. 39, Unconscious Fraud.

medium shows by it his morbid eagerness to display his abnormal power.

This eagerness is even regarded as necessary to success. Eusapia, when she wanted to produce a phenomenon, said that she must wish it ardently.[1] Willy, when he is entranced, evinces the wildest ambition to prove to the persons who attend the séance that he is really possessed of hyperphysic powers.[2] D. D. Home cared so much for his mediumistic gift that, when he thought he had lost it (1856), life had no more zest for him, and though he had promised his confessor, Father de Ravignan, to leave off spiritualistic practices, he could not help resuming them at the least intimation of renewed power.[3] "Vanity," says F. Podmore of this medium, "seems to have been the permanent element of his character; he basked in admiration. . . . The malignant side of his nature showed but rarely, and then chiefly in his attitude towards rival mediums. *But it flashed out when vanity was injured.*"[4]

The ambition to convince those around them of their extra-natural power is so unrestrained in some neurotic persons that a failure in this respect may be enough to upset their mental balance. De Rochas says, according to Chardel, that a young somnambulist (she was fourteen) had declared in a mystic [sic] gathering that she would be lifted into the air at Easter by the fervour of her prayers. As the announced miracle failed to occur, she nearly went mad.[5]

The same haunting eagerness for a supernatural faculty engrossed the pseudo-mystic recently studied by Professor P. Janet. She also is devoured by the craving for levitation: "At certain moments," she says, "I no longer tread the earth. My sandals are not wet, though the ground is damp with rain. . . . I do not walk, I fly. . . . I understand, I know that God is willing to give through me a

---

[1] Grasset, pp. 399-400.
[2] Schrenck-Notzing, p. 169.
[3] *D. D. Home*, pp. 67 ff. It must be recalled he had been converted to Catholicism in the same year. Father de Ravignan's censure of his relapsing (Feb., 1857) was received with a violent show of remorse witnessed by Father de Ponlevoy, whose record of the scene is as follows: " Coming in unexpectedly, I saw him rolling about on the floor and writhing like a worm at the feet of the indignant priest " (*Vie du R.P. Xavier de Ravignan*, vol. ii, p. 299). The author adds that Home wrote down his sworn promise to give up his spiritualistic practices. On Home's early fresh relapse, Father de Ravignan thought he had better leave off acting as his spiritual adviser (*ibid.*).
[4] F. Podmore, vol. ii, p. 228. (The italics are mine.)
[5] Rochas, *Recueil*, p. 28 (quoting Chardel's *Essais de psychologie physiologique*, 1844, p. 293).

LEVITATION

sensible sign of his power by doing for me a little of what he did for Mary, by lifting me up above the clouds. . . . I have promised not to leave the Salpêtrière and to be back in due time. I want to keep my word, but I warn you, if a superior force carries me up suddenly over the roofs, you should not say that I have broken my word. I have tried for a long time to persuade myself that it is a foolish notion, but now everything happens as I foretold. I am more and more lifted up; the miracle is undeniable. I am off. Good-bye ! Good-bye ! "[1]

Another common feature of mediums is their more or less explicit adhesion to the tenets of the spiritualistic doctrine.

" It is noteworthy," writes Dr. Richet, " that nearly every time an experiment is tried, the mediums, even when they have a superficial knowledge of spiritualistic literature, even if they do not know anything of it—as it happens when they are beginners—ascribe to another person than themselves the origin of the thoughts transmitted by the table, planchette, or writing. . . . In almost every experiment there is a personification. There are sometimes several personalities, but as a rule one is predominant. It is what is called in spiritualistic language a guide. The remarkable phenomena produced by Eusapia Palladino were said by herself to be due to the agency of John King. Likewise, Mrs. Piper said that Phinuit was responsible for her phenomena."[2]

This general remark of the French metapsychist holds true of

[1] P. Janet, *De l'angoisse à l'extase*, p. 98. The illusion of levitation seems with this neurotic woman to be connected with a muscular contraction that compels her to walk on tiptoe, a position she regards as foreshadowing a mystic favour. Still, it would be interesting to investigate other cases of the kind in order to know whether the shammed levitation of certain so-called hysterical people does not originate from the imitation of the genuine mystical phenomenon, of which they may have heard more or less. It might then appear that the parallel between the levitation of the mystics and the acrobatic feats of some neurotics is wholly inadequate, the real cause of the latter being found in an imitation of the former. It may be recalled in support of this supposition that, according to the theory formerly advocated by the school of Nancy, of which Dr. Bernheim was the chief, and afterwards confirmed by the observations of Dr. Babinski, hysteria is nothing but an artificial creation of the psychiatrists, who, like Charcot, unconsciously trained their subjects to exhibit the manifestations of a systematic malady of their own making. So that so-called hysteria has practically disappeared as a definite disease, and the various symptoms that made it up are now designated under the term *pithiatism*, to denote the ape-like tendency of the former hysterical subjects.
[2] *Traité*, p. 83.

204

the principal mediums who are known to have experienced aerial raisings: D. D. Home, Stainton Moses, Eusapia, Willy. The latter ascribes his power to a spirit named Mina.[1]

(b) Psychological Occasion of the Phenomenon

Not only does the medium believe in spirits and in his personal intercourse with them, but he is convinced of the necessity of making them propitious. " In all our harder experiments," said Reggazzoni once to Gougenot des Mousseaux, " there is a little invocation, but to benign spirits."[2] One should not think that the practice of the famous magnetist has grown obsolete, in spite of the scientific get-up of modern experiments. It is said that Ochorowicz was unable, in his numerous experiments with Stanislawa Tomczyk, to dispense with the co-operation of the " guide " of the medium, *Little Stasia*, who had to be entreated for help, if any phenomenon was wanted.[3]

Now it often happens that the experimenters regard these entities as merely symbolic, but in order to get results they are very careful not to ruffle the intimate feelings of their subjects and compound with their own positivism.

Indeed, the co-operation of the persons present at a séance seems to be an indispensable condition of success. This co-operation should be moral and physical.

" The tradition," says M. Sudre, " which is justified to a certain extent by experience, at least as far as physical phenomena are concerned, requires that the subject be placed in a set of people in ' fluidic harmony.' Which means, in spiritualistic parlance, that there must be among the persons present a temporary common feeling and perhaps, too, a certain congeniality. It has been ascertained that the presence of certain persons was an obstacle to the production of the phenomena, either because they were disliked by the medium or anybody else in the company, or because their physiological condition prevented the metapsychical forces from working freely.

" The creation of a favourable moral atmosphere is one of the most important elements in metapsychic observation. Spiritualists are careful to select the members of their circle, never to change their positions, not to admit strangers too easily and never more than one or two at a time; lastly, to start the séances with invocations, religious

---

[1] Schrenck-Notzing, p. 155. [2] Gougenot, *La magie*, p. 276.
[3] Schrenck-Notzing, p. 12.

songs, and soft music. These practices, which may seem ridiculous, are indeed very effective and create the necessary communion between the members of the company."[1]

I must here interrupt the quotation to mention that the said practices are not carried out only in spiritualistic circles. Metapsychists have to comply with them, as was shown above with Ochorowicz, as it would be easy to show with many others.

The experiments of Dr. von Schrenck-Notzing with Willy are conducted very much on the principles set down by M. Sudre:

" We should be careful that the controllers are not disliked by the medium, and that he has met them before. As soon as Willy does not feel his neighbour congenial to him, Mina (the medium's guide) invites him to give his place to another person. The medium asks the company to form a chain by holding each other's hands; he wants them not to talk too noisily and to sing some song, because too intense attention interferes with the phenomena. It is recommended in this respect to play softly on the piano, violin, or to have the musical-box playing. The regularity and rhythm of the singing and playing seem to be here, as in the ecstatic exercises of Oriental monks, of utmost importance."[2]

The mediums are said to be informed by telepathy of every feeling among the company. They know if some persons have come with a purpose of criticism or even of scientific research, and this is enough to paralyse their faculties. Hence the failure of the séances conducted under the control of official committees made up of over-critical and even hostile persons.[3]

During a séance, the best plan for the inquirers is not to be intent on a definite subject; they should remain as far as possible in a musing state of mind, or while away the moments in idle, subdued chatting. The number of the bystanders should be inferior to ten. A person should be appointed to supervise the séance and conduct it, to hypnotise the medium and wake him up, if need be, and put him necessary questions. The bystanders form a chain by holding each other's

---

[1] Sudre, p. 64. This author adds that the spiritualistic interpretation of the phenomena is purely accidental. Spiritualism is, according to him, but an artificial system dependent on a certain type of civilisation: it is " exclusivement un produit de culture " (p. 342). The universality of the spiritualistic hypothesis, through time and space, proves, on the contrary, that it is forcibly suggested by experience. It is quite a *natural* product. Which, indeed, does not prove the truth of it.

[2] Schrenck-Notzing, pp. 169-170.
[3] Sudre, pp. 64-65.

hands. The presence, among the latter, of persons whom the medium wishes to please, either through pride or sexual attraction, is said greatly to help in bringing out the mediumistic phenomena.[1] It is on these principles that Dr. von Schrenck-Notzing conducted his séances with Willy, in Munich, 1922, where the number of by-standers was from seven to ten, and " where it was thought advisable to admit ladies, in order to create an atmosphere harmonious and not too scientific [sic]."[2]

Another condition of success seems in certain cases to be not to pay too keen an attention to the manifestations, at least in their first stage of production. Home himself, so prodigiously gifted, wanted not to be taken much notice of when he felt he was going to be levitated.[3]

I have dwelt a little on these conditions of mediumistic efficiency because they are indispensable to know if one is to establish a comparison between the levitation of the mystic and that of the medium. The organisation and progress of a séance show that, practically, the spiritualistic faith—and even what may be rightly called spiritualistic cult—are a necessary condition of the phenomena.

W. James writes in his work on religious experience that he has not to mention levitation in it because this phenomenon is to be met with in persons who have nothing mystic about them.[4] If the word "mystic" is taken here in the rather loose acceptation that the author himself seems to impart to it, his assertion is open to discussion, for it remains to be proved that levitation was ever experienced by persons entertaining an attitude of pure indifference towards the invisible world. At any rate, such is not the case with saints, mystics—Catholic or not—and sorcerers. As to mediums, we have just seen that all of them are more or less imbued with spiritualistic faith.

---

[1] Sudre, pp. 64-65.
[2] Schrenck-Notzing, pp. 169-170.
[3] This is how Home announced a levitation of his at a séance described by Robert Bell in the *Cornhill Magazine*, in August, 1860: " . . . Presently he said in a quiet voice, ' My chair is moving—I am off the ground—don't notice me—talk of something else.' " (Quoted in *D. D. Home*, p. 144, with the following comment: " In explanation of these words, it may be remarked that Home's experience of the phenomenon of levitation was that, until he had risen above the heads of the circle, any movement or excitement on the part of the persons present appeared to have the effect of checking the force at work to produce the manifestation.") *Cf. Report*, declaration of Mr. H. D. Jencken about materialised spirits vanishing as soon as the inquirers gave the phenomenon too lively attention (sitting of April 14).
[4] *The Varieties of Religious Experience*, p. 408.

LEVITATION

But it is not, perhaps, enough to speak of *faith*. A faith may be merely speculative, practically inactive. Here it makes itself known by definite practices, by a kind of cult—nay, by a mystical worship. Indeed, the medium not only believes in spirits, he not only pays them religious homage; he is confident of having actual intercourse with them, of being helped, loved, possessed by them—all of which is the very essence of mysticism. Moreover, as we have found above, he exacts from all inquirers an outward adhesion to his tenets that has to manifest itself—whatever their intimate conviction may be—as a co-operation of an almost liturgical character.

CHAPTER VII

COMPARISON BETWEEN CATHOLIC MYSTICS AND MEDIUMS IN THE MATTER OF LEVITATION

AFTER this double analysis of the characteristics and circumstances of levitation among Catholic mystics and mediums, it is necessary to compare carefully the two orders of phenomena in every detail in order to discern whether they should be likened to each other or, on the contrary, discriminated as to their nature and origin.

§ 1. ANALOGIES

(a) Physical and Physiological Characters

The analogies are in the following points:

1. *Direction of the Movement.*—In both cases vertical elevation and horizontal or oblique translation of the body are to be observed.

2. *Position of the Body.*—The body is lifted in any position.

3. *Sphere of Influence.*—Inanimate objects may be lifted up into the air with the levitated person without the latter clutching them.

4. *Ascensional Power.*—The levitated person is sometimes able to carry up with himself into the air a weight equal or even superior to himself.

5. *Sinking Back to the Ground.*—The body sinks usually back to the ground in a gentle, gradual way, but a sudden, swift descent is also to be met with.

6. *Organic Condition.*—A special organic condition of the body seems in the great majority of cases to be a necessary condition—or accompaniment—of the phenomenon. This physiological state is not altogether similar in both cases. Differences will be pointed out later on.

7. *Rarity.*—The phenomenon is of exceptional rarity in both cases.

209

LEVITATION

(b) *Psychological Characteristics*

The analogy—indeed superficial—is here that both mystics and mediums are convinced that they communicate with an invisible power that reveals its force in their persons. The differences concealed under this analogy will be marked further down.

§ 2. Differences

(a) *Physical and Physiological Characteristics*

1. Regarding *height, distance,* and *quickness* (the last two elements in case of transport of the body), the mediumistic phenomenon appears as a diminutive variety of the hagiographic manifestation. Even Home, who, among mediums, seems to be a replica of Joseph of Copertino, was far from producing as conspicuous and intense phenomena as the Brother Minor. Nothing is to be found in his life or in Eusapia's, or Stainton Moses', or any other's, that is comparable to the impetuous flights of Joseph of Copertino or Peter of Alcantara.

2. The *lightness* of the body of the ecstatic has been ascertained in different instances by its being swung to and fro by the slightest breath of air. Never—to my knowledge—was the same experiment made with levitated mediums, who do not seem freed from the force of attraction, but lifted up as if with a lever, as has been observed by M. Sudre.[1]

3. *Luminosity.*—Different luminous phenomena have been mentioned in accounts of mediumistic séances. Balls of light, stars, flitting flames, have been seen issuing from or playing about the medium, but this manifestation does not seem usually connected with levitation, nor can it be compared to the steady, dazzling light which has so often been seen surrounding the body of the levitated mystic.

4. *Atmospheric Chilliness.*—The chilling sensation so usually felt by the investigators of metapsychical phenomena has never been mentioned in any account of hagiographic levitation. Now, it could hardly be objected that the phenomenon might have escaped the notice of even the most casual observers, as the latter had so often the opportunity of witnessing a levitation in a confined space, like a cell (Bernardino Realino, Suarez), and have shown that they were able

[1] P. 249.
210

to give very accurate and detailed accounts of what they had seen. So it may be inferred with great safety that no levitation of a mystic has ever been attended with those " ice-cold blasts of air " that regularly recur in the accounts of séances held with Home. Not only nothing of the kind has ever been observed, but Catholic mystics have often presented a reverse phenomenon, which is called by mystical theologians the fire of divine love. What is referred to by this is not a subjective impression of inward heat mentioned by the mystic himself, but a manifestation which has been attested as real and objective by serious witnesses. Among the levitated saints who are said to have experienced this feeling of intense corporeal heat the following may be mentioned: Leonard of Lettere, Nicholas Factor, Passitea Crogi, Angelo of Acri,[1] John Colombini, Colette of Corbie, Lucy of Narni, Francis of Paula, Louis Bertrand, Catherine of Ricci, Philip Neri, Magdalen of Pazzi, Peter of Alcantara, Mary Villani, Veronica Giuliani, Paul of the Cross.[2]

With some of them it is not certain that the burning fire they felt inside was capable of manifesting itself outwardly, but with some others a positive heating up of the atmosphere around them has been emphatically asserted. The confessor of Sister Mariangiola Virgili (who died in 1734 at Ronciglioni) deposed on oath that it was sometimes very hard to stay near this mystic, even in the cold season, so hot became the air around her.[3] And similar facts are reported of another Italian mystic, Gemma Galgani, who died in 1903.[4]

[1] *La stigmatisation*, vol. ii, pp. 40-41.
[2] *Les stigmatisées*, vol. ii, ch. x, *passim*. As regards Philip Neri, *cf.* the quite remarkable biography by L. Ponnelle and L. Bordet (*Saint Philippe Néri et la société romaine de son temps*), p. 82.
[3] This is the original attestation: *Attesta il signor D. Ostillo Riccioti che essendo andato un giorno a confessare la serva di Dio inferma, nel primo porre il piede nel di lei povero stanziolino osservò che ella stesse tutta circondata da vive fiamme. Parimente l' ultimo suo direttore attesta anche con suo giuramento, que soventi volte il Signore communicava alle persone, che trattavano con suor Mariangiola qualche scintilla di quel fuoco sagro e divino, da cui era accesa, tanto che, quantunque fosse nel piu rigido verno, non si poteva quasi resistere per il gran caldo, che nella di lei stanza si provava.* (*Della vita della serva di Dio suor Mariangiola Virgili terziaria carmelitana, scritta di Francesco di Simone, Roma,* 1737, quoted by Imbert-Gourbeyre, *Les stigmatisées* vol. ii, p. 135, n. 1).
[4] *E la serafina di Lucca l' ebbe si intensa questa fiamma (fiamma d' amore) che se fosse durata piu di due mesi o tre, quanto duro, il cuore le si sarebbe incendiato nel petto. Io non racconto favole, ma fatti reali e ben accertati dall' esperienza. Quel cuore era come una fornace; non si poteva accostarvi la mano senza sentirsela scottare. . . . (Compendio della Biografia della serva di Dio Gemma Galgani,* by P. Germano di S. Stanislao, p. 94.) The

5. The *duration* of the phenomenon with mediums is usually very short. Many instances are recorded of mediumistic levitation having lasted but a few minutes, and even a few seconds. No medium was ever seen suspended three hours in mid-air, like Mary of Agreda, or two hours, like Joseph of Copertino.

6. This transient mediumistic manifestation requires for its production definite conditions of *locality* and *lighting*. As we have seen, not only must the room where the séance is held offer a cheering appearance, but—as a most general rule—it should be in the dark, or at best in a very subdued light. Now it appears that no conditions of the kind are a requisite for the levitation of mystics, which takes place indifferently in a cell, in a garden, or in a church, in the dark, by daylight, or by artificial light.

7. With a few rather doubtful and therefore negligible exceptions, levitation never occurs in the cases of mystics outside *ecstasy*, and in those of mediums it is attended by a similar physiological condition called *trance*. This organic condition has been mentioned under the head *analogies*, because it implies in both cases common symptoms such as insensibility, low temperature in the extremities, slackening of the breath.

Some theologians and Catholic doctors—like Imbert-Gourbeyre —have endeavoured to point out physiological differences between the ecstatic rapture of the saint and the trance condition of the medium or hysterical person, whereas rationalist doctors have attempted as sedulously to prove their identity. Both of them had ample scope for their demonstration, for they were dealing with an indeterminate physiological condition. Not only do the symptoms of ecstasy and trance vary with every subject, but in the same individual.[1] Under these circumstances, he who wants to maintain

---

phenomenon was even tested by means of the thermometer: *Questo prodigioso fenomeno fu da me piu volte comprovato con la esperienza del termometro, che appena applicato a quelle carni, vedeasi di tratto la colonna del mercurio ascendere fino alla sommita del tubo, come se fosse stato esposto al fuoco ardente* (*ibid.*, p. 96). The development of an abnormal heat of the body as a result of asceticism is to be met with in Tibet, where some anchorites, according to Mme. Alexandra David-Neel, are able to stand, half-naked, the coldest winter temperature in the caves where they live, on mountains 15,000 feet high. The name of these ascetics, *reskyang*, means that they wear only a flimsy cotton garment. The author says she has observed the phenomenon (*Le Thibet mystique*, pp. 870, 895).

[1] *Cf.* about saints, Imbert-Gourbeyre, *La stigmatisation*, vol. ii, ch. xvi; about mediums, Sudre, *Introduction*, par. 31 *ff.*

one of the theses has just to build up two similar or contrasting types, by picking the required symptoms out of the never-ending series offered by concrete instances. Indeed, it seems to me that an unbiassed examination of the matter reveals rather a general similitude than sharp differences. The said sharp differences could only be brought out by comparing extreme and not average cases.

The differences that may be pointed out are the following: the mystic is spontaneously and rather suddenly thrown into ecstasy; the medium has very often to be hypnotised or he produces the trance condition by artificial means of his own. Nevertheless, cases of sudden trance are mentioned.[1] The ecstasy of the mystic is usually accompanied with complete insensibility—such was the case, among others, with Joseph of Copertino—whereas the entranced medium is not usually so fully anæsthetised. Now it might be objected that complete anæsthesia may be obtained by hypnotisation. . . .

8. *State of Health.*—Health does not seem to have the same influence in both classes of phenomena. With the medium a poor physical condition, sometimes even a trifling discomfort, is said to be able to upset his faculty. With the saint no kind of disease seems to interfere with the power of levitation. Indeed, as was pointed out before, the saints who have enjoyed the gift of levitation submitted themselves to the severest ascesis, and deprived themselves of food and sleep. Therefore, the phenomenon of levitation was always experienced by them in a condition of extreme physical weakness; nor did malady proper exert any influence on the production of levitation, as appears from the examples of Joseph of Copertino and Alphonsus Liguori.

9. The same holds true of great *age*. Indeed, it has been said that mediumistic power was independent of years; but this assertion has not so far been tested by experience: no medium, to my knowledge, has ever lived long enough for it. On the other hand, it has been said by those who had experimented with Eusapia that this medium's power had greatly declined with age. . . . With the saints the case is not doubtful. Not only did some of them preserve the power of levitation to a great age, but others do not seem to have enjoyed it before an advanced age (Andrew Hubert Fournet, for instance).

10. *Sex.*—It has not been observed that sex has anything to do with mediumship.[2] But the inference is not based on a sufficient

[1] Sudre, p. 58.   [2] Sudre, p. 51.

number of cases. As to the saints, it appears, on the contrary, that there is a greater number of ecstatics among men than among women, and the same proportion holds true of levitated saints who have been at the same time ecstatics.

11. *Heredity.*—The author of the study on levitation published in the *Quarterly Journal of Science* (Jan., 1875) believed he had found an instance of hereditary transmission of the faculty of levitation in the royal family of Hungary. Speaking of the levitated saints in general, he says: " the hereditary nature of their gifts is shown by the Hungarian royal family." It is, I think, needless to urge the vanity of this assertion, founded not only on a unique case, but on one of very slender historic evidence. With mediums the case is said to be different, and heredity appears to play a certain part in the origin of the power. As a matter of fact, I mention the difference for memory's sake, for I am far from being convinced of a physiological law being instrumental in the transmission of mediumistic power.

(b) Psychological Characteristics

We have noticed in this respect a general analogy between mystics and mediums, and have shown that indeed mediums are nothing but a category of mystics. The analogy, however, is far from being a deep or extensive one. It consists essentially in both classes of persons entertaining the same belief regarding a possible intercourse between man and supernatural powers. Essential differences underlie this apparent similitude, and are to be pointed out now.

1. Whereas the moral life of the saint is all-informed by an ideal of perfection whose attainment requires constant heroic efforts, and consequently implies in him an extraordinary tension of the will, the medium's is *at its best* insignificant. Whereas the saint, throughout the variety of individual and social types, remains the man of one great idea served by an indomitable energy,[1] the medium usually suffers from mental disaggregation.[2]

2. To achieve the purification that he deems necessary to his union with God, the saint enforces on both body and mind an unrelenting ascesis. The average type of medium does not think he has to undergo any such process to deserve the friendship and help of spirits.

[1] Delehaye, *Sanctus*, p. 239.   [2] Sudre, p. 55.

3. The saint feels the fiercest aversion to any outward manifestation of his mystical state. The medium is morbidly anxious to exhibit his hyperphysical faculties.

4. The mystic believes that his prodigies are wrought in his unworthy self by the pleasure of the Almighty; he remains in constant fear lest these charismata may impair his humility, and he earnestly prays to God that his favours remain interior. The medium ascribes his power to the help of spirits whom he invokes and causes to be invoked by those who investigate his manifestations.

The existence of these psychological differences leads us to this alternative: either levitation, despite contrary appearances, has nothing to do with its moral circumstances, or the phenomena experienced by mystics and mediums offer but a seeming analogy concealing essential differences, suggesting a different origin for each class of facts.

Before passing on to the third book of the present work, which will be given up to a review of the theories imagined to account for levitation or simply for the belief in it, it may be useful to gather in a synoptic table the differences physical and psychological observed in the preceding analyses between the two kinds of levitation.

§ 3. Synoptic Table showing the Differences between the Levitation of Mystics and that of Mediums

(a) *Physical Differences*

Mystics.	Mediums.
1. Conspicuous and sometimes intense phenomenon.	Generally coy and elusive phenomenon.
2. The body seems to have partially lost its weight; it may be swung to and fro by a feeble breath.	The body does not seem to escape gravitation, but to be lifted by some lever or leaning on a support.
3. A steady and sometimes dazzling irradiation of the body often accompanies the phenomenon.	Luminous manifestations rarely attend levitation; they lack intensity and assume flickering forms.
4. Duration always sufficient to admit of a careful observation of the fact, and extending in some cases to several hours.	The phenomenon is in most cases of a fleeting kind.

215

Mystics.	*Mediums.*
5. Locality is immaterial.	The place where séances are to be held should be carefully accommodated.
6. The phenomenon takes place in daylight, artificial light, or in the dark.	Mediumistic power usually requires for its manifestation complete or semi-darkness.
7. No alteration (unless it be a rising) of the ambient atmospheric temperature.	Frequent lowering of the ambient atmospheric temperature.
8. Disease is no obstacle to the occurrence of the phenomenon.	Disease and even discomfort often paralyses the medium.
9. Spontaneous ecstasy.	Provoked trance condition.
10. No co-operation of those present.	Phenomenon seemingly obtained with physical co-operation of those present.
11. Often private occurrence of the phenomenon.	Public occurrence of the phenomenon.
12. Purely personal faculty.	Assumed hereditary transmission of mediumistic faculties.

(b) Psychological Differences

1. Moral life set towards an ideal of perfection.	Dubious or indifferent morality.
2. Life ruled by severe ascesis.	No ascetic practice indispensable.
3. Marked repugnance to any outward manifestation of the mystical state; special prayers to be deprived of them.	Eager pursuit of hyperphysical powers; invocation of spirits in order to obtain them.
4. Phenomenon always unexpected by those present.	Phenomenon produced in the so-called condition of expectant attention in the bystanders.

BOOK III
THE THEORIES

CHAPTER I

NEGATION

§ 1. Its Varieties and Arguments

THE historical evidence for the reality of hagiographic levitation being as reliable as I have tried to show it to be, it may be supposed that all who agree as to the facts themselves, will only be at variance as to their causes. It is not so. Some, *a priori*; some, after a research which one cannot help deeming superficial, dismiss a phenomenon that fails to fit into their general conception of the world, of its nature, and of its laws.

How do both of them make good—on what principles, on what observations—a position historically so paradoxical?

(a) *Historians and Sociologists*

Some content themselves with this assertion—express or implicit: levitation would be a miracle; as there was never such a thing as a miracle, levitation is a fiction. This was Littré's attitude, which met with Renan's warm approval.

" As M. Littré has so aptly said, a never belied experience has taught our own time that every miraculous fact has always had its origin in self-deluding imagination, in blind credulity, in the ignorance of natural laws. No research has ever been able to detect a miracle that had taken place where it could be observed and verified. . . . Never was a heavy body raised, against the law of gravitation, into the regions of the air in the presence of physicists, thus proving that the properties of such bodies are capable of being temporarily suppressed. . . ."[1]

And Renan adds this comment:

" Everybody is not able to verify a fact. Doing it requires a strong mental discipline and the practice of scientific experiments. In the

---

[1] Renan, *Questions contemporaines*, p. 222. His quotation of Littré is from the preface by the latter to the 2nd edition of *Vie de Jésus*, translated from Strauss, pp. v-vi.

miracles that are said to have taken place in the past, none of the conditions is fulfilled. Not only are the texts where they are mentioned very much open to criticism, but the public before whom they occurred were foreign to science and unable to judge whether the laws of nature had been actually violated."[1]

The anthropologist E. B. Tylor expounds a similar view in a way of his own. According to him the Christian belief in levitation is connected with Buddhist folk-lore through Neoplatonist superstition.[2] So there is no need for a very careful investigation of the nonsense which is talked about the matter. For instance, Dom Calmet has referred somewhere to a monk and a nun who used thus to be lifted up into the air when they prayed with special fervour. Unfortunately, the eminent commentator quite forgot to mention the witnesses of these prodigies.[3]

G. Sorel had found another reason for the belief in levitation. It was not, according to him, due to an illusion of the mystics, nor even to a sensory delusion as to their surroundings, but it was an imaginary inference drawn from ascetics being usually extremely thin:

" The ghastly leanness of ascetics," he says, " originated the notion that the godly are light; hence the many legends on the levitation of saints who are said to have remained suspended in the air, legends which have been absorbed by Catholicism."[4]

" Very likely," adds the sociologist, " this prejudice was in some degree responsible for the adoption by criminal law of the cold water ordeal, in which the accused was acknowledged innocent if he floated on the surface."[5]

(b) Society Scepticism

Scepticism regarding levitation is peculiar neither to philosophers or scientists, nor to our time. We find it entertained quite naturally by society people in the seventeenth century. Indeed, when Nicole ventured to recount at Madame de Longueville's the anecdote of a discalced friar, Father Dominic, who had been lifted up into the air before the King of Spain, the Queen, and all the Court, " et que l'on faisait remuer comme une bulle de savon rien qu'en soufflant dessus," the story was received with a general guffaw.[6]

---

[1] *Ibid.*, p. 226.
[2] *Primitive Culture*, vol. i, pp. 149-151.   [3] *Ibid.*, p. 155.
[4] *Introduction à l'économie moderne*, p. 406.
[5] *Ibid.*
[6] *Essais*, lettre xlv. Nicole refers certainly to the levitation of Dominic of Jesus-Mary mentioned above (Bk. I, pt. ii, 2nd sect., ch. v, p. 82).

NEGATION

A hundred years earlier the authors of the *Centuries de Magdebourg* (1552-1574) were jeering at those who were simple enough to believe that Mary the Egyptian could ever have been raised from the ground when she came across Zosimus in the desert.[1] Nearer to us, Goethe, from whom a keener curiosity might have been expected, scorned to account in any plausible way for the prodigy of the same kind he had found recorded in the Life of Philip Neri—a saint to whom he had taken a fancy. He simply assumed that the people of that time who had been foolish enough to conceive there was such a place as a hell might well imagine so strange a piece of marvellous—nay, so impossible (*ja das Unmögliche*)—as the flying up of human bodies.[2]

(c) Objections of Psychiaters

Other minds, though they are likely to have shared in this spontaneous incredulity, thought it their duty to seek after the origin of such a queer tradition. Some of them believed that it came from an illusion of these neuropaths, the mystics of every kind.

" Ecstatics," says A. Maury, " think themselves suspended in the air, like Blessed Joseph of Cupertino, St Thomas of Villanova, St Teresa. This delusion is also to be found among the Buddhist monks, and it is to be accounted for by the power of some hysterical persons to stand firmly on tiptoe and to keep their balance in the most exhausting attitudes."[3]

Dr. Baillarger also explained the same belief by an illusion of the would-be levitated persons:

" Some hallucinations," he said, " are difficult to classify, but they seem cognate to those of general sensitivity. I mean the strange sensations experienced by some persons under the influence of certain drugs, or by some lunatics, that they have grown exceedingly light, that they are lifted into the air, that they are wavering or tossing about. . . . These hallucinations are frequent in dreams, and nearly everybody has experienced them, but they are also produced by datura, opium, hashish; lastly, they are to be met with in ecstasy and acute madness. Some maniacs think themselves so light that they believe they hardly tread the ground. I have known a woman who often felt as if she was lifted off the ground by an invisible hand."[4]

[1] Quoted in Bayle's Dictionary, *s.v.* Marie l'Egyptienne.
[2] *Italiänische Reise*, vol. i, p. 504 (Stuttgart, 1862).
[3] *Magie et Astrologie*, pp. 416-417.
[4] *De l'influence de l'état intermédiaire*, etc., p. 350.

LEVITATION

This psychiatrist had known a lunatic at the Salpêtrière who fancied she was so uplifted. " This is," he says, " how she leaves the ground and what she performs every moment. She takes a wooden shoe in each hand, a wooden bowl or any other object; then she crouches a little, draws in as much air as she can, blows out her cheeks, and begins to get up again with her arms raised. Presently she touches the ground only with her toes, and often stands thus on one foot. She remains one moment suspended in this way, keeping her breath in, lifting her eyes to heaven. . . . A few minutes later she sinks down again. . . ."[1]

Dr. L. R. Regnier thinks that the sensation of being lifted is derived from a temporary loss of the muscular sense:

" Sometimes the ecstasy is preceded with a special illusion that causes the ecstatic to lose the sense of gravity. He thinks that his feet no longer touch the earth, that he is walking in the air, is rising into it. This sensation accounts for the Brahmins' professing to be able to rise into the air and be borne at once through it from one place to another."[2]

This thesis has been taken up again lately by J. H. Leuba, according to whom the levitation of mystics is nothing but a subjective sensation of lightness, as is proved by the instances of the German mystic Suso and of St Teresa. That the latter's levitation is only a delusion seems to this author to be proved by the following passage of her autobiography:

" My body seemed frequently to be buoyant, as if all weight had departed from it; so much so that now and then I scarcely knew that my feet touched the ground."[3]

And J. H. Leuba finds a confirmation of his inference in the experiments he has tried with subjects whom he has caused to inhale ether and nitrous oxide. Both of them, he says, experienced the feeling of levitation.[4]

A Belgian doctor, Nestor Charbonnier, accounted for levitation in a more simple way. What people had mistaken for upliftings or ecstatic flight were merely powerful jumps performed in fits of lunacy:

" From what we have read of these phenomena, we believe that it was usually a more or less extraordinary leap, a movement as impulsive as it was violent, all the more powerful—according to Esquirol—as the neurotics believe it produced by the Deity. We are led to this

[1] *De l'influence de l'état intermédiaire*, etc., p. 350.
[2] *Hypnotisme et croyances anciennes*, pp. 187-188.
[3] *Life*, ch. xx, p. 169.
[4] *Extase mystique*, p. 673.

222

opinion by the fact that their power is soon exhausted. When Joseph of Copertino jumps up to pretty high branches of a tree, he wants a ladder to get down again, just like the lunatics whose strength is exhausted in a supreme effort."[1]

(d) Indirect Negation

Lastly, besides negation proper there are the omissions of some believers who, even in works of edification, fail to mention levitation among the prodigies of the saints, either because they do not believe it themselves or because they fear lest such a gaudy kind of marvel should jar on the sober taste of their readers. As an instance of this state of mind, I will mention the Dictionnaire hagiographique, by Abbé Pétin, published by Abbé Migne, a considerable work which contains about eight thousand biographies and has served as a guide to a number of similar books in England, France, and Germany.[2] Now, the biographies in the said dictionary seem to make it a rule never to refer to levitation, not only in cases when this omission would be commendable—as in St Francis of Assisi's and Dominic's instances—but when it is actually garbling the facts, as in St Joseph of Copertino's Life. Indeed, this saint is simply mentioned as having experienced " raptures as frequent as they were extraordinary,"[3] which may be regarded as an over-discreet allusion to the real facts, and entirely fails to account for the abjuration of John Frederick of Brunswick, or, in general, for the prodigious popularity of the Franciscan Brother.

§ 2. EXAMINATION OF THE PRECEDING OPINIONS

(a) Historians and Sociologists

1. *Littré and Renan.*—The implicit argument of Littré and Renan may be resolved into this:

Gravitation is a constant law.
Levitation means an exception to this law.
Therefore, levitation is impossible.

The circle is obvious.

[1] *Maladies et facultés diverses des mystiques*, p. 40.
[2] *Book of Saints*, by the Benedictines of Ramsgate, London, 1921; *Biographical Dictionary*, by Mgr. F. G. Holweck, London, 1924; *Dictionnaire d'hagiographie*, by Dom Baudot, Paris, 1925; *Vollständiges Heiligen Lexikon*, by J. Stadler and J. Heim, Augsburg, 1858.
[3] *Dictionnaire hagiographique*, vol. ii, col. 162.

LEVITATION

If history proves levitation to be genuine, it shows at the same time that the law of gravitation is open to exceptions, as regards certain bodies, in certain circumstances; though its constancy remains unimpaired in ordinary circumstances.

This brief and general argument will seem exceedingly feeble to those who have taken the trouble to go through the historical file of levitation. If the reality of the phenomenon is to be discarded, it should not be according to a general view of the possibilities of nature, but on a searching inquiry into the evidence about it.

Some, indeed, deny the necessity of any discussion in a case of the kind:

"When critics refuse to believe accounts of miracles," says Havet, "they need not afford any proof for their negation. What has been recounted cannot have happened."[1]

This reasoning has no value, unless the word *miracle* is made a synonym of absurd event, intolerable to reason, like the miracle that has been quoted above about Buddha;[2] but it is certainly not so regarding levitation. That a human body be lifted off the ground and remain floating between heaven and earth is certainly unusual, and consequently jars on our experimental knowledge of the world, but logic is not concerned in it. To scorn the evidence for the genuineness of the fact reveals an exaggerated trust in the formulæ of physics or a remarkable lack of curiosity.

Littré, indeed, though his attitude has a metaphysical origin, makes a show of positive justification of it; if he does not believe in levitation, he says, it is because such a phenomenon never took place in satisfactory conditions: "never was a heavy body raised into the regions of the air in the presence of physicists."

Those who have read the account of the levitation experienced by Joseph of Copertino before the surgeon and the physician who looked after him know, on the contrary, that history has recorded at least *one* case where a heavy body was lifted from the floor and remained suspended in mid-air a quarter of an hour, just in the conditions required by Littré. But even if such a relevant answer was not made to Littré's reasoning, this would nevertheless be void of the least cogency.

Supposing that no levitation had ever taken place in the presence of physicists, it might indeed be surmised that the fact was due to physicists having neglected to verify a fact that they presupposed impossible.

[1] *Le Christianisme et ses origines: Nouveau Testament*, Préface.
[2] *Supra*, p. 149.

Supposing, again, that the said physicists had tried to investigate the phenomenon, they might have failed to be witnesses of it by reason of its exceptional rarity and of the very peculiar circumstances of its occurrence. Or if in the course of a long period a few of them had been lucky enough to come across a case of levitation and had attested it, it is plain that the new-comers would have refused their evidence, charging them with ignorance and credulity. In a contemporary instance of praeternatural phenomena, do we not see doctors at variance about the cures of Lourdes ? If these cures cease to occur, are the doctors' certificates regarding them likely to overcome the scepticism of other doctors in the future ?

Indeed, a physicist, like any other person, may admit the supernatural or not. If he admits it, his evidence may be rejected as a believer's. If he rejects the supernatural *a priori*, he is a believer of another kind, more firmly established in his creed than the believer proper; for the latter, if he admits the possibility of the supernatural *in abstracto*, is not ready to believe *any* unproved prodigies that are proposed to him. The former, on the contrary, has made up his mind to believe *no* prodigy at all. Ready as he is to deny his own senses, if they happened to contradict his scientific tenets, how could he be expected not to deny others' senses in the same occurrence ?

Lastly, it might be objected that science has little to do with the verification of a fact like levitation. It is not necessary to be deeply versed in the law of gravitation to make sure of a thing as obvious as the spontaneous rising of a human body into the air and its suspension there without any stay for a considerable length of time. The most ignorant peasant is quite as fit as the most learned meteorologist to see that a shower is falling.

Practically the phenomenon of levitation, to be observed in conditions that Littré would declare satisfactory, should be regular and even reproducible at leisure. Now, it happens to be capricious and spontaneous. To say, " I will believe it only when physicists attest it," is the same as saying, " I will believe it when it is different in nature from what it is."

2. *Tylor.*—Though Tylor had plainly neglected to examine the reasons for or against levitation, he feigned, like Renan, to base his scepticism on historical grounds. Renan declared he rejected miracles, not on philosophical principles, but because history fails to show any.[1] Tylor does not actually say that he does not believe

[1] *Nous repoussons le surnaturel par la même raison qui nous fait repousser l'existence des centaures et des hippogriffes, cette raison c'est qu'on n en a jamais vu.* (*Vie de Jésus*, preface to the 13th edition, p. vi). If we want to know the

225

in levitation for historical reasons, but he gives a hint in that direction when he reproaches Dom Calmet with having omitted to mention the names of the persons who had witnessed certain feats of levitation. Indeed, if Dom Calmet does not afford sufficient evidence for the facts he has recorded, it is only prudent not to give credence to them; but if one wants to form a serious opinion on levitation, it is advisable not to let the matter stand there, and to ascertain whether other authors do not provide more circumstantial evidence of similar facts.

If Tylor did not investigate the question any further, he, who was such an intrepid reader—witness the copious footnotes in his books—shall we not be entitled to suppose that it was due to his mind being made up before as to the reality of the fact?

To him, to believe in a fact like levitation is essentially a primitive way of thinking; it is a savage notion to be carefully noted by the folk-lorist, but one whose experimental foundation need not be investigated by the historian.[1]

This way of reasoning derives its seeming value from the ingenuous desire of the civilised to be altogether different from savages. In other words, this value is of a purely emotional nature and cannot resist argument; indeed, the savages' belief in levitation has nothing to do with the genuineness of the phenomenon. The errors committed by them in the interpretation of other phenomena, the occult causes by which they think them to be produced, their manifold and queer superstitions, should not induce us to reject a priori and in a lump everything they believe. At that rate, are we to scorn the notions of a Thomas Aquinas, of a Leibniz, of a Newman, on God and his action in the world, for the simple reason that they are not unlike enough to those of an Andamanese?

3. G. Sorel.—Though G. Sorel's account of the belief in levitation cannot be dealt with very seriously, it may be interesting to revert to it if only to show how a quite exceptionally powerful mind is apt to fall into mere nonsense if it indulges in talking at random on any question unknown to it. G. Sorel has shown by his remark about the extreme spareness of the ascetics that he did not even suspect the historical side of the problem of levitation. He felt a priori quite confident that he was entitled to treat the question as a myth. Besides, his assumed relationship of the belief in levitation and the

exact experimental value of this position, we should remember the author had adopted it when he was twenty-two (cf. Cahiers de jeunesse, 1er cahier, No. 49, p. 38).

[1] Primitive Culture, vol. i, p. 155.

practice of water ordeals applied to witches is grounded on a rather un-
happy blunder. Indeed, the *culprit*, and not the innocent, was often
supposed in those ordeals to float on the surface . . .; which James I
curiously accounts for in his *Demonologie* by saying that witches who
have shaken off the water of baptism can hardly be expected to be
received afterwards by this element.[1] I shall add that this widely
diffused belief[2] is pretty likely to have had some experimental basis,
as is suggested by the strange buoyancy of the *Seeress of Prevorst*,
and by other similar cases recorded in some official documents in
witchcraft trials.[3]

(b) Psychiatrists

Other writers have endeavoured to justify their scepticism about
levitation by more concrete considerations. They have shown us
the reasons why people had been led into such a belief by tracing
it back to different self-delusions of the mystics. Neurotics—says
Leuba, following many others—feel themselves so light that they
have the feeling of floating in the air. Their descriptions of this
subjective phenomenon have suggested to their readers the reality
of the fact. And Leuba quotes a well-known text of St Teresa in
support of his thesis. It must be admitted that on the basis of this
text Leuba is quite entitled to question the reality of levitation;
but then we may, in our turn, question the validity of the method,
consisting here in quoting but one text in support of his theory or
building up his theory on this one text, when there are so many
others available which positively disprove his assertion; when ex-
traneous evidence shows that—at least in some cases—the saint's
impressions were not illusory; not to mention the vast number of
saints whose levitation was never known by their own impressions,
but only by those who had been witnesses of it.

The experiments that the author refers to, to ascertain the hallucinatory power of divers drugs, were quite superfluous; that ether
or any other stuff may give to those who absorb it a feeling of

---

[1] Quoted *ibid.*, pp. 140-141: " It appears that God hath appointed for
a supernatural signe of the monstrous impietie of witches, that the water
shall refuse to receive them in her bosom that have shaken off the sacred
water of baptism."
[2] Cf. *ibid.*
[3] *Cf.* Le Brun, *Histoire des pratiques superstitieuses*, vol. ii, pp. 293-301.
According to a report drawn up by a notary on June 5, 1696, at Montigny,
near Auxerre, several persons charged with witchcraft were thrown into the
river Seine, bound hand and foot, and " n'enfoncèrent nullement dans l'eau,
non plus que des gourdes."

buoyancy is a long-established fact, but it entirely fails to account for the delusion of those who beheld the levitated persons.

As to the assertions of Dr. Nestor Charbonnier, they hardly deserve criticism. To think that simple leaps—dizzy as they may be—were taken for forty years for feats of levitation, is to admit a miracle far more wonderful than the feats themselves, by supposing that all that time Joseph of Copertino's companions were all lunatics.

On the whole, the remarks of the psychiatrists are not altogether void of interest, but their purport is strictly limited to the pathological field from which they have been drawn. Their extension to hagiographical facts cannot be obtained without a rash ignorance of all historical evidence. To deny that Joseph of Copertino ever rose above the earth because a neurotic person at the Salpêtrière has experienced such an impression, is a type of reasoning which is hardly worth impugning. It just amounts to rejecting the possibility of the inventions of genius because a number of lunatics have fancied themselves inventive geniuses.

*   *   *   *   *

So whether they have merely denied levitation in behalf of constant natural laws, or have tried to derive the belief in the phenomenon from the misinterpretation of actual facts, the sceptics do not appear to have cared for a close investigation of the matter, and all of them have completely scorned the historical side of it.

Those who seem to form an exception, like Leuba, have simply juggled the problem away, by questioning facts that were questionable indeed, and then unduly generalising their partial solution.

None of them, I believe, earnestly wished to base on a solid induction a doubt whose philosophical validity seemed to them so obvious.

None of them has seen that the one means to establish that levitation was a fiction consisted in subjecting to severe historical criticism a few of the best averred cases and in bringing out in full light their error or their fraud.

CHAPTER II
NATURALISTIC THEORIES

I SHALL group under this head the theories that, while admitting in some cases the reality of levitation, attempt to explain the phenomenon by the working of a natural power without the agency of any intelligent free cause.

The first endeavours to give a rational account of levitation were made a long time ago. In the first half of the seventeenth century Zacchias, the physician of Innocent X, already referred to them, though he said he could not agree with them. Indeed, he thought it impossible to admit that the suspension of a human body in mid-air, by an invisible agency, was not contrary to the laws of nature.[1]

I do not know who are the authors Zacchias is alluding to. They cannot have been very well known, for Nicole, the theologian, thirty years later, was not aware of their existence. Speaking of those who, in his time, denied the possibility of levitation, he wrote: " They have not enough wit to say that a body may remain naturally suspended in the air a quarter of an hour."[2] So he was marking that, to his knowledge, there were but two attitudes towards the phenomenon—rejecting or accepting it in the lump, with its praeternatural connotations.

It was normal that the rationalistic solution of the problem should be taken up again in an epoch when a methodical exploration of natural forces had disclosed their number and complexity. And so it was. Such endeavours are of themselves commendable. They originate from a desire not to hurt common-sense by excluding from history a series of facts for which we possess solid evidence, and at the same time from the rational want to account for them, if possible, by means most consonant with a determinist conception of the universe.

[1] *Quaestiones medico-legal.* (Amsterdam, 1651),l. 4, tit. 1, q. 6, n. 10: *Alii praeterea sunt ecstatici qui a terra in ecstasi elevantur, et quasi in aere librati permanent ; hoc autem (quicquid conati fuerint nonnulli affirmare) in naturali ecstasi est ab omni veritate alienum ; contra naturae enim propensionem omnino est corpus grave a centro propria virtute sublevari et in aere sustineri.*
[2] *Essais* (published 1678), lettre lxv.

LEVITATION

I will not try, in the following account, to mention every author who, in books or articles, has proposed a positivist explanation of levitation, but simply to give a cursory view of the types of such explanation.

Some will find, no doubt, that I have attached too much importance to hypotheses of slender scientific value. I have thought it indispensable to mention them in a general work on levitation. If their interest is small from the aetiological point of view, it is far from being so for the historian and psychologist.

§ I. Account of some Hypotheses

(a) Electricity

Dr. Fugairon, in his book *Essais sur les phénomènes électriques des êtres vivants*, supposes that levitation might be accounted for by the well-known electric phenomenon of the power of points:

" Everybody knows," he writes, " the motions produced by the flowing out of electricity from points, which is shown in lectures on physics by means of the tourniquet. If the apparatus is connected with the conductor of an electric machine, it begins turning round in an opposite direction to the flowing out of electricity. This motion is explained by the point being driven back by the electrified air. The revolution takes place also in oil, a bad conductor, but not in water.

" Similarly, is it not possible that a perelectrogenous subject, particularly gifted, standing on tiptoe on a floor or on a pavement, bad conductors, and letting a great flow of electric fluid out of his toes, may be lifted from the ground ? Could not the same result be obtained if the subject, rapt in ecstasy, let his fluid flow out of both of his feet and bent knees ?

" . . . The bodies of animals are known to be diamagnetic and the earth to be a magnet. Now, just as heavy bodies are raised off the earth when they weigh less than an equal volume of the surrounding medium, so a magnet repulses the body which is less magnetic than the medium in which it is plunged. This principle, found by Becquerel, works perhaps in levitation."[1]

De Rochas, from whom I have borrowed the citation, finds Fugairon's hypothesis quite plausible, and he completes it with these remarks:

" This seems all the more probable as levitation has been shown, in the above quotations, to be like an extension of supernatural

[1] Rochas, *Recueil*, pp. 98-99.

NATURALISTIC THEORIES

agility—that is, the consequence of the lightness of the subjects, and that experiments made at the end of the last century seem to prove that electricity lessens the weight of the bodies."[1] The said experiments are those of a professor of physics at Ingolstadt, Steiglehner, who thought he had been able to ascertain that a brass vessel full of water and the body of a bird had lost a few grains' weight after being electrified. The Abbé Nollet, in 1747, sent a report about similar facts to the Académie Royale des Sciences.

(b) Nondescript Forces

The same de Rochas has said elsewhere[2] that levitation might be due to a physical force developing in the body of the subject and acting like a magnetic or odic current which repulses a similar current in the ground.

Indeed, the subtle, mysterious agent that Reichenbach named *od* has, according to him, among other properties, a considerable mechanical power. It is, he says, through the agency of these odic effluvia that tables are set moving and whirling.[3]

Under the same head should be classed, I think, the so-called magnetic or electro-telluric forces referred to in the following lucubration by a vague Indian theosophist quoted by de Rochas:

" Levitation cannot be explained except by the theory of universal attraction and repulsion. If the mediums are uplifted, it is because they have been made for a time positive as regards earthly magnetism, which is supposed to be positive. There are in every human organism, as in all nature, two kinds of magnetism, the positive and the negative. . . . If we were altogether negative, we should be rooted to the ground like trees; if we were altogether positive, we could not stay one moment on earth, and we should always be driven off its surface, because of the mutual repulsion of positive forces. . . ."[4]

This magnetism, which has only the name in common with the power studied in textbooks of physics, is—according to the same author—dependent on the will, at least among yogis and occultists, whence their faculty to rise up into the air at leisure; they have but to make themselves magnetically positive.[5]

This result is obtained in the yoga system of breathing, called *prânâyâma*, by drawing the air in and out according to certain rules. According to M. E. Bosc:

[1] Rochas, *Recueil*, pp. 98-99.   [2] *La lévitation*, pp. 19-47.
[3] *Le fluide des magnétiseurs*, ch. xiii.
[4] Rochas, *Recueil*, pp. 18-19.   [5] *Ibid.*

231

LEVITATION

" Levitation is the result of the control of breath practised by Oriental ascetics in order to gain spiritual peace, as a preparatory stage to spiritual illumination. When the yogi has reached a certain degree of spiritual progress by the control of breath named *prânâyâma* his purified spirit is saturated with a spiritual knowledge of the highest order. . . . When the training of the fakir is applied to the ethereal organism of man, they put him in connection with electro-telluric forces and give him a very effective control over them."[1]

The practices of yoga are to be found again in Taoism:

" The air," says Father Wieger, " should be breathed in through the nostrils very slowly, so gently that no noise is audible, and till the breast is filled to its utmost capacity. Then the air should be kept in as long as possible, at least the time of counting to one hundred and twenty. Then it should be completely breathed out, so softly that a swan's feather hanging before the mouth is not swung about. Then the same process is to be gone through all over again. . . . To be assimilable, the air must be *alive* and not *dead*; that is, the exercise must take place between midnight and midday, a period during which the air is *yang*; and not between midday and midnight, during which the air is *yinn*. The diet of those who practise this exercise must be vegetarian, for on meat diet the body would be too excited to be managed in the proper way."[2]

Animal magnetism has also been supposed to be able to produce attractive phenomena where the body of the subject is lifted off the ground by the extended hands of the magnetist. Phenomena of lightness and weight have even been said to be caused by simple suggestion of the hypnotist. De Mirville says that he saw a subject who, on a simple sign made by himself to the magnetist, became extremely light or heavy. He experienced the fact himself by carrying the hypnotised person on his back and ascertaining his seeming change of weight.[3]

Lastly, some say that levitation is caused by the dilatation of the fluidic or astral body, a subtle medium between the material body and the immaterial soul, an organism that is normally enclosed in the body proper, but is able to radiate from it. One Abbé Petit, mentioned by de Rochas in his essay in the *Annales des sciences psychiques*,[4] said he had twice been levitated in a church, and accounted for the

[1] *Yoghisme et fakirisme hindous*, pp. 111-112. The reader will excuse me if my respect for the original prevented my being more clear.
[2] *Histoire des croyances* . . ., p. 393.
[3] *Des esprits*, pp. 295-295.
[4] No. 1, 1901.

first of these upliftings by the occultist principle just referred to. The second phenomenon, he said, seemed different, for he had felt as if he had been carried away by an exterior power.

(c) Teleplastic Pseudopods

W. Crawford thought he had found in his experiments with the medium Kathleen Goligher the secret of telekinesis, which would at the same time account for the levitation of the human body. He said that the table lifted by the medium was supported on a sort of cantilever sprung from his body, made of an elastic and resisting matter, but invisible, stayed or not on the ground. " From a theoretical point of view," writes M. Sudre, " the levitation of a person is as easy to understand as that of an object. The teleplastic levers have naturally their fulcrum on the floor. Their shape is not definite; it may be that of a simple stay, of a cloudy cushion, or even a complete human materialisation. The force of gravity is not eluded, but simply opposed by a contrary upward power. The spent amount of energy is not above that required for the production of a fair phenomenon of telekinesis."[1]

(d) Fascination

L. Jacolliot, whose account of a fakir's levitation I have reproduced above,[2] declared that he could explain the prodigy only by a suggestion of the Indian, " par un sommeil magnétique le laissant lucide tout en lui laissant voir par la pensée du fakir tout ce qui pouvait lui plaire."[3]

It was in the same way that Count Spada accounted for the strange feats he had seen performed by Home. " Nous pensons," he said, " que Home exerce sur les personnes présentes une fascination qui leur fait voir ce qui n'est pas."[4] The same supposition has been made by an author who had examined the problems of mediumship with a peculiar attention, Frank Podmore:

" There are," he says, " some grounds for supposing that the habitués of Home's séances exhibited a suggestibility and a tendency to hallucination above the common. Partly this was due, it is likely, to peculiarities of temperament in the witnesses. *But it seems possible that in part it may have been due to some power possessed*

---

[1] Sudre, pp. 248-249. [2] Supra, Bk. I, pt. i, ch. i, par. 2.
[3] Quoted by de Rochas, *Recueil*, pp. 10-11.
[4] Gougenot des Mousseaux, *Les moyens et les médiateurs de la magie*, pp. 27-28.

233

by *Home* in common with other mediums. Madame Blavatsky appears to have possessed on occasion the power of causing the persons in her train to see visions and dream dreams. And two or three persons have testified to having seen hallucinatory figures and heard sounds, which may also have been hallucinatory, in company of Miss Freer. There is, then, some evidence for the view that a medium's equipment may include a faculty of inducing false perception in his clients."[1]

This hypothesis might be, theoretically, extended to all kinds of levitation.

§ 2. Criticism

The reader must have found the above survey rather delusive. Without going into details, he has already noticed that none among the proposed theories affords at best an explanation of levitation available for every class of the phenomenon. The criticism I shall give of them will be generally short, and in some cases is solely for form's sake.

(a) Electricity

It is surprising that de Rochas, who might have found in his scientific culture an antidote to his native credulity, has allowed himself to be misled by the so-called electrical explanation. Indeed, if electric effluvia are emitted by the feet and knees of the levitated person, why do they repulse the ground instead of getting lost in it ? And if it is supposed that the body is not repulsed from the ground, but attracted from above, where is the electric source from which the attraction issues ?

As Father Poulain observes, why do not the champions of the electrical theory try to test it by means of some experiments ? A statue provided with an electrogenous apparatus should be lifted up into the air just like a levitated human body.[2]

Others do not speak of repulsion or attraction, but of reduction of weight by electrisation. And de Rochas quotes in support of this theory, which he seems again very eclectically to patronise, the experiments of a German physicist of the eighteenth century and of the Abbé Nollet at the same epoch. The choice of such obsolete authorities, especially in a science as progressive as electricity, cannot pass for very fortunate. At any rate, it should be observed that no modern

---

[1] F. Podmore, *Modern Spiritualism*, vol. ii, p. 268. Professor Balfour Stuart also believed that Home managed to influence those present at his séances, by what he names " electro-biological power " (*D. D. Home*, p. 339).

[2] *Des grâces d'oraison*, ch. xxi, § 5.

physicist's experiment has ever confirmed that electrisation was able to alter the weight of anything.

Besides, it is remarkable that if the vertical uplifting of the body could be accounted for by electric repulsion, the same explanation could not apply to a movement of horizontal or oblique translation.

Lastly, if all these objections were removed, we should be still confronted with another problem: in levitation, why does the electric phenomenon take place only in psychical circumstances which every physician is regularly entitled to ignore in his laboratory?

(b) Nondescript Forces

Nondescript forces may be named od, vital fluid, magnetic fluid, or otherwise: the common fault with them is not only that which is implied by their epithet, but to have been imagined with the purpose of accounting for numerous, heterogeneous, and often doubtful phenomena. The uncertainty is not only about their existence, but about some of the facts that it is their special office to explain. Indeed, they are like a powerful and capricious *deus ex machina*, whose action has nothing to do with the forces usually dealt with in experimental science. They are so subtle, so varied and whimsical in their effects, their working seems dependent on such immaterial conditions that, classing them among natural forces—even with the acknowledgment of their indeterminate character—is suggestive of a tendency to sloppy-mindedness in those who resort to them.

Supposing any such fluid as the odic to be existent, it is to be observed that its emission is in close dependence on the health of the subject, and on many other minute details, which are to be taken into account in the experiments.[1] Now, levitation has been shown to be a less delicate manifestation with the mystics, as far as the material conditions of its production are concerned.

As to the magnetised persons who are said to have been lifted from the ground as a seeming consequence of magnetisation, it is difficult to know the truth about it by reason of the very small number of cases and of their private character. As I have observed before, this effect of animal magnetism has not been mentioned by the most famous magnetists, and this is enough to make us suspicious about the few assertions we have met with regarding the levitation of magnetised subjects. Besides, even if the few instances quoted were genuine, it is doubtful if they should be classed under the head levitation; indeed, this term denotes nothing but an uplifting of the

[1] Reichenbach, pp. 47 *ff*.

235

LEVITATION

body effected without any visible agency. In the levitation of the
saints, nobody is magnetised, nobody is submitted to any passing
of hands, nobody is to be seen from whom the attractive force might
be issuing. And if one admits that an invisible being plays the role
of magnetiser, the action of magnetism has become superfluous,
as we are no longer on naturalistic ground.

Lastly, it is to be noticed that the classing of so-called magnetic
levitation under the head magnetism may be regarded as arbitrary
as long as each of the cases has not been searchingly investigated.
It may be true that the subjects were magnetised, but the inference
that magnetisation was the cause of levitation may be erroneous.
J. Kerner thought that his passes were the cause of the buoyancy
of the Seeress of Prevorst, but the latter had another theory of her
own; she believed, like any other medium, that she enjoyed the protection of a familiar spirit (*Schutzgeist*), who freed her from the influence of natural laws.[1] The attribution of her faculty to mediumship, possession, witchcraft, or magnetism depends, after all, much
more on the general philosophy of the observer than on scientific
induction.

(c) Teleplastic Pseudopods

To simplify the discussion, we will regard the reality of the cantilever of Crawford as established, and we will admit that some organ-
isms are endowed with the faculty of developing out of themselves
invisible but strong tentacles by means of which they are able to take
hold of, and remove, distant objects.

Possibly this mechanism accounts satisfactorily for the phenomena of telekinesis, and even for human levitation, such as they are
experienced in mediumistic séances; but it is obviously inadequate
as far as the levitation of the mystics is concerned. Indeed:

1. The growing of the said tentacles is known to be checked
by full light. They develop only in the dark or in subdued red
light. Nay, their substance is so exquisitely delicate that the simple
act of gazing at them with too much inquisitiveness is apt to jeopar-
dise their existence.[2] Now, we know that those present at the levitations of the mystics never bethought themselves of such precautions.

[1] J. Kerner, p. 17.
[2] I may seem to exaggerate, but I do not, as the reader may satisfy
himself by reading the observations of von Schrenck-Notzing on the question
(p. 211). Even in the case of so powerful a medium as Home, it is said
that his manifestations were sometimes checked by people present being
" too positive " (*cf.* Podmore, *op. cit.*, vol. ii, p. 263).

236

2. The teleplastic formations—unless they escape the general law of metapsychical phenomena—depend more or less on the health of the subject; they cannot be expected to grow out of an exhausted body. On the other hand, we know that a condition of extreme weakness not only does not put a check on the phenomenon with the mystics, but seems rather to promote its production.

3. According to Dr. von Schrenck-Notzing, the teleplastic organs necessary to levitation are very short-lived formations; the force that produces them is soon exhausted. Besides, their power is limited, and the phenomena are no longer possible at a certain distance from the medium. Practically this distance should not exceed seven feet.[1] If it is so, one cannot help thinking that the pseudopods necessary to throw up Joseph of Copertino into the air and keep him suspended there several hours, would have been teleplastic excrescences of quite an abnormal character.

4. These organs, according to metapsychists, are nothing but the materialisation of implements intensely wanted by the medium to perform the prodigy which is expected of him. They are grown out of himself by a process of *ideoplasty*. The theory fits in admirably with what we know of the psychology of the medium, whose eager wish for success in the experiments is a common—and even necessary—feature; but it fails to account for the levitation of the saint, who infallibly distinguishes himself by a positive abhorrence of any such physical manifestations.

5. Some ecstatics were mobile in the air. Pushed upwards, they would keep the new position given to their body, and they would oscillate in a soft breeze like feathers. Such a phenomenon seems hardly compatible with the existence of a material support, fluid and elastic as it may be.

(d) Fascination

The criticism of this supposition need not go into details. In fact, it is not proved that suggestion is possible on a normal person, in a waking condition, without a previous training. Then far more improbable is it that such influence may be exerted on a whole crowd. Besides, even if it were possible, the hypothesis of fascination should be rejected in the case of the mystics, because they do not

[1] Schrenck-Notzing, p. 432.
237

want to be seen levitated, but actually loathe it. Lastly, we know that several saints were seen in this condition when they thought they were alone.

*   *   *   *   *

From the above survey and criticism, it appears that the theories proposed to explain the phenomenon of levitation in general are far from satisfactory. When they are not totally inadequate, they are partly so. None of them affords a shadow of an explanation regarding the levitation of the saints, which we are bound, from a purely positive point of view, to regard as a special type of phenomenon requiring an explanation of its own.

CHAPTER III

QUALIFIED SUPRANATURALISM

I CALL supranaturalist the theories according to which levitation is a phenomenon produced directly or indirectly by an immaterial intelligent free cause. Now, this cause is supposed to act through an unknown natural force which it sets working, and then the phenomenon remains in relationship with the determined course of natural laws through its instrumental cause. This is qualified supranaturalism. Now, the phenomenon is supposed to be wholly independent of any natural property of things or any unknown faculty of the soul; it is beyond nature both through the cause itself and the manner of its action. This is absolute supranaturalism.

§ 1. A Survey of the Theories

(a) J. J. von Görres[1]

The way in which the German writer has tried in his well-known treatise to account for levitation may be given as an instance of seminaturalism or qualified supranaturalism.

Görres supposes that levitation has its source in the human organism. It may be produced by a pathological process or by a mystical disposition of the soul, but in every case a natural mechanism pre-existing in the levitated person is responsible for the production of the phenomenon. Even if it has a supranatural origin, as in the case of the saint, it is an infallible result of definite conditions of

---

[1] It may be useful to remind some readers that Görres is not a religious, as Dr. Richet seems to believe (*Traité*, bk. iii, ch. iv, p. 693), but a political writer who became professor of physics, then of mythology and folk-lore, which he professed in Heidelberg (1806). His treatise on mysticism, *Die Christliche Mystik*, was published when he was a professor in Munich (1836–1842). This work is marred by daring and sometimes hardly intelligible theories, and also by a shocking lack of criticism. Nevertheless, it has the merit of being the first attempt to give a general history and explanation of the phenomena of mysticism.

239

body and soul. These conditions are for the body an ascetic training and for the soul a special gift of the Holy Ghost.[1] The levitation
of the saint is supranatural because its mechanism has been set
working by his holiness, a supranatural fruit of divine grace, but it is
natural as far as this mechanism had been provided by nature and
was ready for use. From the last point of view, mystical levitation
does not differ essentially from somnambulistic agility. The reason
why Görres requires a special operation of the Holy Ghost in the
case of the levitation of the saint is not very clear, for the same phenomenon may take place in a person who is neither a mystic nor a
demoniac nor a witch as the result of a somnambulistic fit,
which he compares to " a kind of interior tempest aroused by the
mechanical forces of the organism being suddenly upset."[2]

(b) Spiritualism

Most spiritualists, though they believe that levitation is wrought
by a spirit, and consequently adhere to a supranaturalist doctrine,
admit that the spirit acts on the levitated body through a means
borrowed from physical nature. So for Allan Kardec, when an
object is lifted into the air, it is because a spirit wraps it up in a kind
of fluidic atmosphere that neutralises the force of gravity just as the
air does with balloons and kites.[3]

§ 2. Criticism

(a) Görres

To be acceptable, the compromise of Görres should be first of all
divested of the masquerade of pseudo-scientific expressions which
makes his thought so perplexing. Secondly, his supposition that
levitation may be the result of a natural condition of the human
organism is far from being proved, and he does not give any convincing
instance of it. It is easy to show that the few cases that might be
invoked in favour of a natural explanation of the phenomenon can be
reduced to the traditional categories of possession or witchcraft.

Mocked by the rationalist, who reproaches him with his credulity,
Görres is not better used by the theologian, who cannot forgive him
for minimising the action of God in the production of mystical
levitation itself, by assuming a natural gear which it only sets working at the right moment. Besides, the necessity of this divine agency

[1] Vol. ii, ch. xxii and xxiii.   [2] Vol. iii, ch. xvii, pp. 273 ff.
[3] La genèse, les miracles et les prédictions selon le spiritisme, p. 326.

might be questioned in his system, as he admits that in the case of a somnambulist the human body may be raised into the air by a natural process. Hence the harsh appreciation of this theory by Abbé Ribet in his treatise.[1]

Still, some elements of it may be construed into a plausible system, if one is patient enough to disentangle them from their context of incoherence and obscurity. This is how it may be done. Some theologians think that the pure mystical fact, the union of the human soul with the divine essence, though it is wholly dependent on God's initiative, has its source in a natural mystical faculty in man. There is no reason why we should not try to adapt this opinion to a physical phenomenon of mysticism like levitation. So, transposing the commentary of Father Maréchal on the nature of mystical intuition, and applying it to levitation, we might say:

Theology has no compulsory doctrine on the nature of levitation. While the phenomenon, in the saints, is certainly supranatural *quoad modum*, by the way they obtain it, it may be thought to be natural *quoad se*—that is, in the forces that are employed to produce it.[2]

I need not say that in proposing this transposition, I do not profess to determine the limit of what a Catholic has to believe on the question. I have neither quality nor competence to draw such boundary line. Besides, Catholic dogma does not make any opinion compulsory in the matter. Father J. Maréchal himself writes about levitation: " Quant à la lévitation, *épisode purement accidentel et secondaire*, très inconstant d'ailleurs, décrit dans les extases profanes de Jamblique ou dans les états bizarres des fakirs indous aussi bien que dans les trances des médiums, *nous avouons n'avoir pas d'idée faite sur* sa nature et ses causes."[3]

(b) Spiritualism

Let us temporarily admit—despite theology and common-sense—that disembodied spirits are actually able to interfere in human affairs;

[1] Vol. iii, ch. xxxii, § vi.
[2] This is the passage I venture to paraphrase and adapt to my case: La théologie, *elle, n'a pas sur la nature de l'intuition mystique de tradition contraignante. On dirait en termes de l'École qu'alors même que les plus hauts degrés de contemplation seraient* certainement *surnaturels (en tant que* gratiae gratis datae *et non pas seulement en tant qu'actes méritoires), ils pourraient encore n'être pas surnaturels* quoad se, *dans leurs éléments constitutifs, mais seulement* quoad modum, *c'est à dire dans leurs circonstances effectives de collation.* (Études sur la psychologie des mystiques, p. 175. Cf. p. 253, 2°).
[3] p. 221.

and let us admit, in particular, that the levitation observed in mediumistic séances is actually due to the direct or indirect agency of such
spirits. Still, it does not follow that the more numerous, better
proved, more characteristic levitations of hagiography are amenable
to the same explanation. Indeed, if the spirits lift up into the air
the mediums who believe in them, pray to them, and have them prayed
to, why should they bestow the very same favour upon the saints,
who do not invoke them—or any other power either—and do not
wish to be granted supernatural faculties ?

So the least that can be said of the spiritualistic theory regarding
levitation is that it is sadly deficient, as it fails to account for a part
—and, indeed, the more important in quantity and in quality—of
the considered phenomena.

CHAPTER IV

ABSOLUTE SUPRANATURALISM

§ 1. *Account*

HERE it is at first admitted that levitation is essentially contrary to natural laws. According to Benedict XIV's expression, *Naturaliter dari non potest ut corpus a terra sublevetur.*[1] No attempt is made to assign a material means to the intelligent free cause of the phenomenon, whose intervention is wholly independent of any deterministic process, whose agency is derived from a transcendent power. This conception is traditionally that of Catholic theology, though it has no necessary relationship to its dogmas. It might assume a spiritualistic form, if the free intelligent cause was supposed to be a spirit other than God acting on the levitated body in a supernatural manner, exclusive of any natural means. Nevertheless, it is where it is practically met with, among Catholic theologians, that it will be examined hereafter. In fact, their theory, despite the unity derived from the above-mentioned principle, does not afford one but several solutions of the problem of levitation, according as the phenomenon is experienced by orthodox mystics or not.

(a) *Levitation of the Saints*

The classical opinion (Lopez Ezquerra, Scaramelli, Benedict XIV) regards levitation of the ecstatic as a miraculous communication of the agility of glorified bodies.[2] As the contemplation of the mystics is the prelude of their eternal beatitude, so their bodies are granted beforehand the effect of their future glorification. This charisma is purely gratuitous; it cannot be automatically obtained by any mode of life, it is not the fruit of any ascesis, it is not even the

---

[1] *De Canon. Sanct.*, bk. iii, ch. xlix, n. 3.
[2] Ribet, vol. ii, ch. xxxii, par. vi, p. 649. The belief in the agility of the glorious bodies is based on the passage in St Paul: (*Corpus*) *surget in virtute* (1 Cor. xv 43). According to the Apostle, the reformed man will have a body πνευματικόν, and no longer ψυχικόν, no longer ruled by the ψυχή, mere principle of life and sensitivity, but by the πνεῦμα, superior part of the soul, whose impulsions are sovereign.

inevitable result of a superior form of contemplation. Thus, though this theory admits the connection between levitation and the divine union of the mystic, it is in sharp contrast with the yoga doctrine according to which the emancipated soul recovers of itself its sovereign power over matter. Here the bodily aerial rapture is wholly dependent on the divine pleasure of God, who symbolises thus the likeness of his saints on earth and of his saints in heaven.

This view of theology fits in with the impressions of the mystics themselves. A famous ecstatic, whom her raptures would at times lift from the ground, Catherine of Siena, has given us the following account of the spiritual propriety of levitation in the form of a revelation: the perfect soul lives in constant union with God, so, says Christ to her, "though still associated with a mortal body, it enjoys the bliss of the immortals, and despite the weight of its body, it is granted the alacrity of the spirit. So the body is often lifted up from the earth as a result of this perfect union of the soul with me, as if it had lost its weight. It is not so, but as the union of the soul with me is more perfect than the union with the body, the power of the spirit fixed in me lifts the body from the earth."[1]

The spiritual efficiency of levitation as a charisma has been brought out into sharp relief by St Teresa:

"His Majesty so manifests itself that the hairs of my head stand upright, and a great fear comes upon me of offending God, who is so mighty. This fear is bound up in exceedingly great love, which is acquired anew, and directed to him, who bears so great a love to a worm so vile, and who seems not to be satisfied with attracting the soul to himself in so real a way, but who will have the body also, though it be mortal and of earth so foul, such as it is through our sins, which are so great."[2]

Still, it should be observed that the saint does not regard levitation as the sign of the highest mystical state. On the contrary, the soul that has reached the intimacy of the seventh mansions no longer experiences such rapturous flights.[3]

As it has been pointed out, the charismatic nature of levitation, though it is commonly admitted by Catholic theologians, is no corollary of Catholic dogma. A modern theologian as penetrating and widely informed as Father Léonce de Grandmaison did not hesitate to class levitation among the phenomena connected with

[1] *The Dialogue*, ch. xlix (79).
[2] *Life of St Teresa*, ch. xx, p. 163.
[3] *The Interior Castle*, Seventh Mansions, ch. iii.

ecstasy, which are " ni un honneur ni une puissance," but simply " un tribut payé par les mystiques à la fragilité humaine." The Abbé Bremond, from whom I am borrowing the quotation, sides in this with the learned Jesuit.[1]

Though they generally believe in the miraculous character of the levitation of the saints, Catholic theologians do not think themselves debarred from hypotheses on the *how* of the fact. Father Seraphin, for instance, accounts for the uplifting of the levitated body by saying that it actually loses its weight. Father A. Poulain, who mentions the supposition, observes that it is physically impossible, for if the body had no more weight it would behave in the air like a piece of cork in water; that is, it would be raised to the extreme limit of the atmosphere. " There is," he concludes, " a more simple explanation. The body is in the same condition as a balloon, which rises, reaches a position of equilibrium, and oscillates. Nothing is destroyed, but something is added; that is, a power equal and contrary to the weight."[2]

(b) Levitation of Witches and Demoniacs

Catholic theology believes that angelic or diabolic spirits have the power to move matter. It explains the levitation of demoniacs and sorcerers by the agency of malign spirits. In the former case it is a plague inflicted on a victim, in the latter case a favour bestowed on an ally.[3]

(c) Levitation of Mediums

If the levitation of the mediums is supposed to be something else than a subtle piece of trickery, a preternatural—but not miraculous—origin should be assigned to it. The intervention of an intelligent entity in the levitations produced in mediumistic séances is—according to Mgr. Farges—an explanation that forces itself on the candid observer, for the phenomena will take place when those present ask, or simply express a mental desire for them. And nothing but an intelligence is able to produce intelligent phenomena and draw physical effects from nature by its commands.[4]

Now, these entities cannot be disembodied souls, because the spirits of the dead are unable—unless through a miracle—to have intercourse with the world of the living and to move matter.[5]

Hence the levitation of the mediums, whenever it is not a cheat, is a diabolical achievement.[6]

[1] *Histoire littéraire*, vol. ii, p. 591.   [2] Poulain, ch. xxxi, par. 7, 1°.
[3] Ribet, vol. iii, ch. vii, par. ix-x.   [4] Farges, vol. ii, ch. iii, art. ii, par. iii.
[5] *Ibid.*   [6] *Ibid.*

LEVITATION

(d) Non-Christian Mystics

Catholic theology does not conceal its distrust of preternatural phenomena the divine origin of which is not vouched for by a life fitting in with its moral and ascetic ideal. So it maintains a prudent reserve regarding the supposed levitations of the mystics of Islamism, Buddhism, Parseeism, Taoism, or any other sect. Still, it does not deny *a priori* the possibility of a miracle in general—and consequently of levitation—in favour of a holiness outside Christianity. It assumes that the prodigies wrought by the devotees of magical cults, like the worshippers of Çakti, are diabolical in their origin, but it acknowledges that sincere ascetics seeking after divine union, in all humility and according to their means, may be the subjects of favours similar to those of its saints. This doctrine is expounded, for instance, by Father J. Maréchal regarding simple ecstasy, and may be extended to aerial rapture.

" . . . Does not Catholic theology teach that supernatural grace, whatever the way in which it is imparted, is not denied to any willing soul ? Then why should we refuse to admit that God may reveal himself still more directly, even outside Christianity, to some fervent ascetic, who searches after him in the dark, with humble, patient energy, perhaps through some queer exotic but moving processes ?"[1]

Father Maréchal expresses here nothing but a commonly accepted, though rather little known, doctrine. " It is a point of Catholic teaching," writes Abbé de Broglie, " that there are graces granted, and consequently prayers answered by the true God outside the external communion of the true Church." And Father de Grandmaison, from whom I am quoting the passage, recalls that this was St Augustine's theory.[2]

§ 2. CRITICISM

If the general *a priori* objection according to which any explanation resorting to spiritual forces, such as God, angels or demons, is invalid, the Catholic thesis offers the advantage of affording an interpretation of levitation that fits in more adequately than any other with the physical and psychological diversity revealed by a close observation of the phenomenon. In this, whatever may be the intrinsic value of its system, it keeps a narrower touch upon reality, and, as a schematic view, may be said to be more scientific and rational than the so-called rationalistic attempts.

[1] *Études sur la psychologie des mystiques*, p. 258.
[2] *Religion et critique*, p. 69. Quoted by L. de Grandmaison, " Le Sadhu Sundar Singh et le problème de la sainteté hors de l'église catholique," in *Recherches de science religieuse*, Jan.-April, 1922, pp. 18-19.

On the other hand, it does not profess to supply an analytic account of the phenomenon. It is content with seeing in the levitation of the saint a visible sign of divine possession that fills him with reverence and love. The marvel has its justification in its symbolism, and the supreme power that produces it dispenses with looking for its instrumental causes.

With this mystic symbolism of levitation may be connected an interpretation of it that has not been expounded, but which is involved in the commentary by E. Baumann on the vision by an English lady of the levitated Dominican on the deck of the sinking ship *Bourgogne*:

"The shipwrecked lady," he says, "*did see* something; but as she was the only one who saw, among the survivors, we are unable to settle whether her excitement created the phenomenon or if God, to enlighten her, revealed to her the anticipated glory of an elect soul."[1]

In such a case, levitation may be supposed to be a non-objective phenomenon, in the common acceptation of the word, but no less fraught with superior reality. It may be termed hallucination, but a divine one, infinitely truer than the short sight of the non-hallucinated people. According to this explanation, levitation is, in some cases, not a charisma of the levitated person, but of him who is granted the sight of it; and this interpretation accounts for some difficult cases, like that of A. H. Fournet, where a very sincere and trustworthy testimony does not receive from other circumstances a satisfactory confirmation.[2] This hypothesis has not to be extended to very definite facts where nothing suggests a resort to it.

An objection to the supranatural interpretation of the phenomenon may arise, in some minds, from the practical connection between levitation and a definite mode of living.

It is to be observed that the necessity of ascesis as a *condition* is not particular to levitation, but to every other phenomenon of the mystical life, including the psychological phenomena. If the soul, which has not gained a full mastery over the body with which it is associated, is found to be debarred from the higher form of contemplation, this does not entitle us to declare that mystical union is but a natural phenomenon, added *ex opere operato* to a mortified life. To do so would be to confuse *cause* and *condition*.

A proof that here the agency is actually foreign to the physical plan may be derived from the fact that the material mode of living

---

[1] Baumann, p. 392; cf. *supra*, p. 133.
[2] I am referring to the levitation at the calvary unnoticed by the parishioners of La Puye (*supra*, p. 123).

is unable to produce phenomena of the kind unless it is enforced by the will. It has already been remarked that there are lives where bitter mortifications are imposed by circumstances without ever winning for the victims the transcendent benefits of ascesis.

It has been remarked that the supranaturalistic interpretation of levitation in orthodox mystics, if traditional in Catholic theology, still remains a matter of personal opinion, and eminent theologians like Father J. Maréchal or L. de Grandmaison did not think themselves bound to adopt the classical view on the question. Far from considering as evident the miraculous nature of levitation, they feel inclined to regard it as a rather uncouth by-product of ecstatic rapture. Some will think that if this attitude is but prudent when it concerns certain physiological concomitant circumstances of ecstasy, like the slackening of the pulse, the cooling of the body or its insensibility, it reveals, in the case of levitation or ecstatic flight, a rather exaggerated contempt of the so-called somatic phenomena. Besides, on practical grounds, this position appears grievously impaired by the meeting—were it unique—with a case like that of Saint John of the Cross. For, after all, can we fairly label " physical taint " a phenomenon experienced by the least morbid of mystics, in whom contemplation was so ideally free from any physiological ambiguity? A strange shortcoming indeed, the rapture that snatches up from the floor the poet of *The Living Flame of Love* along with Teresa listening to him, in the parlour of the *Incarnacion* !

The assimilation of mediumistic levitation to a diabolic prodigy has a striking cohesion with the rest of the system. Indeed, it should be recalled that *the Catholic Church does not show less severity in the appreciation of the charismata of its own mystics*; any preternatural favour occurring in an ordinary life and not accompanied with a strong feeling of unworthiness seems utterly suspect to it. Whosoever avails himself of a revelation should be supposed self-deceived; according to Gerson: *deest enim pondus humilitatis.* Nay, prayers and orthodox practices (fasting, confession, communion), if they were resorted to with a view to gaining supernatural power, should be regarded as equivalent to an invocation of the Evil One.[1]

[1] *Summa*, II-II, q. 96, a. 1 (quoted by Ribet, vol. iii, pp. 318-319). It may be interesting to point out that this opinion is not peculiar to the Catholic Church. A sect of Darvishes like the Mâlamiûn regards as a sin the wish for supernatural faculties. The teaching of Buddha was in the same direction, and the modern ascetic Râmakrishna was averse to every theurgic power. (*Cf. Râmakrishna : His Life and Sayings*, London, 1910; Collected Works of Max Müller, xv.)

ABSOLUTE SUPRANATURALISM

Why should theology prove more lenient to mediums ?
It is vain to draw an objection against this doctrine from the respectability of any particular medium. D. D. Home displays his magic in every capital in Europe; Thomas of Villanova leaves off preaching so as not to be seen rapt in his pulpit. This is quite enough to go by. . . .

The theological point of view does not seem to have been understood by some metapsychists. They cannot help smiling or feeling indignant at the thought of this particular person, whom they are acquainted with, whom they are experimenting with, regarded by the Catholic Church as implicitly a witch or a latently possessed person.

Though the notion may seem distasteful to a non-Catholic, it is necessary to be aware of it, and to endeavour to gain a sufficient comprehension of it. Now, as it has just been shown, if certain premises are accepted, it presses itself upon the mind with impeccable logic.

So it would be childish to object that this or that amateur or professional medium has nothing to do with witchcraft because his manners are correct, his language is decent, and his life not scandalous. What is in point here is an inner attitude essentially unknown to, and practically unascertainable by the layman, which theology cannot appreciate otherwise than it does, and which it thinks to supply with a precious test for the trying of supernatural facts.

Even if it were probable or proved that there is no wilful participation in a malign power, the hypothesis of possession would not be eliminated of itself for those who adhere to this doctrine. In fact, it was the one explanation that forced itself upon the mind of a non-Catholic who had known D. D. Home for thirty years, who loved and thought highly of him, Dr. Thomas Hawksley, of London. Dr. Thomas Hawksley, asked for his opinion on the faculties of his former patient and friend, expressed himself as follows:

" After very careful study of the facts, I came to the conclusion that in all probability they were due to an intelligent spirit which possessed the body of my friend, and was able to leave his body for the purpose of enacting various things at a distance from him. . . . Assuredly, in the case of Mr. Home, though I am driven to think he was possessed, my knowledge of his life and habits made me a profound believer in his truth, honesty, warmth of heart, kindness, generosity, and goodness."[1]

[1] *D. D. Home*, pp. 188-189.

249

CONCLUSIONS

IT is now time to draw from this work the chief conclusions. They may be summed up in the following form:

1. According to very old traditions of various origins, the human body is apt, in certain circumstances, to elude the law of gravity.

2. Catholic hagiography alone is in possession of an ancient written tradition, continuous and varied, based on verified and accurate documents, on levitation. Still, every fact recorded elsewhere, as those regarding demoniacs, mediums, and non-Catholic mystics, may not be imaginary.

3. Catholic hagiography, among doubtful or even seemingly interpolated facts, presents a number of cases where the evidence for levitation offers the security usually required from historical documents.

4. Those who reject these facts as *impossible* meet an historical assertion with a denial which it behoves them to make good on the ground of historical criticism. The most efficient process seems to pick out one of the best-established cases—that of Joseph of Copertino, for instance, to start with—and to demonstrate its weakness by exposing fraud or error in it. Such a test has never been tried.

5. Those who account for the belief in levitation by an illusion of the mystics or witnesses betray a superficial knowledge of the question. Their arguments can satisfy only a prepossessed mind. Practically these deniers do not form a category different from the preceding ones.

6. If the levitation of mediums is regarded as genuine, the analysis of its physical characteristics and the description of its psychological circumstances preclude any likening of it to that of Catholic mystics.

250

CONCLUSIONS

7. The problem of levitation presents itself in terms that do not fit in with the method of physics. The pseudo-scientific solutions proposed to account for the phenomenon are valueless, at least as a *general* explanation, and there is no sign that something better may be found out in the future. Indeed, levitation is always connected with moral circumstances: a certain way of thinking, of feeling and living. The conjunction of two distinct orders, " cet effet qui excède la force naturelle qu'on emploie," as Pascal would say, does not suggest the agency of an *unknown* natural power, but of a cause that is *heterogeneous* to every natural force.

8. Traditional Catholic theology does not admit a natural cause for levitation—though this attitude has no necessary relationship with its dogma. It regards it as a divine marvel or a diabolic trickery. The levitation of demoniacs or mediums is a parody, dismal or ludicrous, of the charisma of its saints. As to that of non-Catholic or even pagan mystics, it does not *a priori* deny its divine origin; the nature of the phenomenon in each case is to be judged after the moral context of the life in which it occurs.

APPENDIX I

INSTANCES OF LEVITATION THAT HAVE NOT BEEN INSERTED
IN THIS VOLUME

I HAVE mentioned hereafter some names of levitated saints or mystics, about whom I had not enough information, or even no information at all. Those of whom chronological details were available might indeed have been placed in their proper place in the second book of the present work, and it has been done for some of them, but I have thought that too great a number of mere mentions without any concrete details was likely to encumber the text without profit. So I made up my mind to defer them to this appendix.

ADELAIDE OF ADELHAUSEN.—Dominican. Görres, *La mystique*, vol. ii, ch. xxii, p. 299.
AGNES OF CHÂTILLON.—*Ibid.*, p. 313.
ALPHONSUS OF HERRERA.—*Ibid.*
ANGIOLO OF MILAN. — Imbert-Gourbeyre, *Les stigmatisées*, vol. ii, p. 234, n. 1.
ANTOINETTE MIET (†1657).—Ursuline of Roanne. Imbert-Gourbeyre, *La stigmatisation*, vol. ii, p. 239, n. 1.
ANTONY OF NARDO.—Franciscan. Imbert-Gourbeyre, *ibid.*, p. 241.
ARMELLE NICOLAS (1606–†1671).—*Ibid.*, p. 322.
CATHERINE TEXADA.—Carmelite. Imbert-Gourbeyre, *Les stigmatisées*, vol. ii, p. 234, n. 1.
CHRISTIAN (*thirteenth century*).—Görres, vol. ii, ch. xxi, p. 289 (probably the Blessed Christian of Perugia, one of the first disciples of St Dominic).
ELISABETH OF FALKENSTEIN.—Dominican. Görres, vol. ii, ch. xxii, p. 311.
FLORA, BLESSED (†1247).—Order of Malta. *La stigmatisation*, vol. ii, p. 239, n. 1.
FRANCES OF SERRONE (1557–†1600).—Franciscan. *Ibid.*
FRANCES OLYMPIA.—Görres, vol. ii, ch. xxi, p. 284.
GASPAR DE BONO, BLESSED (1530–†1604).—Minim. H. Thurston, p. 335.
GUILLEMETTE OF LA ROCHELLE (*fifteenth century*).—She came to live in Paris by Charles V's order. Christine de Pisan says "she was sometimes seen, in contemplation, raised more than two feet above the ground" (*Le livre des faits et bonnes mœurs du sage roi Charles V*, p. 228).
HUMILIANA, BLESSED (1219–†1246).—Franciscan. *A.S.*, May 19, p. 395.
HUMILIS OF BISIGNANO, BLESSED (1582–†1637).—Franciscan lay-brother.

252

APPENDIX I

Shown levitated in an old engraving reproduced in the article by de Rochas, "La lévitation," in *Annales des sciences psychiques*, 1901, No. 1, fig. 10.

IGNATIUS BALSAMO (*seventeenth century*). Jesuit. *Revue d'Ascétique et de Mystique*, 1921, No. 6, p. 163, n. 1.

ISABELLA SANCHEZ.—Franciscan. *La stigmatisation*, vol. ii, p. 262.

JERONIMA CARVALHO (†1585).—Dominican. *La stigmatisation*, vol. ii, p. 239, n. 1.

JOAN MARY BONOMI, BLESSED (1606-†1670).—Benedictine. *Ibid.*, p. 239, n. 1.

JOAN MARY OF MAILLÉ, BLESSED (1332-†1414).—Franciscan. *Ibid.*

JUANA DE LA ENCARNACION (†1705).—H. Thurston, p. 335 (referring to *Passion de Christo*, by L. J. Zevallos, pp. 23-24).

LEO OF CATANA.—De Bonniot, *Le miracle et ses contrefaçons*, p. 364.

LIBERATO OF CIVITELLA (†1479).—Franciscan. Görres, vol. ii, ch. xxi, p. 284.

LORENZO DA BRINDISI, BLESSED (†1619).—Capuchin. H. Thurston, p. 335 (*Ristretto*, B. da Coggaglia, pp. 136, 196).

LOUIS OF MANTUA (*sixteenth century*).—Franciscan. Görres, vol. ii, ch. xxi, p. 288.

LUKE OF CIRAMO (1543-†1603).—Franciscan. *Les stigmatisées*, vol. ii, p. 285.

MARGARET EBNER (1291-†1351).—Dominican. *La stigmatisation*, vol. ii, p. 239, n. 1.

MARIA MINIMA STROZZI (†1672).—H. Thurston (referring to *Vita*, anonymous, p. 19).

MARIANNE OF JESUS (1555-†1635).—Clare. *La stigmatisation*, vol. ii, p. 268, n. 1.

MARTIN OF PORRES, BLESSED (1579-†1630).—Dominican. Shown levitated in the reproduction of a painting by La Piccola in de Rochas' "La lévitation" (*Annales des sciences psychiques*, 1901, No. 1, fig. 2).

MARY GOMEZ.—Görres, vol. ii, ch. xxi, p. 284.

MARY OF BLONDEAU (1573-†1635).—Dominican. *Ibid.*, vol. i, p. 252. *La stigmatisation.*

MATTHEW OF BASCIO.—Görres, vol. ii, ch. xxi, p. 284.

MICHAEL LAZAR (1570-†1602).—Dominican. *Ibid.*, ch. xxii, p. 313.

NICHOLAS FACTOR, BLESSED (1520-†1585).—Franciscan. *Ibid.*, ch. xxi, p. 284. *Vida*, by Moreno, pp. 128-129 (quoted by H. Thurston, p. 335).

PAUL OF SOGLIANO.—Imbert-Gourbeyre, *La stigmatisation*, vol. ii, p. 274.

PETER OF GUARDA (1435-†1505).—Franciscan. Görres, vol. ii, ch. xxi, p. 284.

PHILIP OF CASTILE.—Franciscan. *Ibid.*, p. 266. *La stigmatisation*, vol. ii., p. 266.

PUDENZIANA ZAGNONI (1608).—Franciscan. *La stigmatisation*, vol. i, p. 197.

RANIERO OF BORGO DI SAN SEPOLCRO, BLESSED (†1580).—Franciscan. *Ibid.*, p. 239, n. 1.

RAYMUND ROCCO (1583-†1655).—Dominican. *Ibid.*, vol. ii, p. 135.

ROSANA BATTISTA (1610-†1663).—Franciscan. *Ibid.*, vol. i, p. 305.

SPERANZA OF BRENEGALLA.—Görres, vol. ii, ch. xxii, p. 300.

VERONICA LAPARELLI (†1620).—H. Thurston, p. 335 (referring to Process, *Summario*, pp. 138, 141).

LEVITATION

VERONICA OF THE HEART OF JESUS (1825–†1883).—Foundress of the *Sœurs Victimes du Sacré-Cœur.* Mentioned in *Dictionnaire pratique des connaissances catholiques, s.v.* " Lévitation " (by L. Roure).

VITO DE MARTINA.—Franciscan. *La stigmatisation,* vol. ii, pp. 247, 282.

WALTHER (†1264).—Dominican. *Ibid.,* vol. i, p. 15.

*   *   *   *   *

To these saints or holy personages should be added the strange prophet Eugène Vintras, who is said by J. Bricaud to have been sometimes levitated in the presence of witnesses.[1] The author has been kind enough to give me some information about the said witnesses, who were, among others, the Abbé Breton and M. Edouard Souleillon, of Lyons, who were on intimate terms with Vintras.

Vintras's sect was condemned by papal brief on November 8, 1843. The visionary answered the sanction by proclaiming himself sovereign pontiff. He would wear a purple robe, carry a magic sceptre, and in his diadem the Indian lingam shone.[2]

New instances of mediumistic levitation are recorded in the communication of Dr. Albert von Schrenck-Notzing to the Third International Congress for Psychical Research held in Paris in 1927,[3] the Proceedings of which have just been published. Dr. von Schrenck-Notzing says he was able to observe no less than thirty-five levitations with the medium, Karl Weber (this is a pseudonym), from the middle of June to the end of August, 1924, either in his own laboratory or at Professor Gruber's. The levitations lasted at most twenty-five seconds. The medium's body was lifted vertically or horizontally four or five feet over the floor. On August 18, 1924, Weber failed in his attempts and even took a fall. The séances took place in the dark, but luminous strings round the medium's body enabled the bystanders to follow all his movements. Weber's psychological idiosyncrasy is quite similar to that of Willy Sch. (cf. *supra,* p. 202). He is said to have undergone a special training in order to obtain abnormal powers.[4]

[1] *L'abbé Boullan,* p. 28.

[2] I borrow these details from Eliphas Lévi's *Histoire de la magie,* p. 487.

[3] " Über einen Fall willkürlicher Erzeugung paraphysischer Phäno-mene," in *Compte Rendu du IIIᵉ Congrès International de Recherches Psychiques,* pp. 92-94.

[4] " Webers Charakter lässt einen stark hysterischen Einschlag erkennen. Ein Gegner der spiritistischen Theorie, versuchte er durch psychotechnische Yogaübungen (Atemgymnastik, Vertiefung und Verdeutlichung des Kör-pergefühls, eidetische Steigerung des Anschauungsvermögens bis zur höch-sten Potenz) seinen Vorstellungen den Charakter der Naturwirklichkeit zu geben, obwohl die ersten Phaenomene bei ihm unter der Form spiritistischer Sitzungen beobachtet wurden."—*Ibid.,* p. 92.

APPENDIX II

W HEN I wrote the passages of the present book referring to the levitation of demoniacs, the phenomena recorded by the Curé of Wickerschwihr (near Colmar) in his work on the possessed boys of Illfurt were unknown to me. It is now too late to alter my text, but I desire to say that the facts mentioned in Abbé Sutter's book seem to me well established enough to require a marked qualification of the opinion expressed by me on the matter. Indeed, the possessed boys, Thiébaut and Joseph Burner, are formally said by divers eye-witnesses to have been actually lifted above the ground in several of their fits. Here are two of the passages of the book referring to the said phenomena:

Page 78 (after the notes of Professor Lachemann): "When the possessed boy was sitting on a chair, the latter was often raised with him into the air, then fell down again with force on the floor; the chair would fly into a corner and the child into another. The latter's mother herself sitting by her child was thus lifted with him and flung into a corner without being hurt."

Page 111 (after the report of M. Werner, Brigadier of Gendarmerie at Illfurt): " In February 1869, in the afternoon, I was with the children. . . . Their mother seated them on chairs near the stove. . . . I was about to leave the place, exchanging some words with M. Frindel, the station-master, on the landing place, when we heard cries coming from the room. We hastily entered and saw Thiébaut lifted by a mysterious force and suspended twelve or fifteen inches over his chair. He remained several minutes in this position. Everyone present was quite excited. A girl took hold of a holy water vessel and besprinkled the boy, who, after a short delay, started coming down again with jerks on to his seat. He looked exhausted and asked to be put to bed. The parents and some bystanders whom I questioned told me that the same thing had already happened several times to the two boys. . . ."[1]

[1] *Le diable, ses paroles, son action dans les possédés d'Illfurt, etc.*, 4th ed., Arras, 1926.

255

BIBLIOGRAPHICAL INDEX

A few of the following works have not been consulted directly by the author, who has still thought it advisable to mention them hereafter to facilitate the checking of his quotations.

AL-HUJWÎRI. The Kashf-al Mahjûb. Translated by R. A. Nicholson. London, 1911.

AMÉLINEAU (E.). Les moines égyptiens. Vie de Schnoudi (Annales du Musée Guimet, Paris, 1889).

AMELOTE (FATHER). Vie de sœur Marguerite du Saint-Sacrement. Paris, 1654.

AMEYUGO (F. FRANCISCUS DE). Novum gratiae prodigium, sive vita venerabilis matris sororis Joannae a Jesu Maria, etc. Coloniae, 1689.

ARNAUD D'ANDILLY. Les vies des Saints Pères des déserts, etc. 3 vols. Paris, 1733.

ARNOBIUS. Adversus gentes. (Migne's Latin Patrology, vol. v.)

ARTURUS. Martyrologium franciscanum. Paris, 1638.

ASIN PALACIOS (M.). La mystique d'al-Gazzali. (Proceedings of Semaine d'ethnologie religieuse, Louvain, 1914.)
Une introduction musulmane à la vie spirituelle. (Revue d'ascétique et de mystique, vol. iv, July to October, 1923.)

ATHANASIUS (ST). Vita sancti Ammoni. (Acta sanctorum, vol. ii of January.)

BAILLARGER (DR. J.). De l'influence de l'état intermédiaire à la veille et au sommeil sur la production et la marche des hallucinations. Paris, 1846.

BARNABEI (JEROME). Vita S Philippi Nerii. (Acta sanctorum, vol. iii of May.)

BARTOLI (FATHER D.). Histoire de saint Ignace de Loyola, etc. 2 vols. Paris, 1844.

BAUDOT (DOM). Dictionnaire d'hagiographie. Paris, 1925.

BAUMANN (E.). Mon frère le Dominicain. (Le Roseau d'Or, 4th no. of chronicles, Paris, 1927.)

BAYLE (P.). Dictionnaire historique et critique. 3rd ed., 4 vols. Rotterdam, 1720.

BELL (R.). Stranger than Fiction. (Cornhill Magazine, August, 1860.)

BENEDICT XIV. De servorum Dei beatificatione et sanctorum canonizatione. 7 vols. Venice, 1764-1767.

BENET (A.). Procès-verbal fait pour délivrer une fille possédée par le malin esprit à Louviers, etc. Paris, 1883.

BERNINO (D.). Vie de St Joseph de Cupertino de l'Ordre des Frères Mineurs Conventuels. Paris, 1856. (Translation of Vita del Padre Fr. Giuseppe da Copertino de' Minori Conventuali, etc. Roma, 1722.)

256

BIBLIOGRAPHICAL INDEX

BERSANGE (ABBÉ J.). Mme du Bourg, Mère Marie de Jésus, fondatrice de la congrégation des Sœurs du Sauveur et de la Sainte-Vierge. Paris and Lyon, n.d.
BERTHE (FATHER). S Alphonse de Liguori. 2 vols. Paris, 1906.
BINI (GIOVANNI E.). Vita della Serva di Dio Maria Domenica Barbagli del Monte San Savino. Firenze, 1873.
BLANC (HIPPOLYTE). Le merveilleux dans le jansénisme, le magnétisme, le méthodisme américains, l'épidémie de Morzine, le spiritisme. Recherches nouvelles. Paris, 1865.
BODIN (J.). De la Démonomanie des sorciers. Paris, 1582.
BOIRAC (E.). La psychologie inconnue, etc. Paris, 1912.
BOLLANDISTS. Acta Sanctorum, January to November, 67 vols. Paris, 1863–1875–1928.
BONNIOT (J. DE). Le miracle et les sciences médicales. Paris, 1879. Le miracle et ses contrefaçons. 5th ed. Paris, 1895.
BORÉ (L.). Les stigmatisées du Tyrol. 2nd ed. Paris, 1846.
BOSC (E.). Yoghisme et fakirisme hindous. Paris, 1913.
BOUCHER (J. B. A.). Histoire de la bienheureuse Marie de l'Incarnation dite dans le monde Madame Acarie. 2 vols. Paris, 1854.
BOUHOURS (FATHER). La vie de saint François-Xavier, apôtre des Indes et du Japon. 2 vols. Paris, 1810.
BOUIX (M.). Vie de Marcelline Pauper de la congrégation des Sœurs de la Charité de Nevers. Nevers, 1871.
BOURDENNE (FATHER). La vie et l'œuvre du vénérable Michel Garicoïts. Paris, 1918.
BOURG (G. DU). Une fondatrice au xixᵉ siècle. Paris, 1914.
BOURRU (H.) et BUROT (P.). La suggestion mentale et l'action à distance des substances toxiques et médicamenteuses. Paris, 1887.
BREMOND (H.). Histoire littéraire du sentiment religieux en France. 6 vols. Paris, 1900–1924.
BRICAUD (J.). L'abbé Boullan. Paris, 1927.
BROGNOLI (CANDIDO). Manuale exorcistarum. Bergomi, 1651.
BROWN (JOHN P.). The Darvishes or Oriental Spiritualism. London, 1927.
BROWNE (E. G.). A Literary History of Persia. 4 vols. London, 1902 ff.
BRUNET (G.). Les évangiles apocryphes, traduits et annotés d'après l'édition de J.-C. Thilo. 2nd ed. Paris, 1863.
BURNOUF (EUG.). Introduction à l'histoire du Bouddhisme indien. Paris, 1844.
BUTLER (ALBAN). The Lives of the Fathers, Martyrs, and other Principal Saints, etc. 7 vols. London, 1756–1759.
BUZY (D.). Vie de sœur Marie de Jésus Crucifié, religieuse carmélite converse morte en odeur de sainteté au Carmel de Bethléem (1846–1878). Bar-le-Duc and Paris, 1922.
CAHAGNET (L. A.). Magie magnétique, etc. Paris, 1854.
CALMEIL (A.). De la folie. 2 vols. Paris, 1845.

257

LEVITATION

CARAMUEL (J.). Caramuelis Dominicus: hoc est venerabilis P. Dominici a Jesu Maria, parthenii ordinis carmel. excalceat., etc. Viennae in Austria, 1655.

CARRA DE VAUX. Les penseurs de l'Islam. 5 vols. Paris, 1921–1926.

CASIMIR DE TOLOSE. La vanité combattue et surmontée par la fille forte ou la vie pénitente de sœur Jaquette de Bachelier. Béziers, 1678.

CATHERINE OF SIENA. See HURTAUD.

CEPARI. Vita B. Aloysii Gonzagae, S.J. (*Acta Sanctorum*, vol. v of June.)

CHAMPAULT (CHANOINE). Une possédée contemporaine (1834–1914), Hélène Poirier de Coullons (Loiret). Paris, 1924.

CHARBONNIER (DR. N.). Maladies et facultés diverses des mystiques. Bruxelles, 1875.

CHARPIGNON (J.). Physiologie, médecine et métaphysique du magnétisme animal. Paris, 1848.

CHÉRANCÉ (L. DE). Sainte Marguerite de Cortone. Paris, 1896.

CHRISTINE DE PISAN. Le livre des faits et bonnes mœurs du sage roi Charles V (*Choix de chroniques*, etc., par J. Buchon, Orléans, 1875).

DARAS (E.). Les saints et les bienheureux du xviii⁰ siècle. 2 vols. Paris, 1867.

DAVID-NEEL (ALEXANDRA). Le Thibet mystique. (*Revue de Paris*, February, 1928).

DAVIS (HADLAND). Among the Adepts and Mystics of Hindustan. (*Occult Review*, December, 1905.)

DEBERRE (ABBÉ). Histoire de la vénérable Marguerite du Saint-Sacrement, Carmélite de Beaune. Paris, 1907.

DELEHAYE (HIPPOLYTE). Les légendes hagiographiques. Bruxelles, 1905. Sanctus, Essai sur le culte des saints dans l'antiquité. Bruxelles, 1927.

DELORME (F. M.). Pour l'histoire des martyrs du Maroc. (*La France Franciscaine*, vol. vii, Paris, 1924.) La Legenda Antiqua S Francisci. Paris, 1926.

DEL RIO (M.). Disquisitionum magicarum libri sex, etc. Lugduni, 1612.

DENIS (M.). Saint Joseph de Copertino. Paris, 1820.

DESNOYERS (M. J.). Le vénérable Benoît-Joseph Labre, etc. 2 vols. Lille, 1857.

DIODATO DELL' ASSUNTA. Vita di S Giangiuseppe della Croce, etc. Roma, 1839.

DOUGLAS (NORMAN). A Pioneer of Aviation. (*North American Review*, July, 1913.)

DUNOYER (FATHER). Vie de Saint Gérard Majella. Paris, 1914.

DU VAL (A.). Vie admirable de la bienheureuse sœur Marie de l'Incarnation, etc. Paris, 1893.

ERNY (A.). Le psychisme expérimental. Étude des phénomènes psychiques. Paris, 1895.

EUNAPIUS. Eunapii Sardiani vitas sophistarum recensuit Boissonade. Amsterdam, 1822.

FABER (F. W.). Notes on Doctrinal and Spiritual Subjects. 2nd ed., 2 vols. London, 1872.

BIBLIOGRAPHICAL INDEX

FAGES (FATHER). Histoire de saint Vincent Ferrier. 2 vols. Paris, 1901.

FAGOT (F.). St François d'Assise raconté par ses premiers compagnons (translation of *Legenda Antiqua*, edited by Father Delorme). Paris, 1927.

FARGES (A.). Les phénomènes mystiques distingués de leurs contrefaçons humaines et diaboliques, etc. 2 vols. Paris, 1923.

FÉLIX DE JÉSUS CRUCIFIÉ (FATHER). Gemma Galgani. Arras, 1910.

FIGUIER (L.). Histoire du Merveilleux dans les temps modernes. 4 vols. Paris, 1860.

FILIPPO DELLA S TRINITA. Vita dell' V. P. Domenica di Gesu Maria. Roma, 1668.

FLÉCHIER (E.). Mémoires sur les grands jours tenus à Clermont en 1665, annotés et augmentés d'un appendice par M. Chéruel, etc. Paris, 1856.

FLEURIAU (B. G.). La vie du vénérable Père Pierre Claver, etc. 2 vols. Paris, 1830.

FONTANA (L. M.). Vita della vittima riparatrice la serva di Dio Suor Maria della Passione, etc. 4th ed. Scansano, 1921.

FRANCIOSI (ERNESTO Mᴬ). Vita di S Giuseppe da Copertino dell' ordine dei Minori Conventuali. Recanati, 1925.

FRANCLIEU (A. M. DE). Vie de M. Claude Dhière, Directeur du Grand Séminaire de Grenoble, etc. Grenoble, 1882.

FRUNGILLO (R.). Vita della ven. serva di Dio suor Maria Crocifissa delle Piaghe, etc. Napoli, 1876.

FUGAIRON (S. L.). Essai sur les phénomènes électriques des êtres vivants comprenant l'explication scientifique des phénomènes dits spirites. Paris, 1894.

GALLONIO (A.). Vita Beati Philippi Nerii florentini, etc. Romae, 1600.

GARÇON (M) ET VINCHON (J.). Le diable. Paris, 1926.

GARINET (J.). Histoire de la magie en France. Paris, 1818.

GERMANO DI STANISLAO. Compendio della biografia della Serva di Dio Gemma Galgani. 10th ed. Roma, 1915.

GIBIER (DR. P.). Analyse des choses, etc. Paris, 1890.

GLANVIL (J.). Sadducismus Triumphatus, or a full and plain Evidence concerning Witches and Witchcraft, etc. London, 1726.

GODARD (CH.). Le fakirisme. Paris, 1910.

GOETHE. Italiänische Reise, herausgegeben von Christian Schuchardt. 2 vols. Stuttgart, 1862.

GÖRRES (J. J. VON). La mystique divine, naturelle et diabolique (translation of *Die Christliche Mystik*, by Ch. de Sainte-Foi). 5 vols. Paris, 1854–1855.

GOUGENOT DES MOUSSEAUX. La magie au xixᵉ siècle, etc. Paris, 1864.

GOUT (R.). La vie de sainte Douceline, texte provençal du xivᵉ siècle (traduction et notes par R. Gout). Paris, 1927.

GRANDMAISON (L. DE). Le Sadhu Sundar Singh et le problème de la sainteté hors de l'église catholique. (*Recherches de science religieuse*, January to April, 1922.)

GRASSET (DR. J.). L'occultisme hier et aujourd'hui. Le merveilleux préscientifique. 2nd ed., Montpellier, 1908.)

LEVITATION

GUÉRIN (MGR. P.). Le Palmier Séraphique ou vies des saints et des hommes et femmes illustres des trois ordres de saint François. 12 vols. Barle-Duc, 1872–1875.

GUILLOUZOU (R.). Vie de la sœur Marie Paret. Clermont, 1678.

GUIRAUD (J.). Saint Dominique. 6th ed. Paris, 1909.

HARDY (R. SPENCE). A Manual of Buddhism in its Modern Development (translated from Singhalese MSS.). London, 1853.

    Eastern Monachism: An Account of the Origin, Laws, etc., of the Order of Mendicants founded by Gotama Buddha. London, 1860.

HÉLOT (DR. CH.). Névroses et possessions diaboliques. Paris, 1897.

HEREDIA (C. M. DE). Spiritism and Common Sense. New York, 1922.

HILARY (ST). Liber contra Constantium Imperatorem (Migne's *Latin Patrology*, vol. x).

HOME (D. D.) Incidents in my Life. London, 1863.

HOME (MME DUNGLAS). D. D. Home, His Life and Mission. London, 1888.

HOWITT (A. W.). The Native Tribes of South-East Australia. London, 1904.

HUEBER. Menologium S Francisci. Monachii, 1698.

HURTAUD (J.). Le Dialogue de sainte Catherine de Sienne. Paris, 1913.

IAMBLICHUS. De vita Pythagorica. Paris, 1878.

    Iamblichi de Mysteriis liber, recognovit Gustavus Parthey. Berlin, 1857.

IMBERT-GOURBEYRE (DR. A.). Les stigmatisées. 2nd ed., 2 vols. Paris. 1873.

    La stigmatisation. 2 vols. Clermont-Ferrand and Paris, 1894.

ISWOLSKY (P.). Un saint russe au xixᵉ siècle, saint Séraphin de Sarov. (*Les Lettres*, October 1, 1921.)

JACOLLIOT (L.). Voyage au pays des Fakirs charmeurs. Paris, 1883.

JALÁLU D'DIN RÚMI. The Masnavî. Book II, translated, etc., by C. E. Wilson. 2 vols. London, 1910.

JAMES (WILLIAM). The Varieties of Religious Experience. London, 1903.

JANET (DR. P.). De l'angoisse à l'extase. Étude sur les croyances et les sentiments. Paris, 1926.

JÖRGENSEN (J.). Saint François d'Assise, sa vie et son œuvre, translated by T. de Wizewa. 28th ed. Paris, 1912.

JUNOD (H. A.). Les Ba-Ronga. Étude ethnographique sur les indigènes de la baie de Delagoa. Neuchâtel, 1898.

KARDEC (ALLAN). La genèse, les miracles et les prédictions selon le spiritisme. 19th ed. Paris.

KERNER (JUSTINUS). Die Seherin von Prevorst, bearbeitet und eingeleitet von Rudolf Lambert. Stuttgart, 1922.

LACORDAIRE (H. D.). Œuvres complètes. 9 vols. Paris, 1894 ff.

LAFITAU (J. F.). Mœurs des sauvages américains comparées aux mœurs des premiers temps. 2 vols. Paris, 1724.

LAFONTAINE (CH.). Mémoires d'un magnétiseur. 2nd ed. 2 vols. Paris and Genève, 1867.

BIBLIOGRAPHICAL INDEX

LAING (F. S.). Saint Joseph of Copertino. Saint-Louis, 1918.

LAMÉ (E.). Vie de Julien l'Apostat. Paris, 1861.

LANG (ANDREW). Cock Lane and Common Sense. London, 1894.

LANTAGES (DE). Vie de la vénérable Mère Agnès de Jésus (a new edition by M. Lucot). Paris, 1863.

LA TASTE (DOM). Lettres théologiques aux écrivains défenseurs des convulsions et autres prétendus miracles du temps. Paris, 1740.

LAVIOSA (D. B.). Vita della beata Maria Francesca delle Cinque Piaghe di Gesu Cristo. Roma, 1843.

LE BRUN (PIERRE). Histoire des pratiques superstitieuses, etc. 2 vols. Paris, 1750.

LEGOUX (A. M.). La vénérable Marie-Madeleine Postel, fondatrice de l'Institut des Sœurs de la Miséricorde, etc. 2 vols. 1906.

LÉON DE CLARY (FATHER). L'auréole séraphique. Vie des saints et des bienheureux des trois ordres de saint François. 4 vols. Paris, 1886.

LERICHE (ABBÉ). Étude sur les possessions en général et sur celles de Loudun en particulier. Paris, 1859.

LE ROY (MGR.). La religion des primitifs. 5th ed. Paris, 1925.

LEROY (OLIVIER). La raison primitive. Paris, 1927.

LE SCAO (FATHER). Au pays de Sette Cama. La religion des habitants, les fétiches, le Bouiti. (Messager du Saint-Esprit, 1908-1909.)

LESCOEUR (FATHER). La science et les faits surnaturels contemporains. Paris, 1897.

LETTRES ÉDIFIANTES ET CURIEUSES, ÉCRITES DES MISSIONS ÉTRANGÈRES. 14 vols. Lyon, 1819.

LEUBA (J. H.). Extase mystique et révélation. (Mercure de France, February, 1911.)

LÉVI (ÉLIPHAS). Histoire de la magie (a new edition). Paris, 1922.

LEWIS (DAVID). Life of St Teresa. 5th ed. London.

LUCA DI ROMA. Breve compendio della vita, virtù e miracoli del beato Padre Tommaso da Cori. Roma, 1786.

MAISTRE (J. DE). Les soirées de Saint-Pétersbourg. 4th ed., 2 vols. Lyon, 1842.

MALINOWSKI (B.). Argonauts of the Western Pacific: Native Enterprise and Adventure in the Archipelagos of Melanesian New Guinea. London, 1922.

MARACCI (L.). Vita della V.M. Passitea Crogi Senese. Venice, 1682.

MARCHESE (D. M.). Diario domenicano. 6 vols. Napoli, 1668-1681.
    Vita della V. Serva di Dio Suor Maria Villani. Napoli, 1674.

MARÉCHAL (J.). Études sur la psychologie des mystiques. vol. i (no other published). Bruges and Paris, 1924.

MARÉCHAUX (DOM B. M.). Le merveilleux divin et le merveilleux démoniaque. 2nd ed. Paris, 1901.

MARTIN (S.). Vie des saints. 4 vols. Paris, 1840.

MASDEU (G.). Vita santa dell novello Beato Giuseppe Oriol. Roma, 1806.

LEVITATION

MASSIGNON (L.). La passion d'al-Hosayn-Ibn Mansour al-Hallaj, etc. 2 vols. Paris, 1922.

MAURY (L. F. A.). La magie et l'astrologie dans l'antiquité et au moyen-âge, etc. 4th ed. Paris, 1877.

MAUSS (M.). L'origine des pouvoirs magiques dans les sociétés australiennes. Paris, 1904.

MAZZARA. Leggendario francescano. Venice, 1721.

MELCHIORRI (S.). Vita di S Pacifico de San Severino. Roma, 1839.

MÉRIC (E.). Le vol aérien des corps. (*Revue du monde invisible*, March-April-June, 1899.)

MIR (M.). Vida de Santa Teresa. Madrid, 1912.

MIRVILLE (J. E. DE). Des esprits et de leurs manifestations fluidiques. 3rd ed. Paris, 1854.

MONNIN (A.). Le curé d'Ars. Vie de saint Jean-Baptiste Marie Vianney. 2 vols. Paris, 1914.

MONTMORAND (M. DE). Psychologie des Mystiques catholiques orthodoxes. Paris, 1920.

MÜLLER (MAX). Râmakrishna: His Life and Sayings. London, 1910.

MURRAY (R. H.). The Oxford Dictionary (*s.v.* Levitation).

NASSAU (R. H.). Fetichism in West Africa. London, 1904.

NEWMAN (J. H.). An Essay in Aid of a Grammar of Assent. New impression. London, 1924.

NICOLE (P.). Essais de morale. Paris, 1714-1723.

NUTI (ROBERTO). Vita del Servo di Dio P. Giuseppe de Copertino, etc. Vienna, 1682.

OLDENBERG (H.). Le Bouddha, sa vie, sa doctrine, sa communauté. 3rd ed. (translated from the 3rd German ed. by A. Foucher). Paris, 1921.

ÖSTERREICH (T. K.). Les possédés. Paris, 1927. Translated from the German by R. Sudre. Paris, 1927.

PASTROVICCHI (A.). Compendio della vita, virtù e miracoli del B. Giuseppe di Copertino, etc. Roma, 1753. (Latin translation by C. Suyskens in *Acta Sanctorum*, September, vol. v.)

PAULINUS (ST). In Natal. S Felicis (Migne's *Latin Patrology*, vol. lxi). De vita S Martini. *Ibid.*

PERRENS (F. T.). Jérôme Savonarole. 2nd ed. Paris, 1856.

PÉTIN (ABBÉ). Dictionnaire hagiographique. 2 vols. Paris, 1850. (Vols. xl and xli of Migne's *Encyclopédie théologique*.)

PHILOSTRATUS. Apollonius de Tyane (translated by A. Chassang). 2nd ed. Paris, 1862.

PICARDA (FATHER). Autour de Madéra. Notes sur l'Ouzigoua, l'Oukwéré et l'Oudoé (Zanguebar). (*Les Missions catholiques*, June 4, 1886.)

PINARD DE LA BOULLAYE (H.). L'Étude comparée des religions. 2 vols. Paris, 1922-1925.

PIO DEL NOME DI MARIA. Vita del Beato Paolo della Croce, etc. Roma, 1853.

PODMORE (FRANK). Modern Spiritualism, A History and a Criticism. 2 vols. London, 1902.

262

BIBLIOGRAPHICAL INDEX

PONNELLE (L.). ET BORDET (LOUIS). St Philippe Néri et la société romaine de son temps (1515–1595). Paris, 1928.

PORPHYRY. De vita Pythagorae. Paris, 1878.

POULAIN (AUG.). Des grâces d'oraison, traité de théologie mystique. 10th ed. Paris, 1878.

POZO (J. DEL). Vita del B. Francesco de Posadas. Roma, 1818.

Quarterly Journal of Science, January, 1875. Human Levitation, illustrating certain Historical Miracles. (Anonymous).

RAESS (A.). Die Convertiten seit der Reformation. Freiburg, 1868.

REGNIER (DR. L. R.). Hypnotisme et croyances anciennes. Paris, 1891.

REINACH (S.). Cultes, mythes et religions. 4 vols. Paris, 1908–1913.

RENAN (E.). Questions contemporaines. Paris, 1868.
     Vie de Jésus. 13th ed. Paris, 1906.
     Les Apôtres. 23rd ed. Paris, 1921.

RIBET (M. J.). La mystique divine distinguée des contrefaçons diaboliques et des analogies humaines. A new edition, 4 vols. Paris, 1902.

RICHET (DR. CH.). Traité de métapsychique. Paris, 1922.

ROCHAS (A. DE). Recueil de documents relatifs à la lévitation du corps humain. Paris, 1897.
     La lévitation du corps humain. (*Annales des sciences psychiques*, No. 1, 1901.)

ROGER (ABBÉ J.). Histoire de Nicole de Vervins, etc. Paris, 1853.

ROURE (L.). Le merveilleux spirite. 6th ed. Paris, 1922.
     Lévitation. (*Dictionnaire pratique des connaissances religieuses.*) Paris, 1926.

SABATIER (P.). Actus beati Francisci et sociorum ejus. Paris, 1902.

SAINT-ANDRÉ (DE). Lettres à quelques-uns de ses amis au sujet de la magie, etc. Paris, 1725.

SAMANIEGO (J. X.). Vie de la vénérable mère Marie de Jésus, abbesse du monastère de la ville d'Agréda. Translated by Father Crozet, Paris, 1857.

SAUBAT (J.). André-Hubert Fournet. 2 vols. Tarbes, 1924.

SCHMIDT (R.). Fakire und Fakirtum. Berlin, 1908.

SCHMÖGER (K. E.). Anne-Catherine Emmerich. 3 vols. Paris, 1868.

SCHRENCK-NOTZING (A. VON). Les phénomenes physiques de la médiumnité. Translated from the German by E. Longaud. Paris, 1925.
     Über einen Fall willkürlicher Erzeugung paraphysischer Phäno-mene. (*Compte rendu du* 111e *Congrès international de recherches psychiques à Paris*, September to October, 1927, Paris, 1928.)

SCORAILLE (R. DE). François Suarez, etc. 2 vols. Paris, 1914.

SELIGMANN (C. G.). The Melanesians of British New Guinea. London, 1924.

SIMPLICIEN SAINT MARTIN (FATHER). Histoire de la vie de notre Père Saint Augustin, des saints, bienheureux et hommes illustres de notre ordre, 1640.

SOREL (G.). Introduction à l'économie moderne. 2nd ed. Paris, 1922.

STEILL. Ephemeriden, etc. Dilligen, 1692.

LEVITATION

SUDRE (R.). Introduction à la métapyschique humaine. Paris, 1926.

SULPITIUS SEVERUS. Hist. and Dialogus iii, vol. xx of Migne's *Latin Patrology*.

SUTTER (P.). Le diable, ses paroles, son action dans les possédés d'Illfurt (Alsace) d'après des documents historiques, 4th ed. Arras, 1926.

TANNOJA (A. M.). Mémoires sur la vie et la compagnie de saint Alphonse-Marie de Liguori. 3 vols. Paris, 1842.

TANQUEREY (A.). Précis de théologie ascétique et mystique. Paris, 1924.

TERESA (ST). The Interior Castle, or the Mansions and Exclamations of the Soul to God, translated from the Autograph by the Benedictines of Stanbrook, 1912.

Life written by herself and translated from the Spanish by David Lewis. 5th ed., re-edited and compared with the autograph text.

THURSTON (HERBERT). Some Physical Phenomena of Mysticism. Levitation. (*The Month*, April and May, 1919.)

TONQUÉDEC (J. DE). Introduction a l'étude du merveilleux et du miracle. 3rd ed. Paris, 1923.

TRILLES (H.). Le totémisme ches les Fân. Münster-i.-W., 1912.

La sorcellerie chez les non-civilisés, féticheurs et sorciers. (*Proceedings of Semaine d'ethnologie religieuse*, Louvain, 1914.)

TROCHU (F.). Le Curé d'Ars, S Jean-Marie-Baptiste Vianney. Lyon, 1926.

TYLOR (E. B.). Primitive Culture. 2 vols, 4th ed. London, 1903.

VACANT ET MANGENOT (E.). Dictionnaire de théologie catholique (*s.v.* Extase). Paris, 1924.

VALLÉE-POUSSIN (L. DE LA). Bouddhisme, opinions sur l'histoire et la dogmatique. 4th ed. Paris, 1925.

VENTURI (FATHER). La vie incomparable de la bienheureuse Mère Passidéc de Sienne. Paris, 1627.

VILLECOURT (C.). Vie et institut de saint Alphonse-Marie de Liguori. 3 vols. Tournai, 1864.

WADDING (L.). Annales ordinis Minorum ab anno 1208 ad annum 1540. Lugduni, 1628.

WIEGER (L.). Histoire des croyances religieuses et des opinions philosophiques en Chine. 2nd ed. Hien-hien, 1922.

ZACCHIAS (P.). Quaestiones medico-legales, etc. Amsterdam, 1651.

INDEX OF THE NAMES OF PERSONS

The names of Catholic saints or mystics have been printed in clarendon letters, unless they are quoted only as authors. The names of authors are in small capitals.

265

LEVITATION

Home (D. D.), 20-26, 145, 146, 193,
194, 195, 196, 197, 198, 200, 201,
203, 205, 207, 210, 211, 233,
249
Howitt (A. W.), 9, 10
Hugh (Bishop), 156
Hugon (Father), 133
Hugues of Digne, 47
Hulst (Mgr. d'), 128
Hume (D.), 155
Hume (D. D.). *See* Home
Humiliana, 253
Humilis of Bisignano, 253
Husson (Dr.), 146

Iamblichus, 3, 4, 241
Iarchas, 4
Ignatius Balsamo, 253
Ignatius of Loyola, 58, 62-63, 163
Ignazio del Nente, 62
Imbert-Gourbeyre (Dr. A.), vi, 11,
43, 50, 56, 60, 61, 62, 66, 68, 74,
75, 80, 83, 87, 88, 105, 106, 119,
127, 128, 129, 132, 133, 135, 141
156, 167, 182, 186, 187, 192, 211,
212, 252, 253
Imolensi (G.), 56
Innocent X, 229
Isabella Sanchez, 182, 253
Iswolsky (P.), 38

Jacolliot (L.), 5, 6, 140, 233
Jahenny. *See* Mary Julia
Jalálu d'Din Rûmi, 7, 8
James I, 227
James (Brother), 48
James (William), 207
James of Illyria, 51, 56, 189
James of Ravenna, 170
Janet (Dr. P.), 203
Jaquette de Bachelier, 73, 82
Jencken (H. D.), 207
Jeremias of Palermo, 51, 55
Jerome da Silva, 78, 80, 176, 177
Jerome de Butis, 56
Jeronima Carvalho, 253
Jesus Christ, 33
Jîlâni, 7
Joan Mary Bonomi, 253

Joan Mary of Maillé, 253
Joan Mary of the Cross, 73, 87
Joannicus, 35, 37, 162
Joan of Arc, 150
Joan of Jesus-Mary, 73, 84, 156
Joan of Orvieto, 51, 52
John Angelo Porro, 58, 59, 162,
163
John Baptist of Mastena, 103, 105,
189
John Berchmans, 191
John Capistran, 168
John Colombini, 51, 53, 211
John Joseph of the Cross, 103, 106-
107
John Leonardo of Lettere, 73, 80-81,
211
John Marinoni, 58, 64, 162
John Mary Baptist Vianney, 118,
123, 175
John Massias, 73, 83, 189
John of the Cross, 58, 66, 71, 181
Jones (Enmore), 25
Jörgensen (J.), 53, 166
Joseph Benedict Cottolengo, 118,
123-124, 174, 176
Joseph of Copertino, 85, 89-102,
145, 156, 158, 167, 168, 169-174,
175, 176, 178, 179, 180, 181, 182,
183, 184, 185, 187, 189, 190, 191,
192, 210, 212, 213, 223, 228, 237,
250
Joseph of Leonessa, 73, 74
Joseph Oriol, 103
Joseph, T., 18
Jousset (Dr.), 159, 167
Juana de la Incarnacion, 253
Juan di Ribera, 73, 74
Judas, 33
Julian the Apostate, 5
Junod (H. A.), 11
Jutta, 39, 44, 162

Kardec (Allan), 240
Karpovitch (Dr.), 197
Kerner (Dr. J.), 29, 236
Keue-Houng, 7
Kia-cheu-fang, 7
King (John), 204
Kleodemos, 4

270

INDEX OF THE NAMES OF PERSONS

271

INDEX OF THE NAMES OF PERSONS

275

Villani. *See* **Mary**
Villani (Father), 175
VILLECOURT (CARDINAL DE), 112, 113,
  114, 115, 116, 117
Vincent Ferrer, 13, 51, 54, 55, 162
  180
VINCENT OF AREZZO, 49
Vincent of Paul, 191
Vincentini (Professor), 145
VINCHON (J.), 19, 186
Vintras (E.), 253-254
Virgili. *See* **Mariangiola**
VISA, 36
Viscardi (Agatha), 157
Vito de Martina, 192, 254
Vivaud (J.), 47
Vollhardt (Maria), 28, 193
Volpicelli (Father), 116
Vughet (A.), 64
Vuillet (V.), 18

WADDING (L.), 57
WAGENSEIL (J.), 33
Walther, 253
Ward Cheney, 20

Watteville (De), 27
Weber (Karl), 254
Werner, 255
WIEGER (FATHER L.), 6, 7, 149, 232
Werner, 255
William, 56
WILLIAM OF TOCCO, 48
Willy Sch., 28, 194, 195, 196, 197,
  199, 200, 202, 203, 205, 206, 207,
  254
WILSON (C. E.), 8
Wynne (Ch.), 23, 24

Xavier (Sister), 126
XIMENES (J.), 66

YEPES (BISHOP), 70, 71, 174

ZACCHIAS (P.), 229
Zagnoni. *See* **Pudenziana**
ZEVALLOS (L. J.), 253
Zita, 167
Zosimus, 35, 36, 221
Zuccarini, 145

www.ingramcontent.com/pod-product-compliance
Lightning Source LLC
Chambersburg PA
CBHW021136090426
42740CB00008B/809